POLARIZED

POLARIZED

The Collapse of Truth, Civility, and
Community in Divided Times
and How We Can Find Common Ground

KEITH M. PARSONS

PARIS N. DONEHOO

Prometheus Books

59 John Glenn Drive
Amherst, New York 14228

Published 2019 by Prometheus Books

Cover design by Liz Mills
Cover design © Prometheus Books

The internet addresses listed in the text were accurate at the time of publication. The inclusion of a website does not indicate an endorsement by the authors or by Prometheus Books, and Prometheus Books does not guarantee the accuracy of the information presented at these sites.

Inquiries should be addressed to
Prometheus Books
59 John Glenn Drive
Amherst, New York 14228
VOICE: 716–691–0133 • FAX: 716–691–0137
WWW.PROMETHEUSBOOKS.COM

23 22 21 20 19   5 4 3 2 1

Library of Congress Cataloging-in-Publication Data

Names: Parsons, Keith M., 1952- author. | Donehoo, Paris, 1952- author.
Title: Polarized : the collapse of truth, civility, and community in divided   times and how we can find common ground / Paris N. Donehoo and Keith M.   Parsons.
Description: Amherst, New York : Prometheus Books, 2019.
Identifiers: LCCN 2018036715 (print) | LCCN 2018048446 (ebook) | ISBN   9781633884557 (ebook) | ISBN 9781633884540 (hardback)
Subjects: LCSH: Political culture--United States. | Polarization (Social   sciences)--United States. | Civil society--United States. | Courtesy--United States. | BISAC: POLIT-   ICAL SCIENCE / Civics &   Citizenship. | POLITICAL SCIENCE / Political Ide-   ologies / Conservatism &   Liberalism. | PHILOSOPHY / Social.
Classification: LCC JK1764 (ebook) | LCC JK1764 .D66 2019 (print) | DDC   306.20973--dc23
LC record available at https://lccn.loc.gov/2018036715

Printed in the United States of America

(Paris): Dedicated to my mother, Peggy Donehoo, who gave me my first Bible, and to the memory of Brantley Seymour—pastor, teacher, mentor, and friend.

(Keith): Dedicated to my mother, Charlotte Parsons, who, at ninety-four, is still going strong and who has strongly encouraged this project. Dedicated also to the memory of the great professors I had at Berry College, in Rome, Georgia, nearly fifty years ago: Bob Sturdivant, Bill Hoyt, Jorge Gonzales, and Gordon Carper, who inspired me to pursue a career in academe, which I finally attained and which has given me so many rewards.

CONTENTS

SECTION I: UNTRUTH AND ITS CONSEQUENCES

CONTENTS

SECTION II: NO CIVILIZATION WITHOUT CIVILITY

How Do We Restore Civility?

Concluding Thoughts on Civility

SECTION III: *E PLURIBUS UNUM*: COMMUNITY IN DIVERSITY

What Is Community in a Pluralistic Society?

How Has Divisiveness Become So Extreme?

What Is the Value of Community?

CONTENTS

THE PURPOSE OF THIS BOOK

So how did we embark on this project? One of us (Keith) lives in Texas and the other (Paris) lives in Illinois, but each holiday season we return to visit family and friends in our home state of Georgia. We always meet a day or two after Christmas to enjoy a good meal and lots of laughs. When we got together in 2016, we were in a more subdued mood. It was in the aftermath of the election that made Donald Trump president of the United States. To us, this event was perhaps the most shocking and puzzling occurrence in our country in our lifetimes. When we got past our initial expressions of incredulity and dismay, we found that we strongly agreed on why this event disturbed us to such a degree.

Donald Trump's 2015/2016 presidential campaign exhibited an utter disregard for truth by disparaging science, expertise, journalism, and religious practices that did not suit his own ends. Instead, he favored crackpot claims and conspiracy theories. Trump also repeatedly displayed extreme incivility toward his opponent, and, more disturbingly, contempt for any critic, even mocking the disability of a reporter he perceived as hostile. Further, the rhetoric of the campaign was bitterly divisive, exploiting ethnic, racial, religious, and gender divides, playing up to extremist and racist elements, and making alarmist and even paranoid claims.

As we see it, the elements of mendacity, incivility, and divisiveness have been metastasizing in our public life for some time, reaching their loudest and most blatant expression in the Trump campaign. We therefore found ourselves in strong agreement about what is wrong and why it is wrong, despite the fact that we come from very different religious and philosophical viewpoints. That is, we found that we shared much common ground and that we could appreciate and learn from each other's thinking on these topics, though one of us is an atheist philosopher and the other is a minister of the Gospel. The discovery of such a basis of agreement, in itself, is an important achievement in these deeply divided times.

We are old enough to remember the terrible divisiveness caused by the Vietnam War. We sat together in August 1968 and watched in horror as cops beat antiwar demonstrators in Chicago during the Democratic National Convention. The demonstrators chanted "The whole world is watching," and what the world saw was America apparently coming apart at the seams. As this is being written, clashes between neo-Nazi white supremacists and counterdemonstrators in Charlottesville, Virginia, were like a flashback to 1968. We as a nation most definitely do not want to go back to those days.

The purpose of this book is to encourage all people of good will, secular and religious, to seek common ground and work together to oppose the dangerous deterioration of our public discourse. At a deeper level, we hope to show that secular and religious thinking is often far more congruent and mutually supportive than is recognized by zealots on either side of the religious/secular divide.

The election to the nation's highest office of a man we both consider utterly unworthy of any public position had for us one salutary effect. Both of us rediscovered patriotism. Patriotism to us had always seemed associated with jingoism, ethnocentric arrogance, maudlin displays of flag waving, and theocratic insinuations that God is an American. Now we both agree that such arrogance, sentimentality, and militarism are not what makes one a patriot. An American patriot is one who thinks that the republic created by the founders, despite its many sins and follies, is the embodiment of ideals necessary to preserve, essential ideals expressed in the nation's founding documents, open to good-faith interpretation.

These ideals are not top-down mandates to honor God and King or to profess the approved ideology, and neither are they mystical appeals to blood, race, and soil. Rather, they are higher-order ideals that allow individuals to follow the dictates of their own conscience and pursue their well-being as they perceive it, so long as such pursuits leave their neighbors equally free to do the same. They must also be willing to defend—through any means conscience will allow—the republic that is based on such ideals from enemies both foreign and domestic.

Astonishingly, this idea, the American Idea, works. It survived perhaps its greatest international challenge when it faced down the Axis forces and their ideologies based on racial purity in the Second World War. The American Idea survived its greatest domestic challenge, the secessionist insurrection of the southern Confederacy in defense of the profoundly anti-American doctrines of racial hegemony and superiority. The defeat of the Confederacy in 1865 should have meant the end of its anti-American agenda. The election of 2016 was a shocking demonstration that its defeat was far from final.

The presidency of Donald Trump, and the forces that gave rise to it, are the greatest domestic dangers to the American Idea since the Civil War. Trump's campaign and presidency are profoundly antithetical to the ideals of the founders. The Enlightenment geniuses who founded this country expressed deep respect for the capacity of the American people for self-government, and that capacity requires that the citizens practice the virtues of reasonableness, civility, and tolerance. Trump and all that he stands for (to the extent that he stands for anything other than Donald Trump) are in direct opposition to these ideals and virtues. We therefore see resisting Donald Trump as our patriotic duty, and this opportunity to write in collaboration with each other, is, among other things, an expression of patriotism.

What follows, therefore, is a back-and-forth set of essays in which we state our concerns and proposals and respond to each other. Of course, we are addressing the reader as well as each other. Because this book is an attempt at achieving a meeting of minds, we begin with autobiographical introductory remarks about our backgrounds, our convictions and how they were formed, and on what basis we can find common ground. We felt that a more personal statement would better convey the nature and depth of our convictions than a bare credo or abstract summary. In the main body of the book we focus on the issues of truthfulness, civility, and unity in diversity because we think that these are crucial ideals and that their abandonment spells grave danger to our society. We state why these ideals are important, how they are under attack, and what can be done to support or restore these crucial values. We approach these topics in different but congruent ways, as will be seen as our dialogue develops. Again, our hope is that people of good will, both religious and secular, will acknowledge the values that we share and work together against those who disdain and undermine these values. We feel that the task is urgent and the time for action is now.

INTRODUCTION

PARIS DONEHOO

One benefit of the internet is its ability to connect people over long distances, many years, and different worldviews. Such was the case when Keith Parsons found my email address and sent me a note expressing nostalgia over our childhood friendship. I think he had just watched the movie *Stand By Me*, had grown a bit wistful, and then reached out to me. I was deeply touched. Like him, I treasured our youthful memories together, and we had connected with each other at various times over the years, but I surmised that our separate paths and perspectives had created a chasm between us that could not be spanned. A close relationship, I assumed, was out of the question. One of my great joys in life was the discovery of just how wrong I was.

Keith and I enjoyed one of those rare childhood connections. We shared very similar interests in almost everything, and we spent as much time as possible exploring them. Unfortunately, those interests seldom intersected with the subjects our teachers wanted us to explore. Why waste time on multiplication tables and diagraming sentences when the jungle gym in my backyard could be transformed into a space ship or jet plane, and a few railroad ties pushed together in Keith's backyard could become a flying carpet or a raft adrift in the ocean? We created an entire alien culture on the planet of Pum, and thrilled to any horror movie we could watch—everything from *Godzilla* to *Dracula*. Mostly, we did a lot of laughing. When I remember our childhood, it comes to me with a rib cage sore from continuous giggling and cackling.

Fissures in our relationship began to form in our high school years. Our families moved away to different suburbs of Atlanta, and our interests began to diversify. Dependent on our busy parents for transportation, our personal contacts waned. By the time we procured driver's licenses we had developed different friendships. Besides, I was going to be a rock star, and Keith had given up on the guitar. Like many teenagers in the sixties, I had an inflated opinion of my musical talents, and I was sure I would soon be performing in stadiums full of buxom females shouting my name. When I entered college I declared a major in journalism, but it was only a cover to keep the adults in my life from raining on my parade.

To say I was a mediocre student would be an understatement. For the most part, I skated through high school academics. The college atmosphere, however, affected me profoundly. I discovered I enjoyed an environment where no one pushed me to study. My professors got paid whether I made an A or an F, and they were not about to cut me any slack just because I was a dimwit. I actually did okay in my math classes (always the bane of my existence), and I did better in the other subjects. By the time I reached my junior year I found my name regularly on the Dean's List.

My freshman year also brought one the most significant experiences of my life, one that continues to shape me even now. Because I was eighteen years old and knew everything, I had regular verbal sparring matches with my Dad. On one occasion I stormed to my room and slammed the door in order to seethe in private. Looking for something to take my mind off my frustration I scoured my bookshelf, and, for a reason unknown to me even now, I picked up my Bible.

Like Keith I had been raised in the church. Our Southern Baptist family never woke up on Sunday morning and asked if we were going to church. It was as much a part of our weekly routine as school and work. My paternal grandfather had been pastor of my home church many years prior. My Dad was a deacon and sang in the choir. My mother worked in the nursery. I was involved in youth group, Sunday School, youth choir, and any other activity that afforded me opportunities to laugh with my friends and secretly lust after the girls. But it was all social. I did not practice Christian discipleship in any substantive way not proscribed by my teachers and leaders.

On that day in my room a new perspective dawned for me. Though I had dutifully carried my Bible with me to Sunday School every week like all good Southern Baptists did, I had never paid much attention to it. That day in my room I began to discover the power of Jesus's words and their capacity for pointing beyond Roswell, Georgia, to the kind of world I had envisioned only in my daydreams. The political turmoil of the sixties had captivated me for some time, but I was at a loss as to how create a world that did not end in dour cynicism. In Jesus's vision of the kingdom of God I found what I had been looking for.

Slowly the possibility of a life in ministry took shape in my mind. I talked with my parents (my mother had suspected I would take this path, although she never breathed a word to me about it), my pastor, my teachers in the church, and others. Finally, I announced my decision to my home church—I believed God had called me into ministry.

I like to say I was raised a fundamentalist, but the word was not spelled with a capital F. Though the basic theology of my upbringing was traditional conservative Christianity couched in a revivalistic mold, my family always encouraged me to think for myself. My pastor, who later became my mentor in ministry, taught me to respect other Christian traditions as well as other religious faiths. During my college years I got involved with Campus Crusade for Christ, played in a Christian folk music group, and made many friends. By the time I graduated, however, I knew I was a poor fit for such hyperevangelical faith. I was grateful for my professors at Southwestern Baptist Theological Seminary who gave me the tools to explore the Bible and theology instead of swallowing a party line. None of this is to say I did not clash at times with my religious tradition. I did, and by the time I received my Master of Divinity degree I already had the reputation for being "a little liberal."

Yet I still wanted to be a good Baptist pastor, so I tried to fit the mold. Then, while still serving in my first church after seminary, the Southern Baptist denomination that had birthed and nurtured me in the faith became embroiled in a fight for its very soul and survival (see my remarks on "Truth" below). Though I grieved the loss of familiar theological surroundings, the rancor within Southern Baptist ranks forced me to take a long, hard look at myself and the ministry to which I felt called. Even though I had been born, raised, and educated as a Baptist, I realized I would always be something of a fish out of water in Baptist life. I entered the Doctor of Ministry program at Columbia Theological Seminary in Decatur, Georgia (not too far from my old stomping ground with Keith), not only for the education, but also for the chance to examine my beliefs within a context other than Southern Baptist.

Columbia Seminary's Presbyterian roots helped me look at faith and ministry with new eyes. I reveled in an atmosphere in which I could leave questions unanswered instead of searching for routes to predetermined conclusions. I learned to appreciate the inconsistencies in the Bible as representative of the paradoxical lives we all live instead of engaging in intellectual gymnastics to explain them away. I discovered a love for the beauty and power of corporate worship done for its own sake instead of as a means to an end. I began to learn the concept of community to describe the church as a living, breathing organism instead of merely an institution. And I was given the freedom to envision the church collaborating with God to create a world of justice and peace instead of saving souls and hoping for the best.

For the first time I seriously entertained the possibility of ministry within a different denomination. I talked with pastors, teachers, and other leaders from Presbyterian, Episcopal, Methodist, United Church of Christ, Disciples of Christ, and probably other churches that I simply cannot recall. I thought about leaving the pastorate and going into teaching. Keith was kind enough to invite me to visit him at the college where he was serving at the time to talk over issues and strategies. Then one day I was perusing an issue of *Christian Century* and saw a notice from a church with roots in the United Church of Christ, located in Park Ridge, Illinois, which was looking for a pastor. I asked for more information and received a document detailing a congregation that prized open inquiry in a nondenominational context. If this church called me as pastor I would not only be leaving the Southern Baptists, but also taking up residence far above the Mason-Dixon Line.

Both possibilities came true in January of 1991. Many ministerial colleagues could not understand why I was abandoning the denomination that had ordained me. When one fellow pastor heard that my new charge was not a Southern Baptist church, he said, "But you're going to change them into a Southern Baptist church, aren't you?" He clearly could not process my no answer. My family, on the other hand, was more upset about the change in location. They said they were not surprised that I was leaving the Baptists, but how could I transplant my family to the wilds of Illinois? My wife's aunt was scandalized to learn her great-grandmother's china would cross into Yankee territory.

It was during my tenure in Park Ridge that I formally made the split with my former tradition. My ordination was moved into the United Church of Christ, where I have found a home ever since. Little did I know that the fissures I had seen in Southern Baptist life were a microcosm of forces tearing the church of Jesus Christ apart all over the country. Although I was grateful for the sense of place the United Church of Christ gave me, it slowly dawned on me what dinosaurs denominations had become. My efforts throughout the 1980s to rescue the Southern Baptist Convention from fundamentalist fanatics turned out to be little more than rearranging deck chairs on the *Titanic*, and the United Church of Christ is still mired in its glory days of the 1950s and 1960s, when mainline Protestantism was on the frontlines of the civil rights movement. These days the UCC passes resolutions that are met with a national yawn.

For various reasons too numerous to elaborate here, churches of all shapes and sizes have been losing membership for decades, and most congregations have slipped into survival mode. I spent my entire ministerial career against a backdrop of religious and ecclesiastical ferment, and I find myself these days feeling more and more like a relic. The modalities of ministry I was taught often do not fit the needs of a church increasingly relegated to the sidelines of society. Additionally, I have watched Christian faith in the United States be slowly hijacked by right-wing politics, special interests, and the worst of American society, as evidenced especially by corporate greed. Granted, the faith tradition in which I was raised has never been a paragon of open-mindedness, and my second home seems reluctant to speak biblically for fear of being mistaken for fundamentalists, but within my lifetime Christian faith in general has come to be associated with intolerance, condemnation, hypocrisy, and fuzzy nostalgia. No matter how much I declare that all Christians cannot be painted with the same closed-minded brush, the perception remains. And far too often, perception is reality.

So why do I still cling to Christian faith? Why do I continue the attempt to order my life according to the example of an itinerant rabbi who lived two thousand years ago? Quite simply, because I choose to. Keith has his rational, intellectual, and experiential reasons for choosing atheism, and I have my rational, intellectual, and experiential reasons for choosing faith. Unlike observable phenomena in a test tube, questions of ultimate reality are not a zero-sum game. Human beings observe life around them and decide what it means. As much as we like to think we have tallied up the evidence and come to the only logical conclusion, none of us can claim to possess ultimate knowledge and omniscience to refute other perspectives once and for all. Keith looks at the wonder of the cosmos and sees marvelous naturalistic forces at work. I look at the cosmos and see a loving God guiding those forces. Neither is right or wrong. Both are complementary.

Besides, in the model of Jesus I find more than a lifestyle. I find a way of life. There is a difference. A lifestyle is a persona one can change like clothing when it becomes boring, inconvenient, or old-fashioned. By contrast, a way of life is a set of values informing all choices and behaviors. A way of life cannot be abandoned any easier than breathing. It has to do with the core principles that form and shape the person one claims to be. I do not believe it was by accident that disciples of Jesus in the earliest centuries called themselves "followers of the way." Jesus did not gather disciples by means of theological arguments or threats of perdition. He simply said, "Follow me." I can only imagine the list of questions those early disciples had. The answers, however, were found in the following, in the day-to-day living of their time with Jesus.

I stay with faith because this way of life puts a frame around experience that is at once comforting and challenging. Anne Lamott says, "God loves us exactly the way we are, and God loves us too much to let us stay like this."[1] There is freedom in choosing to believe in a God who is not in heaven with a tally sheet, but instead loves me unconditionally. "We're all bastards," said the late Will Campbell, "but God loves us anyway."[2] Some Christians believe they will be punished *for* their sins in eternity. I believe we are punished *by* our sins in this life. My mistakes (some of which have been whoppers), have consequences that rebound on me, on those around me, and on society in general. But those mistakes do not follow me beyond the grave. God has no interest in keeping lists.

On the other hand, God is no lenient grandparent leaving me to fend for myself. God does not want me running wild like a naughty toddler loose in a grocery store. I want to live the way of life called Christian faith because God's unconditional love is such an incredible gift. I am motivated to live according to the radical tenets of Jesus not because I fear being the main course at an eternal barbecue but in gratitude for God's loving hand on me. When my daughters were growing up I did not want them to do what I asked because they feared my wrath, but because they knew I loved them. To expect anything less from God is to label God's morality inferior to my own.

Dietrich Bonhoeffer spoke of the difference between cheap grace and costly grace.[3] For me perhaps the most powerful illustration of the difference between those two is the image of a great banquet in heaven. Seated next to me at the table is the person I injured most deeply during my earthly life. At that moment I am overcome by the grace of God that forgives the wrong I did to that individual. Seated next to me on the other side, however, is the person who most injured *me* during my earthly life. Suddenly grace has become costly. I want that person to pay for what was done to me, but God's grace does not play favorites.[4] The struggle between those chairs on either side of me is illustrative of the consolation and the confrontation of Christian faith. Within that struggle I find a context for positive living.

At a lecture at the Furman University Pastor's School I heard pastor and author Charles Poole say, "Most of us fear we will go too far with grace, when the truth is, we haven't gone far enough." Such unfathomable grace led me to a new understanding of Jesus's crucifixion and resurrection—new for me, at least. I had always been taught that humanity's sins were offensive to God and required a sacrifice in order appease divine righteousness. Therefore, when Jesus died on the cross he was paying the penalty that all humankind should have paid, and his resurrection on Easter demonstrated his power over death. The older I got, and the longer I dealt with the human condition, the less satisfied I became with such an interpretation. When I discovered that this theory was first outlined by Anselm of Canterbury in the late eleventh century, I decided it made sense within the context of feudal Europe but not in my own milieu.

The grace of God points me in a different direction. I see Jesus in the world with a message of a God whose love knows no bounds, who is radically inclusive, and who strips away the lies fomented by the status quo to keep their perks and power in place. He was crucified because humanity has never trusted anyone who does not play by the rules. History is replete with stories of people who proclaimed a vision of a better world and were destroyed by those who had too much invested in the existing state of affairs. Jesus, therefore, was rejected. But God loves us too much to let us have the last word. The empty tomb of Easter is God's flat rejection of humanity's rejection.[5] It is God's way of saying, "I love you exactly the way you are, and I love you too much to let you stay that way."

And why do I stay with the church? Given that I will make some disparaging remarks in these pages about the current state of Christ's church, some will claim my commitment is nothing short of hypocrisy. Some wags will claim my real motive is economic—I stayed in ministry for forty years because the church paid my salary. But the truth is this: I stay because of the grace of God I have experienced through my fellow faith pilgrims. As a shy, overweight teenager who felt like a fish out of water most days, I was graced by the support of teachers, youth leaders, and peers who gave me opportunities to discover myself and my talents. When I was a wet-behind-the-ears pastor fresh out of seminary, with absolutely no idea how to lead a congregation, I was graced with an elderly man who would visit me, invite me to walk with him through the church graveyard, and gently suggest ways I could best lead that particular church. When my second daughter was born with a cluster of birth defects called Klippel Feil Syndrome, and I was feeling abandoned by God, I was graced with the friendship of a fellow pastor, as well as a man from my home church whose young adult daughter, unbeknownst to me, had been born with the same anomalies. When my first marriage was falling apart, unlike some churches, who treat divorce as the unpardonable sin, I was graced with people in the church who called me, invited me to meals, gave me hugs when I most needed them, and helped me rebuild my life. When I was working as a hospice chaplain, I was graced with a pastor who, without the subject ever being broached by me, challenged me to consider returning to my first love—ministry in a local congregation. I love the church because, on its better days, it can truly be the "light of the world" Jesus talked about. If I am critical, it is because I believe the church can be much more than a mere institution in society. I believe ordinary people of faith, unsullied by conflicting loyalties, can turn the world upside down.

Some will claim this is wishful thinking, and they could be correct. I choose, however, to see glimpses of God's love and grace in the world around me, and especially in the people who walk the way with me— some for the duration, others for a time. Joshua's challenge to the children of Israel could be my watchword: "Now if you are unwilling to serve the Lord, choose this day whom you will serve, whether the gods your ancestors served in the region beyond the River or the gods of the Amorites in whose land you are living; but as for me and my household, we will serve the Lord" (Joshua 24:15).[6]

When Keith and I were young adults we often clashed over our different viewpoints. Looking back on it now, I realize how much of the conflict stemmed from us being two males feeling like we had something to prove to the world. I am thrilled, to say the least, that we are past that stage of life. Perhaps the most telling evidence of our new phase of life was the night we sat down and read *One Fish, Two Fish, Red Fish, Blue Fish* out loud to each other like we did when we were boys. Whatever rivalries we had in the past evaporated in our laughter that evening.

Unfortunately, childish playground enmities have become the norm in America. But they are luxuries our society can no longer afford. The chasms between Americans grow deeper every day, and nothing is served by shrieking at one another across the divide. It is time for people of good will to come together and celebrate our commonality while honestly acknowledging our differences without acrimony. I, for one, still hold out hope. Long ago I heard John Claypool declare, "Despair is the ultimate presumption."[7] For a Christian like myself, despair means believing God is powerless to change a situation. For an atheist like Keith, it means believing humanity has reached the limit of its creative skill. Either way, Keith and I will not give in to it. There is too much at stake.

INTRODUCTION

KEITH PARSONS

Paris Donehoo and I have known each other for nearly sixty years. My recollection of how we met is this: During recess one day in first grade our activity was kickball, a pursuit, like all such team games, that seemed pointless to me. Perhaps recognizing my lack of enthusiasm, the teacher put me far back into the outfield, where I stood daydreaming and hoping that the ball never came my way. My outfield post happened to be close to a small copse of trees, so, when the teacher was not looking I sidled off to the trees. Another kid was already there. It was Paris. Pleased to find another kickball shirker, I immediately approached him and we began to plan our own fun. Of course it was not to be. The teacher soon spotted us and, with minatory words and looks, led us back to our assigned outfield posts. So, a friendship was born out of mutual disregard for kickball.

We soon found that we had many other things in common. Neither of us was the least athletically inclined, but we had vivid imaginations, and we acted out pretend adventures that we plotted as seriously as novels. We loved monsters, science fiction, Ancient Greece, and whatever struck our fancy that day. Mostly we loved a good laugh. I remember getting a copy of Dr. Seuss's *One Fish, Two Fish, Red Fish, Blue Fish* and reading it with Paris until we were both so choked with hilarity that we could hardly proceed. When Paris got a reel-to-reel tape recorder we began to record our own comedic skits, some of which had a Monty Python-esque flavor. We recorded *The Adventures of Captain Zoom*, a parody of the horrible space operas, like *Lost in Space*, that network TV inflicted upon us.

As young adults we were caught up in the so-called "Jesus Movement" of the early seventies, where "Jesus Freaks" practiced fundamentalist Christianity with a countercultural flair. Each of us took different paths from fundamentalism. I will let Paris tell his own story. For me, the exit was pretty rapid. For about six months I tried hard to be a fundamentalist, but I just could not do it. Try as I might, I just could not disbelieve in evolution or accept that the earth was only six thousand years old. Another stumbling block was the idea of an eternal, punitive hell. The idea that sincere nonbelievers such as Muslims or Jews would be eternally punished for remaining true to their deepest convictions seemed flatly inconsistent with the concept of a loving God.

Then I took some courses in biblical studies in college where, for the first time, I was exposed to critical studies of scripture. I learned that the Gospels were not written by four stenographers—Matthew, Mark, Luke, and John—who followed Jesus around writing down everything he said. Something like this: "What was that, Mark, 'Blessed are the cheese makers?'" "No, Matthew, 'peacemakers.'" "Okay. That makes more sense." Rather, the Gospels were composed by persons unknown forty or more years after the time of Jesus. They certainly were not eyewitness accounts, nor were they historical narratives composed in accordance with modern standards of scholarship and objectivity. Instead, they were highly redacted and reworked composites of earlier materials, largely of unknown provenance and of dubious historical reliability. The facile literalism of fundamentalism and its doctrine of scriptural inerrancy are simply untenable in the face of what is known about the Bible.

Biblical fundamentalism is therefore flatly refuted by science and by biblical scholarship. Its defenders try to prop it up with creationist pseudoscience and junk apologetics, but the Bible is not, and cannot be made into a textbook of science or history. I also found fundamentalism viscerally repellent. It allied with the most extreme political conservatism, while I leaned toward the antiestablishment, anti–Vietnam War radicalism of the day. Also, fundamentalism, despite its glib proclamations of God's love, seemed (and still seems to me) basically mean-spirited and intolerant, with inherent tendencies toward fanaticism, hypocrisy, and self-righteousness.

I therefore tried to rethink my Christian commitment in terms inspired at various times by Rudolf Bultmann's demythologizing, Camus and Sartre's existentialism, and Paul Tillich's philosophical theology. In the fall of 1974, looking for answers, I took off to Emory University's Candler School of Theology in Atlanta, Georgia. Paris remained on the conservative side and went to Southwestern Baptist Seminary in Fort Worth, Texas. Geographically separated and finding ourselves irreconcilably theologically divided, we had little contact with each other during those years.

Unfortunately, I found the kind of Christianity taught and practiced at Candler to be no more intellectually or spiritually satisfying than the fundamentalism I had fled. While I deeply admired the intellect and scholarship of my professors at Candler, I simply could not understand what Christianity meant to them. It seemed to me that once the supernatural element had been taken out, all that remained of Christian belief was a free-floating attitude of reverence with no clear referent or intentional object. *What* was the object of belief? Put another way, they seemed to be practicing a kind of secular humanism that was "Christian" only in the sense that they continued to respond emotionally to elements of Christian preaching and liturgy. One professor explained that he "resonated" to the words and symbols of Christian worship (like a struck bell, I guess). So, Christianity now appeared to me as a choice between hateful, crackpot fundamentalism and vapid, pointless "liberalism." There are alternatives between these extremes, as Paris explains above, but at the time there seemed to me to be no viable *via media*.

At this point two things happened to me: personal crises (the usual young-adult *Sturm und Drang*) and intellectual awakening in the form of the discovery of the writings of Bertrand Russell. In Russell I found an intellect of astonishing power, penetration, and clarity. After the turgid German theology and fuzzy French existentialism that I had been reading, Russell's pellucid prose was like the voice of reason. Russell led me from the dark groves of theology into the brilliant yet harsh light of analytic philosophy. Finding that theological obscurity and cant could not survive in that light, and that my personal problems were not salved by religion, but only by my own efforts, the remnants of my faith crumbled like rotten wood. At age twenty-four I became an atheist, and my intellectual and personal experiences in the forty plus years since have only strengthened that commitment.

What is the intellectual basis of my atheism? For me, atheism is part of a more inclusive commitment to what is normally, but somewhat vaguely, called "naturalism." I take "naturalism" in a minimalist sense. As I understand it, the thesis of naturalism is that the physical universe is causally closed—that is, the only causes are physical causes. Thus, whatever happens in the physical universe happens due to physical causes and conditions. Full stop. There are no miracles, no supernatural interventions into nature, and no supernatural agents to do the intervening. In principle, therefore, physics can explain everything that happens, from the explosion of a supernova to the passing of a transient thought.

Naturalism in the minimalist sense that I accept does not rule out the existence of nonphysical things or abstract objects, such as possibilities, meanings, patterns, numbers, or sets. However, it denies that anything nonphysical has causal powers. Doing math might give you a headache, but the number seven cannot. The set of even integers cannot vote Republican (or Democratic or independent either). By implication, therefore, naturalism rules out any and all putative supernatural agents or actors, and so it rejects ghosts and goblins as well as gods. In particular, naturalism opposes theism, since theism claims that the natural world, and at least some events in that world, have a personal, supernatural cause—i.e., God.

This causal closure of the physical is not dogmatically asserted; it is a default position, a null hypothesis that can be rejected in the light of argument or evidence. If it can be shown that any event has occurred that (a) *requires* an account or explanation (i.e., it is not reasonably regarded as a brute fact), and (b) that no physical cause or causes can be sufficient for that occurrence, and so only a supernatural cause will do, then naturalism is false.

Of course, many in have in fact tried to prove naturalism wrong. I find that their arguments typically share a standard *modus operandi*. First, the opponents of naturalism conjure a faux sense of mystery, claiming that something is in principle inexplicable in physical terms. Mind, life, objective morality, or the "fine tuning" of the basic physical constants, for instance, are said to present deep, insoluble mysteries for the naturalist. Such realities, or putative realities, cry out for explanation, but the naturalist allegedly can offer none. God is then introduced as the tailor-made solution to the alleged mystery.

My replies to such arguments are always along the same lines: (a) The alleged mystery is no mystery, or (like the origin of life) there is no reason to think that natural science cannot provide a satisfactory answer; and (b) invoking God or some other spiritual entity, like souls, does nothing to solve the supposed problem, but, on the contrary, only makes the mystery final and absolute. For instance, some philosophers, generally theists, argue that, being physical systems, brains cannot think, and that we must therefore posit spiritual souls or disembodied minds to account for mental phenomena. And just how does

30

a soul think, feel, or imagine? Nobody knows; indeed, the question is in principle unanswerable. Gods and souls are simply posited to have the occult powers of doing whatever they are supposed to do. In other words, saying "God did it" or "a soul did it" seems to me a roundabout and ax-grinding way of saying "I have no clue."

As for "fine tuning," the argument is that, of all the possible ultimate, uncaused physical realities that might have been, we were, given naturalism, impossibly lucky to have one that permits our existence. Therefore, there must have been an a supernatural intelligent designer to actualize life-friendly conditions out of those vastly numerous possibilities. My reply is that, by precisely the same reasoning, of all the possible ultimate, uncaused supernatural entities that conceivably could have been, we were impossibly lucky to get one that both wanted our existence and had the power to create and control a physical universe so that it would produce us. *Any* posited ultimate (logically) contingent fact—natural or supernatural—will necessarily be only one of infinitely many alternative realities that were equally logically possible. Sauce for the gander. The upshot, on my view, is that it is meaningless to speak of objective probabilities of ultimate posits. Whatever exists as the ultimate, uncaused reality is neither probable nor improbable. It just is.

The arguments against default naturalism therefore seem to me to fall into two categories—bad and really bad. A further reason that I am an atheist is that there are many, many phenomena, like pediatric cancer, that *prima facie* are not what you would expect to find in a universe supposedly created by an all-powerful and perfectly benevolent being. In general, there is very much undeserved and undesired suffering in the world, both by human beings and nonhuman animals. There are, in other words, very many apparently gratuitous evils—i.e., evils that appear utterly pointless and senseless in that, so far as we can tell (or even imagine), they serve no higher purpose as necessary conditions for redeeming goods. For some evils *no* conceivable good seems good enough to justify them, as Dostoevsky's Ivan notes in *The Brothers Karamazov.*

Also, what kinds of necessary conditions can be imposed on God, an allegedly all-powerful being? Well, even God cannot do the logically impossible; even God cannot make an odd number into an even number. So, is the theist willing to claim that *every* instance of undeserved, undesired, and seemingly pointless suffering is necessary, that is, that *no* such instance could have been omitted by God without necessarily sacrificing the ultimate good (whatever that might be)? The theist would appear committed to such a claim because a *single* genuine instance of gratuitous, irredeemable evil would rule out the existence of an all-powerful and all-benevolent being—i.e., God. After all, an all-benevolent being *would* prevent that evil and an all-powerful being *could* do so. I therefore place my bet that one or more of the innumerable apparently gratuitous evils actually *is* gratuitous, and hence that an all-powerful and perfectly benevolent being does not exist.

Considerations such as these—here expressed very succinctly and roughly—are sufficient to convince me of atheism. For book-length, detailed defenses of atheism, see Nicholas Everitt, *The Non-Existence of God*; J. L. Mackie, *The Miracle of Theism: Arguments for and against the Existence of God*; or Michael Martin, *Atheism: A Philosophical Justification.* For a defense of naturalism in the minimalist sense I support, see Graham Oppy's *Naturalism and Religion.*[1]

It seems to me, then, that there are no good reasons supporting theism and several good ones supporting atheism. Should the arguments for atheism be persuasive for everyone? Can we conclusively rule out any transcendent reality or dimension? No. Reasons such as the above are sufficient for me, but I cannot assume that they would be sufficient for every rational person.

Consider John Hick, who is, in my not-so-humble opinion, the top philosopher of religion going back at least to Hume. Hick's very important book, *An Interpretation of Religion*, argues that the universe is religiously "ambiguous." That is, it may be reasonably interpreted in either a naturalistic or religious way.[2] Hick readily concedes that reality may be viewed as I view it, as physics all the way down. He regards the theistic arguments, in their classical and recent forms, as devoid of cogency, and offers detailed critiques of them.

On the other hand, Hick argues that a religious interpretation of human experience is equally valid—that is, one that acknowledges transcendence. This acknowledgment arises from an encounter with the numinous, a sense of standing in the presence of the holy. Perhaps, if I may add my own gloss, it is the awareness that Wordsworth described best in *Tintern Abbey*:

> . . . And I have felt
> A presence that disturbs me with the joy
> Of elevated thoughts; a sense sublime
> Of something far more deeply interfused,
> Whose dwelling is the light of setting suns,
> And the round ocean, and the living air,
> And the blue sky, and in the mind of man,
> A motion and a spirit, that impels
> All thinking things, all objects of all thought,
> And rolls through all things.

Such experiences occur across cultures and throughout history. They appear to lie very deep in human nature, and are of fundamental significance to those who experience them.

Indeed, many who subscribe to no religious beliefs have such experiences. You do not have to probe far into the reflections of the greatest scientists to find expressions of awe and wonder in the presence of the cosmos, responses that may rightly be termed "religious." How we interpret these experiences will differ from person to person, depending upon the individual and his or her cultural milieu. However, Hick's claim is that it is perfectly reasonable to take these experiences as exactly what they appear to be to many people, that is, as encounters with a transcendent reality, perhaps as an experience of the very presence of God. Speaking personally, I have had such experiences of the numinous and interpreted them in a pantheistic rather than a theistic sense (as I will explain later on), but I can find no epistemic fault in those who take such experiences differently.

Hick's point is that there is a significant degree of interpretive latitude in whether we take a religious or naturalistic view of reality. Neither the atheist nor the theist can offer conclusive proof or decisive evidence that rules out rational disagreement. Where reason can make no final determination, interpretive choice must step in. That is, each of us, guided by our deepest convictions and values and strongest intuitions, must make choices about our fundamental interpretive categories. This should be a rational choice, an informed choice, but it is still a choice.

I choose to interpret the world in a naturalistic way, because my most basic and compelling experiences and cognitions point me in this direction. I could choose differently. I could persist in trying to take the world in a religious context despite all doubts, but eventually such a commitment would become very costly in time, effort, and mental energy. If I tried to be a Christian now, I would be waging a constant battle against cognitive dissonance. I would constantly be patching holes, plugging leaks, and propping up—and perhaps inevitably engaging in some degree of self-deception. Put simply, atheism is the authentic stance for me.

Recognizing, then, that reasonable people of good will will differ deeply in their religious commitments—or lack thereof—provides us with a basis for understanding and a search for common ground, and that is what Paris and I intend to do here. We will pursue a path that, we hope, will converge in the discovery of shared values, thereby showing just how much secular and religious people can have in common. We see this as a very important message in a cultural milieu that is badly polarized and balkanized.

Perhaps at rock bottom all human beings share basic concerns and values. Like Aristotle, I think that they do. We value the health, security, and well-being of ourselves and our loved ones. We recognize standards of basic decency, justice, and fairness, and we have capacities for empathy and benevolence. Yet the words we use are all too often filled with anger and contempt. Extremist ideologies and overheated rhetoric dominate our public discourse, making it easy to sneer and hard to empathize.

In the often acrimonious confrontations between religious and nonreligious people, both sides energetically fan the flames. I contribute to a blog called the *Secular Outpost* that promotes discussion of religious and philosophical issues. Recently, the site had to impose a strict policy of moderation because discussions between atheists and Christians all too often degenerated into mutual insult and abuse. The "religious right" has long demonized atheists and secular people, and militant atheists have returned the favor.

In the past decade or so we have seen the rise of what is called the "new" atheism, which encompasses the writings of such authors as Sam Harris, Richard Dawkins, Christopher Hitchens, and Jerry Coyne. While I think that, with some revision and logical tightening, many of the arguments of the "new atheists" are solid, they seem to me far too quick to tar all believers with the same brush. It is true that fundamentalists, fanatics, creationists, theocrats, and religious bigots all deserve criticism and often condemnation. However, it simply is not the case that all religious believers are either fools or knaves, yet this is the impression that the new atheists often convey. Further, I know from personal experience that some atheists are as "fundamentalist" in their attitudes as any Bible-beating street preacher, and are viciously hostile to any atheist who is not as hardline as they.

I am an unapologetic defender of the "old" atheism—that is, atheism that is long on argument and does not waste time on calumny or ad hominem. I developed my atheist convictions under the tutelage of such philosophers as J. L. Mackie, Antony Flew, Kai Nielsen, Wallace Matson, and Michael Martin, authors who were content to refute theistic arguments, and felt no need to add dollops of insult. As I say, it seems obvious to me that many religious believers are rational and decent people who, like me, are following their best lights in traversing this vale of tears. If we truly acknowledge this fact, and do not merely pay it lip service, then we have a basis for mutual understanding.

SECTION I
UNTRUTH AND ITS CONSEQUENCES

WHAT IS TRUTHFULNESS?

KEITH PARSONS

> *Truth is saying of what is, that it is, and of what is not,*
> *that it is not.*
>
> —Aristotle, *Metaphysics*

think we should begin by asking, "What is truthfulness?" Why "truthfulness"? Why not "What is truth?" After all, we are talking about the value of truth, so why not begin by defining "truth"? The reason is that philosophers have struggled mightily to define truth and, though theories have proliferated, there is no consensus.[1] Philosophers have proposed that truth be understood as the correspondence of propositions with facts, or as a state of maximal coherence among a body of propositions, or as the efficacy of beliefs in satisfying our long-term desires. Other philosophers propose the radically deflationary view that any assertion of the form "p is true" is just a redundant way of asserting "p." Thus, "It is true that snow is white" is just a verbose way of saying "snow is white." Still others see the whole idea of truth as vacuous and irrelevant. Unsurprisingly, these debates quickly become very technical, and, to non-philosophers, seemingly arcane.

Why has it been so hard to reach agreement about so basic a notion as truth? The reason is that the most basic notions—like truth, love, or goodness—are always the hardest to define precisely. Also, philosophers set a very high standard for definition. A completely satisfactory philosophical definition would have to specify a set of necessary and sufficient conditions that would apply in every conceivable case. It may be impossible to provide strict criteria for truth, except for artificial languages of the sort developed in formal logic. It may be that in natural languages, like English, French, or Russian, the use of locutions such as "true" and its cognates is irreducibly diverse and that there can be no rigorous definition that would not entail conditions that unduly restrict what we are allowed to say. Sometimes we just have to put up with a degree of ambiguity or vagueness, and depend upon context and good sense to keep things straight. As a philosopher, I naturally think that philosophical debate, with its emphasis on rigor and precision, is important and illuminating even when, as is generally the case, it does not lead to consensus. However, the details of the technical issues concerning the definition of truth need not detain us here.

For my money, the most useful and plausible definition of truth is the one given by Michael P. Lynch in his insightful book *True to Life: Why Truth Matters.*[2] Lynch offers a "functional" definition of truth. Some things exist to perform particular functions; that function is *why* they exist, whether they are natural things like kidneys or artificial things like generators. A kidney is something that filters the blood and a generator is something that produces electricity. The specific design and physical constitution of a kidney or a generator is not what primarily defines such things, but, rather, the *job* that they do.

Consider a proposition, which, for our purposes, we will just equate with a declarative sentence—e.g., "Austin is the capital of Texas." What is the function of a proposition? A proposition has the function of informing. It does its job when it *does* inform—i.e., when it correctly tells us what is or is not the case. A true proposition is therefore one that performs its function of "telling it like it is"—of accurately informing us of what is or is not the case, as Aristotle noted in the quote at the beginning of this section. For instance, by telling us that Austin is the capital of Texas when (and only when) Austin *is* the capital of Texas, the proposition "Austin is the capital of Texas" is true. True propositions, then, like kidneys or generators, are things that do their assigned jobs. So what is truth? "Truth" is an abstract noun, but it really is just the property of *being true* that propositions have in virtue of doing their job of representing accurately.

I think that for our purposes here, we may simply assume Lynch's definition of truth. It seems to accord very well with our commonsense and ordinary understanding of truth and falsehood. For one thing, we know that functions can be performed fully, partially, or not at all. A proposition, then, might be wholly true, partially true, or not true at all, depending upon the degree to which if performs or fails to perform its function. This is consistent with our recognition that the simple binary opposition of true and false is not sufficiently nuanced. For instance, in addition to propositions that are simply true or simply false, there are half-truths, prevarications, and equivocations. There are statements that, while technically true, are more misleading than outright lies. On the other hand, a satirical representation, while not strictly accurate, can sometimes convey truth more deeply and vividly than a straightforward description.

In most contexts we know with tolerable clarity what it is to speak truly and what it is to speak untruly. We know what it is to report things fully, fairly, and accurately or, on the other hand, to misrepresent, mislead, or obscure. Therefore, what we need to know here is not so much how to define truth, but what makes it so valuable—and this will be our emphasis. In that case, what we need to get clear about is not truth *per se*, but the virtue of truthfulness and the vice of untruthfulness. Why speak of "truthfulness" as a virtue when there is already a perfectly good word—"honesty"—for the virtue of being truthful? Because if you value truth it is not enough merely to embrace honesty as a personal habit; you must also hold others accountable when they lie or mislead. A respecter of truth will neither lie nor tolerate lies.

One who practices truthfulness will become familiar with the many tricks and sophistries used by those who want to hide, distort, or slant the truth, such as the fallacies listed in textbooks on informal logic. For instance, a defender of truth should learn to recognize when a speaker distracts attention from an argument by attacking the arguer (ad hominem) or muddies the waters by employing emotionally charged or biased terms. Everyone who values truth over obfuscation should carefully study George Orwell's classic essay "Politics and the English Language."[3] That essay shows how ax-grinders can drape the naked truth behind obscuring layers of pretentious verbiage. You don't kill your enemy; you "neutralize hostile elements." Finally, those who seek truth must become aware of the many ways that we can deceive ourselves, even with the best of intentions. Researchers such as Daniel Kahneman and Amos Tversky have shown that humans have built-in tendencies to succumb to a variety of cognitive illusions that require extra diligence to escape.[4]

Those who respect truth also uphold the methods, standards, persons, and institutions that generate knowledge; in short, they honor and defend science and scholarship. In our day, scientists and scholars have produced a mass of facts and well-confirmed theories that tell us more than we have ever known about the universe and ourselves. We are potentially the best-informed society that has ever existed. Yet in recent years we have seen ideologically motivated attacks from both the political left and right on the integrity of scientists and scholars. In the 1980s and '90s, under the banners of postmodernism, social constructivism, and radical feminism, leftist scholars attacked the methods and findings of natural science. From the right, creationists and "intelligent design" theorists have waged a long and bitter campaign against evolutionary science.

Such movements have done enough damage, but the real danger arises when big money joins the fight. Big Tobacco pioneered the way.

In the 1950s, strong scientific evidence was building linking cigarettes to lung cancer. What do you do if the science says that your product is killing hundreds of thousands, yet this very product is making you rich beyond the dreams of avarice? You attack the science, of course. The comic *Dilbert* shows how easy this is. In one strip, evil CEO Dogbert enters a business called "Rent a Weasel." He tells the weasel behind the counter, "I need three bitter and unsuccessful scientists and a hundred lazy journalists." The final frame has Dilbert reading the headline, "Toddlers Thrive on Pollution."[5] Great news if you make money by polluting! We are now in the dire situation described by Naomi Oreskes and Erik M. Conway in *Merchants of Doubt*, where it is big business to generate junk science to protect profits.[6]

Since most members of the public are scientifically ignorant, they cannot tell the difference between junk science and the real thing. What is a layperson to think when one PhD says that adding large amounts of carbon dioxide to the atmosphere is dangerous and another PhD says it is not? In such a case, you are highly susceptible to believing what ideologues tell you. In recent years, right-wing ideology allied with Big Oil and Big Coal to oppose climate science, particularly the evidence for human-caused climate change. Fossil-fuel interests have lavishly funded right-wing "think tanks" that spew misinformation, skewed statistics, and bogus research intended to discredit the inconvenient discoveries of climatologists. Climate-change "skepticism" became a litmus test for true conservatives. Powerful members of Congress, and Scott Pruitt, Trump's former head of the Environmental Protection Agency, deny human-caused climate change, though the overwhelming majority of qualified scientists hold that it is real.[7] When big-money interests ally with ideology to undermine science, they compromise a society's fundamental ability to reach rational decisions.

They say that we live in the Age of Information. Really, we should call it the Age of Disinformation, or, in earthier terms, the Age of

Bullshit. Because we are hyperconnected by the internet and electronic media, bullshit today enjoys advantages vastly greater than in the past. It is an old saying that a lie goes around the world while the truth is still pulling up its trousers. The speed of dark has always been faster than the speed of light. These days, fake news, rumor, pseudoscience, and every form of irrationality and falsehood bounce around online echo chambers and instantly become so deeply entrenched that truth hardly has a chance. For instance, the idea that vaccines cause autism is as thoroughly debunked as any bogus claim can be, but anti-vaccine activists keep it alive on their blogs and websites.[8]

This is not the worst of it. Those whose livelihoods depend upon your beliefs, such as politicians and advertisers, have perfected techniques that are wickedly effective in manipulating opinion. Most politicians are adept at spin. Spin is not a simple lie; anybody can lie, but it takes real cleverness to spin effectively. Spin is telling something that, technically, is the truth, but telling it in a way that misleads. George W. Bush was a master of spin. Donald Trump does not even bother to spin; he goes straight for the big lie. Big liars loudly repeat blatant falsehoods until, by sheer repetition, they become accepted as truth. Finally, catch phrases, code words, buzz words, and slogans fill the air, and, if you let them, they will do your thinking for you. You will start mouthing things like "Make America great again!" and come to think that you are actually saying something.

In conclusion, truthfulness is the virtue of being vigilant for truth. Of course it involves being scrupulously honest in what you say and do. You have to have a visceral hatred of lies. More than that, truthfulness motivates you to require others to respect truth, especially pundits, politicians, and everyone who contributes to public discourse. You will not be silent when the purveyors of lies and claptrap do their dirty work. You call them out in no uncertain terms. When spin doctors and message managers try to excuse such lies, you call them out too.

Further, you oppose the merchants of doubt who serve big-money interests by generating junk science and undermining legitimate research. You should oppose ideologues on either the left or the right who denigrate science in order to promote their doctrinal infatuations. Finally, you become aware of all the subtle ways that bullshit can permeate and vitiate our thinking, and you determine to oppose irrationality in all of its forms.

WHAT IS TRUTHFULNESS?

PARIS DONEHOO

"What is truth?"

When Pontius Pilate addressed his question to Jesus (John 18:38), he expressed more than mere frustration at a peasant Galilean who was interrupting his day. He framed an issue that has puzzled people of integrity throughout the centuries. In an era when the difference between "real news" and "fake news" depends upon who shrieks the loudest, a working definition of truth seems as elusive as capturing the wind. In addition, the old rules, traditions, and standards of behavior have broken down, leaving our culture without a sense of mooring and balance, or, at least, without an illusion of mooring and balance.

So "What is truth?" Perhaps the place to start is by defining what sort of truth we seek to address. Can our truth claim be examined under a microscope, viewed through a telescope, or recreated in a test tube? Some realities appear to be self-evident or can be objectified. My boyhood Superman costume was careful to print this disclaimer on the shirttail: "Remember: This suit will NOT make you fly. Only Superman can fly." Evidently, the manufacturers had observed enough of the effects of gravity to affirm what would surely happen if I donned my costume and jumped off the roof of the house.

I doubt, however, that Pilate's question was prompted by a confusion regarding physics. His was a search for meaning, which is, of course, more elusive. Religious truth claims have historically attempted to shape meaning for human beings by giving them a focus for life, and Christian faith is no different. For more than two thousand years, Christian theology has tried to make sense of this world by defining truth for its adherents.

For a Christian, the question *"What* is truth?" cannot be answered until one addresses the question of *"Where* is truth?" I was reared in a Christian tradition that located truth within the pages of the Bible. One prominent preacher, decrying what he perceived as a liberal drift within the denomination, balanced his Bible on the tips of his fingers and shouted, "These seminary professors say they're looking for truth. Well, I'm holding it in my hand!" A careful reading of that book in his hand, however, reveals that the Bible never makes such claims about itself. Yes, certain biblical writers wrap their words in the mantle of truth, but they are either claiming words given to them by God (i.e., the prophets proclamation of "Thus says the Lord . . .") or they are writing to particular people in particular situations (see the Pauline epistles).

A truth claim nestled in the pages of one biblical book cannot be taken as authoritative for the whole. The Bible is a library, a collection of many books written over many centuries to different people in different circumstances. Since the early fourth-century, Christians have considered the books of the Bible to be authoritative for faith and practice, but there has never been agreement over just which books belong in the canon of scripture. When the writer of 2 Timothy 3:16 said, "All scripture is inspired by God," some of the New Testament books had yet to be written, and few were widely accepted as canonical throughout the various Christian communities.

I must stress that I am speaking here from a Christian perspective. Other religious traditions (such as Islam) *do* locate truth within a book. I want to make the case, however, that, for a Christian, truth is not located in a book but in a person—Jesus Christ. Every truth claim must be measured against the teaching and example of Jesus. His was not an invitation to philosophical, theological, or doctrinal assent, but a simple call to walk in his way. He bade those who were interested in following the way to "follow me," and in that living—sometimes blatantly countercultural—they learned the truth:

> "And the Word became flesh and lived among us, and we have seen his glory, the glory as of a father's only son, full of grace and truth." (John 1:14)
>
> "Jesus said to him, 'I am the way, and the truth, and the life.'" (John 14:6)
>
> "This is the Spirit of truth, whom the world cannot receive, because it neither sees him nor knows him. You know him, because he abides with you, and he will be in you." (John 14:17)

I realize this sounds like a circular argument—i.e., the Bible is not truth but we know about Jesus from the Bible. I answer in two ways. First, Christians believe one can have a relationship with God in Christ through the presence of the Holy Spirit: "When the Advocate comes, whom I will send to you from the Father, the Spirit of truth who comes from the Father, he will testify on my behalf" (John 15:26). The nonbeliever may discount such a relationship as wishful thinking or self-delusion, but Christians have always claimed the promise of Jesus in Matthew 28:20, "I am with you always, to the end of the age." This personal relationship with Christ means one can never drop anchor in faith. Truth is always evolving and changing to meet the needs of a new day, while remaining firmly rooted in the Jesus model. The United Church of Christ captured the spirit of this dynamic truth when it adopted as its slogan the words of the late Gracie Allen, "Never place a period where God has placed a comma."[1]

Second, the church *at its best* can be a truth-practicing community. I emphasize the words "at its best" because I am under no illusion about the church's checkered past. Like non-Christians everywhere I am appalled and embarrassed by the Crusades, the Inquisition, the Salem witch trials, and the legacy of racial violence and hatred perpetrated by American Southerners who, like myself, claimed to be Christians. As a pastor, I have seen parishioners behave in ways diametrically opposed to the example of Jesus. And yet I have also seen the congregations actually become the Church from time to time. I have seen them support one another through times of difficulty and doubt. I have seen them encourage one another to explore new thinking and risk challenging forms of service. I have seen them hold one another accountable, ensuring that one of their number does not depart for the nether regions of theology or practice. During my student days I became convinced God was leading me to transfer away from my secular college to a more Bible-based school. My pastor and others in my home church gently persuaded me of the error of such a path. To this day I remain grateful for their guidance. What I believed to be truth would have been a terrible mistake for me.

So I will not excuse the church's sinful actions, nor will I apologize for the constructive effect it can have on a Christian's practice of truth. Of course, all these musings would be merely esoteric ruminations to those outside Christian faith, as well as "in-house" language to Christian believers, were it not for the current intersection of public policy and religious truth claims. Donald Trump claims to be a Christian. I cannot look into his heart and judge his relationship with God, but I can listen to his speech as well as watch his actions, and I can measure them against the example of Jesus. When queried as to whether he ever asked God's forgiveness for his actions, Trump said, "I am not sure I have. I just go on and try to do a better job from there. I don't think so . . . I don't bring God into that picture. I don't."[2] How does that square with Jesus instructing us to ask God for forgiveness of our sins (Matthew 6:12)? More importantly, what does that say about humility and decision-making in the White House?

When the president signed an executive order banning Muslims in seven countries from entering the United States, he ignored Jesus's rebuke to his disciples who advocated draconian action on those who were different (Luke 9:52–56). Trump's refusals to pay workers hired for his construction projects (sometimes because he says he did not like their work) cannot be polished to look Christlike when compared to Jesus's parable about laborers who were all paid the same for different amounts of work (Matthew 20:1–16).

Such examples could be written off as the "same old same old" in politics—after all, Trump is not the first president with questionable morals and religious bona fides—if it were not for his embrace by scores of persons who identify themselves as Christians. Somehow a man who brags about groping women, who publicly refers to opponents as "loser," "stupid," and "dummy," who makes a mockery of a reporter's menstrual cycle, and who mocks a disabled reporter has become the standard bearer for Christian truth in the minds of many. Apparently, some who claim to be followers of Jesus decided they can put the example of Jesus aside as long as they get what they want out of Washington. In essence, they have sold their souls for two Supreme Court justices, an embassy in Jerusalem, an assault rifle, and white privilege.

The Bible has a word for all this: Idolatry. When the truth embodied in the life and teaching of Jesus is set aside in favor of "making America great again," we have fooled ourselves into thinking we can serve two masters equally, even though Jesus clearly taught that is not possible (Matthew 6:24). Yes, I am concerned about the policies endorsed in Washington. Yes, I am concerned about the drift toward extreme nationalism. Yes, I am concerned about the rise of winner-take-all politics and scorched earth campaigns. But, at a deeper level, I am more concerned about the lack of integrity that has become commonplace among many of my fellow believers. The church has always had its charlatans and miscreants, but the current situation feels different. As the church in the

West shrinks in size, and as the millennial generation drifts farther and farther away, the time for complacency is over. If nothing else, perhaps this era will force Christians to decide where their real loyalties lie. Is our allegiance to Christ, who embodies truth and bids us to follow in his footsteps? Or is our allegiance to a vision of an America that caters to our convenience? We cannot have it both ways.

ARE WE IN THE POST-TRUTH ERA?

KEITH PARSONS

> *Facts aren't facts; truth isn't true; reality isn't real. This is where we are [in Trump's America].*
> —Kathleen Parker, columnist,
> *Washington Post*, May 12, 2017

> *Power unconstrained by facts is unconstrained by anything.*
> —Leonard Pitts Jr., columnist,
> *Miami Herald*, May 26, 2017

> *Who is this that darkeneth counsel by words without knowledge?*
> —Job 38:2, King James Version

Paris, I think we have a good start. Let me lay out how it seems to me that our approaches are different but congruent. I speak of truth as telling it like it is. Truth, then, is something you speak. You approach truth as something you practice. As you say, "the Church *at its best* can be a truth-practicing community." These sound divergent, but they are not. Truth must be both spoken and lived. One who speaks the truth but does not live it is a hypocrite, and one who speaks lies is doomed to live them. You also talk of truth as meaning, and this is right. Truth always matters, but some truths, deep truths, matter the most. These are the truths that tell us why we live, the truths that make our lives *our* lives by giving them coherence, significance, and direction. Without such truths, life would be trivial and superficial—one damn thing after another. The deepest truths are truths about value, about what is truly worthwhile.

For you and other Christians, the paradigm of the meaningful life is found in the life and teachings of Jesus of Nazareth. The teaching of Jesus is powerful, even for a nonbeliever like me. Here is one of the most powerful things Jesus said: "For what is a man profited, if he shall gain the whole world, and lose his own soul?" (Matthew 16:26, KJV). When you lose your integrity, you lose your soul, and this is a bad bargain, even if what you gain is the presidency of the United States. What is true of an individual is true of a nation. When a people are willing to subordinate truth to ideology, when science and rationality do not matter, and "true" in practice reduces to "what my side wants," then the nation's soul is lost. As you trenchantly put it, they become idolaters, worshipping false gods of greed, nationalism, bigotry, and partisanship: "In essence, they have sold their souls for two Supreme Court Justices, an oil pipeline, an embassy in Jerusalem, an assault rifle, and white privilege."

Are we there yet? Are we in a post-truth age? I think so. Let me justify that claim by telling part of the history of that descent.

Of course, politicians have always lied, deceived, and resorted to dirty tricks. As you know, Herodotus was called the "Father of History" by his admirers, and the "Father of Lies" by his detractors. He tells a terrific story about Pisistratus, the tyrant of Athens in the sixth century BCE. Whether this story is historical or not, it tells us a lot about how politicians operated, even more than 2,500 years ago. Having been booted out of Athens once, Pisistratus schemed to get back in power. He found a beautiful and unusually tall young woman, whom he decked out in fine clothes, a war helmet, and shining armor. She rode with him into Athens in a gilded chariot. Runners preceded the duo, calling out to the gaping Athenians that Athena herself was bringing Pisistratus back to assume his rightful position. Though even Herodotus doubts that the Athenians would have been that gullible, whatever Pisistratus did, it worked, and he returned to power.[1]

A century later, at the height of the Athenian democracy, Athens was rife with "sophists," such as Protagoras and Gorgias. The sophists were professional teachers of rhetoric who, for a fat fee, would teach ambitious young men how to speak eloquently and persuasively in public. Athens was a democracy, so to be in charge you had to get a majority of the suckers—er, voters—on your side. According to their harshest critic, Plato, the sophists were sleazy characters who employed what today we call "sophistry," that is, the use of specious arguments to "make the worse appear to be the better cause."[2] If there is any truth in Plato's charges, there is no question that aspirants to high public station in Athens would have gladly paid the sophists' fees to learn all the tricks of demagoguery. Lies and trickery for political gain are therefore as old as politics, and the techniques of deception were already well advanced by the fifth century BCE.[3]

Yet things are worse now than ever. Lies are now weaponized, as Daniel J. Levitin puts it in his excellent exposé of the tactics of manipulation in the post-truth era.[4] Liars now know how to employ many advanced techniques that exploit the discoveries of psychology and neuroscience to make us unwitting accomplices in our own deception. Mass manipulation of public opinion is now a science. Manipulators know our weaknesses and that is where they hit us. For instance, we humans are remarkably bad at the comprehension and analysis of large quantities of numerical information.[5] We are visual thinkers. We need graphs, charts, and pictures, not tables of data. A good graph or chart can make complex data comprehensible, but a dishonest chart can create a visual impression that is the opposite of truth. For instance, suppose there has been a 5 percent rise in crime. You can graph that 5 percent rise so that it looks terrifying or like no big deal, depending on your motives. Today's society, unlike ancient Greece, is heavily dependent upon numerical information, and we are particularly vulnerable to the manipulation of such information.

Yet the manipulation of statistical information is only one small item in the well-stocked toolkit of today's liars. A few years ago I wrote a book called *Rational Episodes: Logic for the Intermittently Reasonable* (please pardon the shameless self-promotion!).[6] Over a third of the book addresses such topics as rhetoric, spin, fallacies, bogus "studies," and pseudoscience. These chapters detail the ways that misinformation and disinformation can be dressed up, like Pisistratus's fake Athena, to look like the real thing. There are some very smart people who know how to push your "belief" buttons and get you (literally or figuratively) to buy into their products. In fact, the manipulation of opinion is big business. Advertisers, public relations firms, politicians, and ideologues invest heavily in the manipulation of opinion. Such persons are not necessarily unscrupulous. On the other hand, they are not necessarily scrupulous, either. When there is a strong enough motivation to control belief, inevitably, all means of persuasion are used, both fair and foul.

Are things worse now? Or is this just the grousing of a confessed curmudgeon? Well, if it is grousing, I am not the only one doing it. Numerous books in recent years have bemoaned, and documented, the "dumbing down" of American culture—that is, the intensification of the anti-intellectualism classically chronicled in Richard Hofstadter's *Anti-Intellectualism in American Life.*[7] Among the recent studies of growing gullibility, deepening ignorance, declining attention spans, deteriorating critical thinking skills, and increasing disrespect for science and expertise are *Unscientific America* by Chris Mooney and Sheril Kirshenbaum, and *The Dumbest Generation* by Mark Bauerlein.[8]

My personal favorite of this genre is *Idiot America* by Charles P. Pierce.[9] Pierce's hilarious and horrifying commentary argues that, while America, with its free speech traditions, has always been a good place to be a crackpot, it used to be much harder to make a career out of it. As long as they remain outsiders, cranks play a valuable role, says Pierce. They mark the boundaries of rational discourse, as the dragons on old maps marked *terrae incognitae*. Besides, every now and then, they have an idea that turns out right. But when cranks are mainstreamed, then, for all practical purposes, there is no mainstream, and consequently no fringe either. All discourse reduces to its market value; it is worth what it will get you. Rationality, logic, evidence, and all the old values of objectivity become irrelevant. Science reduces to opinion. The expert's judgment carries no more authority than a radio loudmouth's. The operant definition of "true" becomes "what my gut tells me," and, as Pierce observes, your gut is your inner idiot.

Pierce is right. Goofiness once relegated to the lunatic fringe is now mainstreamed. The Republican Party now countenances the sort of nuttiness that, fifty years ago, emanated only from the likes of the John Birch Society. In our lifetimes, we have seen the Republican Party go from a moderate/conservative party, to a very conservative party, to a party of ideological extremism, to a party of downright lunacy, tolerant even of wildly irrational claims, such as the "birther" nonsense, conspiracy theories about the "deep state," and the "alt right" neo-fascism.

Here is an incident you may have heard about: When the US Army conducted exercises codenamed "Jade Helm 15" in Texas during the summer of 2015, far-right conspiracy sites exploded with paranoid fears. Instead of laughing at this preposterousness, Greg Abbott, the governor of Texas, played up to it by saying that he would ask the Texas State Guard (a volunteer organization) to "keep an eye" on the Army.[10] Apparently, there is no right-wing silliness so extreme that Republican politicians will not at least play footsie with it. By the way, no one needs to take the word of a sour old liberal like me on the lurch of the GOP to crazy town. Mike Lofgren was a Republican staffer for twenty-eight years in Washington before he quit and wrote the book *The Party Is Over* about how the party he once knew has taken a sharp right turn into extremism and irrationality.[11]

Do only Republicans lie? Of course not. Politicians are politicians, and even a Pericles, a Lincoln, or a Churchill can play a mean shell game with truth. I tell my classes not to accept *any* statistics from *any* politician until they have checked them out from independent sources. Lyndon Johnson's manufacture of the Gulf of Tonkin "incident" may have been the most damaging lie in the history of the United States since it was used to justify the escalation of American involvement in Vietnam. Yet that was a clumsy lie and would never have been bought a few years later when the public had been made more cynical by Vietnam and Watergate. When the public becomes more cynical and skeptical, liars have to improve their game, and more effective techniques have to be developed. Lies have to be weaponized.

When it comes to the deployment of weapons-grade lies, nobody does it better or with more deadly effect (literally) than recent Republican presidents. The Constitution grants the president of the United States vast, though limited, executive power, but his cultural impact is now virtually unlimited. The 24/7 cable news cycle means that the president is literally in the news all day every day. He has an ability to influence opinion that no pope ever enjoyed. When George H. W. Bush made a disparaging remark about broccoli, hundreds of millions of people instantly heard about it, to the understandable alarm of broccoli growers. In a hyperconnected world, whatever the US president says today can be breakfast conversation in Botswana tomorrow. Thus, when the president lies about important things, this is a very, very serious matter. The presidency is a pulpit like no other in history. So, let me trace our national descent into the post-truth era by outlining the recent history of presidential mendacity.

Let's begin with Ronald Reagan or St. Ronnie as he is portrayed in the hagiography of the right. Actually, when it came to zeal for truth, Reagan was not exactly a saint. His remarks frequently were rife with "stretchers," as Huck Finn would have called them. Though Reagan's admirers called him "the great communicator," author Mark Green suggests "the great prevaricator."[12] Reagan's most infamous untruth was his tale about the "Welfare Queen," as the *Chicago Tribune* dubbed her. In 1976, as quoted in the *New York Times*, Reagan, in highest dudgeon, reported on a Chicago woman who, he claimed, had eighty aliases, thirty addresses, twelve Social Security cards, and collected veterans' benefits from four nonexistent deceased husbands. She had Medicaid, food stamps, and collected welfare under each of her names, giving her a tax-free cash income of $150,000 (over $600,000 in today's inflation-adjusted dollars).[13]

Wow! What an outrage! Hard-working Americans were understandably livid. Clearly, if the welfare system permitted such egregious abuses, it had to go. The problem is that Reagan had stretched the truth so far that his tale bore little relation to reality. As Josh Levin reported in a 2013 story in *Slate*, Linda Taylor, the woman who was the basis for the "Welfare Queen" story, was a genuinely despicable criminal, and was sent to prison for welfare fraud after her 1977 trial.[14] However, as of 1976, when Reagan was spreading his tale, Taylor had not yet been convicted, and she was charged with having four aliases, not eighty, and of fraudulently collecting $8,000, not $150,000. This was bad, of course, but nothing of the outrageous proportions of Reagan's fable. More importantly, even if Reagan's anecdote had been 100 percent true, it could not have shown that welfare cheating was common or widespread. In fact, it was classical rabble rousing, intended to inflame resentment toward welfare recipients, and, since welfare recipients were stereotyped as African American (Taylor's race was ambiguous), the racial subtext was clear. That saint's halo is looking a bit lopsided and tarnished in retrospect.

Reagan's misinformed (to put it charitably) assertions got really scary when dealing with nuclear weapons. In 1981 he said that the United States had "unilaterally disarmed" in the 1970s. In fact, the reverse is true.[15] In 1982 Reagan said that ship-borne nuclear missiles can be recalled. They cannot. When you are talking about thermonuclear weapons, you really, really need to know what you are talking about.

Reagan sometimes intentionally misled, as, perhaps, with the "Welfare Queen," but, generally, his departures from truth seemed to be sins of omission, products of intellectual laziness rather than deceitful intent. Instead of checking the facts, he just relied on ideology, hazy memories, and wishful thinking. Compared to the weaponized lying of later presidents, Reagan's falsehoods look relatively venial.

Fast forward to the administration of George W. Bush and Dick Cheney. Here, Machiavellian ruthlessness replaces Reagan's lazy fantasies and fibs. For the Bush administration, lying was a martial art. Cheney is often depicted as the spider at the center of the web of lies, but so pervasive, deep, and proficient was the mendacity of the Bush administration, that no one person, however malignant, can be held responsible. Even fundamentally decent people, like Colin Powell and Condoleezza Rice were suborned. When Rice would publicly testify in the lead-up to the Second Gulf War, you could see on her face the struggle as her innate honesty fought against her will to lie. Each time I would silently urge her not to give in to the dark side and to repudiate the lies, but she always lied anyway.

Deception was the dark heart of the Bush administration. It had to be. To see why, consider the one most honest thing George W. Bush ever said. When speaking to a group of wealthy supporters, the "haves and have mores" as Bush quipped, he stated frankly, " I call you my base."[16] Exactly. The one overriding and consistent goal of the Bush administration was to help the rich get richer. However, you cannot tell the American voters that this is your goal, since "No billionaire left behind" is not a slogan that plays in Peoria. You must, for instance, disguise tax cuts for the wealthy as tax cuts for the middle class. Every break for the über-wealthy and large corporations had to be spun as a benefit for ordinary Americans.

Then there was the war against Saddam Hussein. The neoconservatives surrounding Bush had been advocating war with Iraq for years. Hussein was a true villain, a tin pot Stalin who would resort to any brutality, but villainy alone was not a sufficient reason to attack him. Bush needed a pretext. Then 9/11 happened. Hussein had absolutely nothing to do with those attacks, which were perpetrated by al-Qaeda, an organization that despised Hussein and was despised by him. The administration endorsed dubious stories of contacts between Iraqi intelligence and al-Qaeda operatives, but even that was not a sufficient excuse for war. Hussein needed to pose an imminent danger, and so his weapons of mass destruction came to be. Only, those terrible arsenals did not exist in reality, but only in the fevered imaginations of Cheney, Bush, and the neocons. Nevertheless, this falsehood was relentlessly promoted, and anyone who cast doubt was viciously vilified. Nor, as was later claimed by Bush apologists, was the administration the victim of bad intelligence. Rather, the intelligence was manipulated and distorted to fit the claim.[17]

What most characterized the untruths of the Bush administration was not merely their pervasiveness, but their sophistication. Anybody can lie. That takes no skill, but it takes a really clever propagandist to spin, to say what is technically true and make it more deceptive than any outright lie. It is possible to say nothing but the truth, but to say it in such a way that it creates an intended misunderstanding. In one of the *Pink Panther* movies, Peter Sellers, playing the bumbling Inspector Clouseau, addresses a gentleman with a dog sitting quietly at his feet and asks, "Does your dog bite?" The man answers "No," and, of course, the dog mauls Clouseau's hand when he reaches to pet it. "I thought that you said that your dog does not bite!" Clouseau angrily remonstrates. "That is not my dog," is the placid reply.[18] The trick is to withhold crucial information, knowing that your listener will make an incorrect assumption, and that assumption is precisely the one you want him to make.

For instance, you sell a tax plan with sumptuous benefits to the top 1 percent by telling a story, technically true, of how a waitress earning $22,000 would pay no taxes on your plan. However, you omit the relevant information that someone making $22,000 a year probably *already* has no income-tax liability. The listener hears only that the plan will help a low-income worker and neglects that its main purpose is to give huge cuts to the rich. Like Rumpelstiltskin spinning straw into gold, the Bush team could spin truth into pure obfuscation.[19]

Another way to spin is to manage images. The most remarkable instance of this was when, on May 1, 2003, Bush landed in a military jet on the deck of the aircraft carrier *Abraham Lincoln*. Alighting in his flight suit to the cheers of the assembled sailors and marines, Bush strutted to the podium. Behind and above his head was an enormous banner reading "Mission Accomplished." This elaborately staged piece of theater, designed to create the impression of decisive and successful war leadership, made Americans want to snap to attention and salute. Of course, the agony in Iraq was just beginning and would drag on for several murderous years.

The nature of presidential lying changed greatly from Reagan to Bush, and again from Bush to Trump. For Reagan, lying was an omission. For Bush, it was a strategy. For Donald Trump, truth is simply irrelevant. Trump says whatever he thinks will help close the deal. For Trump, truth is not even an inconvenience; he does not even bother to dissemble, spin, or equivocate. His lies are weaponized, but not by clever subterfuges, as they were for Bush, but simply by their sheer volume, repetition, and the promiscuity of their utterance. If Trump thinks that it useful to say that Mexican immigrants are criminals and rapists, then that is what he says. The fact that first-generation immigrants, whether here legally or not, have a *lower* rate of criminality than US citizens could not matter less to Trump.[20] When called out for his lies, he just lies louder. His first press secretary, Sean Spicer, used all the classic techniques of double-talk to deflect criticism of his boss—changing the subject, ad hominem attack, word-salad gibberish, verbose misdirection, feigned incomprehension, and so on. Trump does not even bother. Truth/falsehood is not for him a meaningful distinction; for him, the only significant distinction is between getting what he wants and not getting it.

To catalog all of Trump's lies during his campaign and presidency would require far more space than we have here. They range from the petty and petulant (the crowd for his inauguration was the biggest ever), to the fatuously egotistical (he knows more about ISIS than the generals), to the demagogic (he will bring back lost manufacturing jobs), to the delusional (Mexico will pay for the border wall), to the paranoid (Obama wiretapped Trump Towers). Once in office, Trump's lying only increased. As of this writing, less than six months into Trump's presidency, two reporters for the *New York Times*, David Leonhardt and Stuart A. Thompson, have attempted to catalog every lie that Trump has publicly spoken since taking his oath of office. My downloaded copy is over five pages long, single spaced, with twelve-point font, and once again we see Trump's propensity to lie about anything and everything.[21]

When you lie for just any reason, even when lying is silly, pointless, or contrary to your interests, then lying has become pathological, and the sickness takes a terrible toll. The pathological liar has lived in lies for so long that he can no longer tell when he is speaking the truth and when he is fabricating. Inevitably, the line between reality and fantasy is blurred. Here is reality: The man with the codes for the thermonuclear arsenal of the United States is prone to mistaking fantasy for reality.

To sum up: Reagan neglected truth; Bush subverted it; Trump has forgotten what it is.

In parallel with this history of presidential mendacity, were the astonishing developments in personal technology. When Reagan was elected to his second term in 1984, personal computers—very crude ones by today's standards—were first getting poplar. The internet, social media, smart phones, email, and text messaging did not exist. One effect of our current obsession with such technology has been to give us instant access to information. Or disinformation. Millions now get their news from internet sources, and this allows them to hear only what they want to hear.

Paris, you may remember that my dad was a newspaperman. Every day when he came home from work, he had copies of the *Atlanta Journal* and the *Atlanta Constitution*. In those days, the role of a newspaper was to print the news and raise hell. The front page of the *Constitution* often carried editorials by the South's leading journalistic hell-raiser, Ralph McGill. McGill would frequently outrage segregationist readers with his uncompromising support of the Rev. Martin Luther King Jr. and civil rights. Mercurial restaurateur (and future governor of Georgia) Lester Maddox used to wield an ax handle to chase black folks out of his establishment. Regularly, though, he would take a break and sit down to write a foaming philippic in reply to McGill, which he would pay to have published in the papers. In those days, when you read the paper you read things you might not like, and points of view that might make you queasy. That was a good thing. Today, ax-grinders have indoctrinated their followers with deep distrust of the mainstream media, and encouraged them to get their news from echo chambers where party lines rule. The result is that people live in information bubbles where they see, hear, and speak nothing but the ideologically pure message. When truth tries to penetrate ideological armor, it is like attacking a battleship with a BB gun. Someone once said of "tea-party" types, "They will believe anything you tell them. Except the truth." Precisely.

So, here we are in the post-truth era.

ARE WE IN THE POST-TRUTH ERA?

PARIS DONEHOO

You and I have both reached the age when we can look back over many decades and assess where our society has been and where it appears to be now. In doing so, I cannot help but agree with you. We are living in a post-truth era. My question, however, is whether things are worse now than they have ever been. Having been raised in the waning days of the Jim Crow South, and the tumultuous years of the Civil Rights movement, we both were no strangers to lies disseminated in the public square. I remember a grainy black-and-white photo of Martin Luther King Jr. sitting in the front row of an interracial crowd "proving" that the civil rights leader had attended a communist training school. In actuality, it was the twenty-fifth anniversary of the Highlander Folk School in Tennessee, where King had been invited to speak.[1] Ergo, "fake news" has always been with us.

So perhaps it is a matter of degree and the mixed blessing of the internet. The false claim about King was plastered on billboards, reproduced on primitive copy machines, or churned out by professional printers with a political axe to grind. Even so, the document never gained much attention outside the Deep South. Imagine what the racists of our childhood could have done if they had access to email, texting, Facebook, Twitter, and the host of other social media available today. Politicians and other leaders have always resorted to what Kellyanne Conway called "alternative facts," but they can now be disseminated worldwide in microseconds. Given Trump's amazing capacity for lighting up the internet with late-night tweets and outrageous speech, a case could be made that things are worse than they have ever been.

From a Christian standpoint, however, the world has been living in a post-truth era almost from the beginning. In the second, and oldest, creation story in the book of Genesis, God tells the first man and woman, "You may freely eat of every tree of the garden; but of the tree of the knowledge of good and evil you shall not eat, for in the day that you eat of it you shall die" (Genesis 2:16–17). Seems straight-forward enough. But then along comes the serpent (Genesis 3) with a leading question: "Did God say, 'You shall not eat from any tree in the garden'?" The woman replies, "We may eat of the fruit of the trees in the garden, but God said, 'You shall not eat of the fruit of the tree that is in the middle of the garden, nor shall you touch it, or you shall die.'" At this point the serpent presents a different slant on reality. "You will not die," he sneers, "for God knows that when you eat of it your eyes will be opened, and you will be like God, knowing good and evil."

At this point, the man and woman have a choice to make. The presence of the tree is not in dispute, but its meaning is in dispute. The man and woman can choose to believe God's version of the facts, or they can choose to believe the serpent's version of the facts. They must decide whether God has their best interests at heart, or whether God is just hoarding the best stuff. The man and the woman eventually select the second option, and act upon it. And in the acting, in the practice of their choice, paradise is lost forever. Theologians have often said that the essence of sin is disobedience to God, but a closer examination of this primeval parable reveals mistrust to be the essence of sinful behavior. The first humans chose the serpent's interpretation of their situation instead of God's and acted accordingly.[2]

In my judgment, the classic doctrine of original sin obscures this connection between truth and choice. By teaching that sinfulness is somehow hardwired into our DNA because our progenitors plucked and ate forbidden fruit (by the way, the Bible never says it was an apple), the practice of truth is divorced from choice because we humans have no choice. We cannot help behaving badly. Thus, when avowed Christian Greg Gianforte body slams and punches journalist Ben Jacobs two days before his election to the House of Representatives—not exactly a Christlike action—his supporters excuse his behavior as the natural consequence of being provoked by a pesky reporter, and Trump goes a step farther by claiming, "Any guy that can do a body slam—he's my kind of guy."[3] But if his behavior is the result of a choice to assume a malignant intention in the situation—just like the man and woman did in Genesis 3—then truth is as much of a casualty as Mr. Jacobs's broken glasses and injured shoulder.

The truth of the Genesis story, therefore, does not lie in its historicity, but in its repetition throughout history. In my work as a pastor I saw it repeated, metaphorically speaking, over and over. Long before I got the latest news out of Washington I had already witnessed actions occasioned by basic mistrust. Truth becomes nothing more than a commodity serving the serpent's worldview.

For this reason, the story of Jesus's temptation becomes even more crucial for a Christian's practice of truth (Matthew 4 and Luke 4). By the time of the New Testament, the serpent in Genesis 3 has become the devil (due to Israel's exposure to Persian dualism), but he still plays the role of the trickster. He continues to introduce variant interpretations of the situation. To address Jesus's hunger, the devil suggests he use his miraculous power selfishly. To gain a following among the people, he suggests Jesus perform a circus trick to gather a crowd. To accomplish his goal of sweeping change, the devil offers him the entire world for only the low price of Jesus's integrity. In each case, Jesus relies on scripture to keep himself focused on God's interpretation of the situation. He chooses to believe God's intentions are right and offer the best possibility for positive change.

Again, the point is not whether this story is historically verifiable, but whether the story is verifiable in human experience. I believe it is. Whenever people choose to trust there are possibilities for good undergirding our existence, rather than forces seeking our harm, our world has become a little more humane, even godly. Harriet Tubman, for example, ignored the voices telling her it was foolish to rescue slaves from the Antebellum South. Mahatma Gandhi and Martin Luther King Jr. refused to believe that violence was the only way to free oppressed people. I have known ordinary folks who decided to believe one does not have to choose greed, anxiety, and mistrust in order to live in this world, and they left this world a better place.

Jesus said, "The thief comes only to steal and kill and destroy. I came that they may have life, and have it abundantly" (John 10:10). Such a juxtaposition, I believe, may account for a portion of our current social situation. Many of those who claim to follow Jesus have, either inadvertently or deliberately, decided that the thief has a better deal for them. They call themselves Christians while buying into the serpent's view of reality. Throughout my years of ministry I encountered scores of kind-hearted, dedicated people who acted in inspiring, Christlike ways when dealing with persons in need, yet refused to apply those same principles in the voting booth or when advocating public policy.

For example, when Bill Clinton ran for president and then ran for reelection, his opponents succeeded in portraying him as "slick Willy." Unfortunately, his own behavior while in office often fed such a persona. As a result, many Christians—particularly those subscribing to a more conservative theology—claimed that a candidate's character mattered and voted for his opponents in 1992 and 1996. When Donald Trump emerged from the Republican pack ten years later, evidently character did not matter anymore. Even though Trump maintained he was allowed to fondle women because "When you're a star, they let you do it,"[4] claimed he could walk out on the street "and shoot somebody and I wouldn't lose any voters,"[5] and refused to acknowledge the blatant sinfulness of refusing payment to workers with whom he had contracted,[6] still 81 percent of avowed evangelical voters cast their ballots for him—a higher percentage than went to George W. Bush, John McCain, or Mitt Romney.[7]

So much for "character matters."

George Bernard Show famously said, "What a man believes may be ascertained, not from his creed, but from the assumptions on which he habitually acts."[8] Though Shaw was not a religious man, his observation is painfully applicable to our current era, especially when it comes to the practice of Christian faith. It is bad enough when anyone sets aside their core beliefs in favor of selfish goals or political expediency (which are usually intertwined), but when Christians do the same we gain the whole world at the cost of our souls.

Our era is not unique in the sense of a disconnect between professed beliefs and actual practice, but our current situation feels more insidious. Today's lies appear to be based in the logic of George Costanza from *Seinfeld*: "It's not a lie if you believe it."[9] Truth is not a matter of speaking (as you affirm), nor is it a matter of practice (as I claim), but simply a matter of repeating one's beliefs over and over while plugging one's ears, closing one's mind, and drowning out differing opinions in the process. You mentioned your dad (of whom I have fond memories), and the editorials of Ralph McGill displayed prominently on the front page of the *Atlanta Constitution*. My dad also read McGill every day. He rarely agreed with him, but he read him every day. When I expressed an interest in writing as a possible career, it was McGill whom my dad held up as a professional role model.

Sadly, such respect seems to have died with both of our fathers. In our current "echo chamber" society there is no cross-fertilization of ideas. And when truth becomes merely a bludgeon to stamp out differing opinions, everyone loses.

WHAT IS THE VALUE OF TRUTH?

KEITH PARSONS

All humans, by nature, desire to know.
—Aristotle, *Metaphysics*

Anyone who has the power to make you believe absurdities has the power to make you commit atrocities.
—Voltaire, *Questions sur les Miracles,* 1765

Truth: It has no alternative.
—Ad for the *New York Times*

That is a remarkable anecdote about your dad, of whom I have many warm memories, and it makes precisely the point I was getting at in my last section. Your dad had conservative convictions as deep as anyone's, but, unlike today's ideologues, he listened, really listened to the other side. I recall having a long discussion with him after Muhammad Ali refused induction into the military. Your dad thought that this was an inexcusable dereliction of patriotic duty. I argued that it was done in response to a higher duty, the obligation to obey conscience. After the discussion neither of us had accepted the other's claim, but we came away with a deep respect for the integrity, honesty, and intelligence of the other. This is precisely what is so sorely missing in what passes for debate these days, and, in reality, is little more than mutual recrimination.

71

The statistics you cite about the percentage of evangelicals who voted for Trump simply appall me. What the hell happened? When the "Grab them by the [bleep]" tape came out, I thought, "Okay. This is it. The evangelicals can never support such blatant and ugly vulgarity." Yet, I have evangelical relatives, people whose intelligence and decency I fully respect and have never questioned, who voted for a man with a gutter vocabulary and an X-rated mentality. I honestly do not understand it.

By the way, I remember the "Martin Luther King Jr. in communist training school" posters and signs. Nowadays, such odious lies are all over the internet and Facebook with thousands of "likes." Liars never had it as good as they do today.

So, we both agree that truth, telling it like it is, as an ideal, and truthfulness as a virtue, have taken their lumps in recent years, victims of weaponized lying techniques deployed by politicians and powerful special interests. Manipulating opinion and public perceptions is now a science and a big business. When big corporations cause major disasters, they call their lawyers first and their PR firms next. Image management, or good "optics" as they now barbarously call it, is essential for any person or any company that is in the public eye. So, powerful persons and organizations have a big motive to control the message, and they have at their disposal highly effective tools for doing so.

Well, so what? Speaking truth is important only if truth is important. Why is truth so important? Why is it so valuable? What is our obligation to honor it? Why should truth stand in the way of getting what I want? As we noted, for Donald Trump truth has no value whatsoever, unless it happens to be the tool that gets him what he wants. It has no intrinsic value for him. Does truth have intrinsic value, value not just as a means for getting us what we want, but as something, perhaps like love or friendship, that is valuable for its own sake?

I think that it definitely does, but to explain why I need to address a possible source of confusion. In what sense of "truth" do we speak of it as having value? "Truth" is multiply ambiguous. Among its various meanings are these: It can refer to a property of *sentences* or *propositions* and how they relate to *things*, or it can refer to the *things* themselves. It was in the former sense that we said earlier that true propositions are those that function properly by accurately representing things as they are. However, when we say that we want to know "the truth" about something we mean that we want to know about those things themselves, which our true propositions are about. For instance, when we say we want to know "the truth" about the Trump administration's ties to Russia, the truth we seek is what events actually transpired between certain individuals.

In which, if either, of these senses does truth have value, either intrinsic or instrumental? Not necessarily in either. There are many true propositions that mean nothing to us, and there is no reason they should because they are truths that are irrelevant or trivial. "There are exactly 5,426 leaves on the tree outside of your office" may be a true statement. I just made it up for purposes of illustration and the number is arbitrary. By sheer coincidence it could be true, but, even if it is, that truth has no value for me, or, presumably, for anyone. Further, there are many states of affairs that, likewise, have no significance for me or anyone, either because they are unimportant or because there is no way to know them. What Julius Caesar had for breakfast on June 5, 79 BCE might be interesting to know, but I know of no way that we can find out, so that fact can have no significance for us.

What, then, do we mean when we assert that truth is valuable? Basically, we mean that some things are good to know. Truth can be valuable for us only if we can know it, so, it is not truth in the abstract that is valuable, but truth as possessed or potentially possessed— known—by us. Further, not everything knowable is valuable, but some things are, either, as I argue below, because having such knowledge is

73

intrinsically fulfilling for rational beings or because such knowledge is instrumentally valuable in alerting us to dangers and opportunities.

Suppose, then, that we can get some truth. Can such knowledge be an intrinsic good for us, independent of its practical or instrumental value? Yes. I saw a photograph one time that showed me why. It showed a beautiful beta fish, resplendent in a bowl on a table, under intense observation by two intelligent creatures, a big tomcat and a human toddler. You could read their expressions vividly. The tom was glaring with the most serious predatory intent, and the toddler had an expression of rapturous wonder. The tomcat was thinking, "How do I get it?" The toddler was thinking, "How can it *be*?" Cats are predators and fish are prey. End of story. Humans, though, perhaps uniquely in the animal kingdom, have a capacity for sheer wonder and the delight of discovery. It is our glory that we can take joy in just knowing. Cats are famously curious, but their curiosity is a means of reconnoitering their environment for threats or useful information. For us, curiosity is an end in itself. As Aristotle said, "All humans, by nature, desire to know." Those who lose their natural curiosity have lost something precious.

Truth—the whole truth and nothing but the truth—is the object commensurate with the human capacity for wonder. Nothing less is fully adequate. Often, indeed, we may have to settle for less than truth. Many of the laws of nature are idealizations, limiting values, or approximations, not literal truths. Galileo's famous law, $d = \frac{1}{2} gt^2$, stating how far an object will fall from a state of rest in a given time, which is equal to one half times the acceleration due to gravity multiplied by the square of the elapsed time, is strictly true only in an absolute vacuum, which does not exist. The actual rate that things fall is very complex and depends on too many factors for us to grasp, such as the shape of the object, the density of the medium through which it falls, and any other forces that might affect the object, such as air currents. Galileo's law is a compromise between truth and simplicity.

When dealing with very complex phenomena, we have to make concessions to the limitations of our minds, and employ simplified or idealized models, formulas, and maps. The whole field of statistics exists to allow us to make the best approximations when precise knowledge is beyond our capacity. Historians dig for truth with all of their might, but all too often they are left with unanswered questions and an account that can be no more than plausible. Yet even when the obscurity, inaccessibility, or complexity of the facts means that we cannot know the whole or precise truth, we still want to minimize error, even in fields like astronomy or paleontology where "practical" concerns are hardly at stake.

When we can know the pure and complete truth, there is no acceptable substitute, nothing else that truly satisfies our curiosity and gratifies our wonder with its highest reward. Discovery, the encounter with truth after a hard quest, is a moment of holy bliss, as Keats timelessly expressed it in "On First Looking into Chapman's Homer":

> . . . Then felt I like some watcher of the skies
> When a new planet swims into his ken;
> Or like stout Cortez when with eagle eyes
> He stared at the Pacific—and all his men
> Looked at each other with a wild surmise—
> Silent, upon a peak in Darien.

"Stout Cortez" (Balboa, actually) would no doubt have been less amazed had he only discovered a statistical probability that a large body of water lay in this direction.

The experience of coming face-to-face with truth can be awe-inspiring even when the truth is terrifying. Prior to the Trinity test on July 16, 1945, the Manhattan Project scientists had only known about nuclear explosions through their theoretical calculations, chalk on blackboards. Many expected it to fizzle. It did not fizzle. At 5:29

a.m., when the countdown went to zero, and the literally blinding light filled the New Mexico desert, some of the scientists prayed, some wept, and some fell to their knees. J. Robert Oppenheimer famously recalled the words from the Hindu scripture the *Bhagavad Gita*:

> If the radiance of a thousand suns
> Were to burst at once into the sky
> That would be like the splendor of the Mighty One . . .
> I am become Death,
> The destroyer of worlds.

More prosaically, physicist Kenneth Bainbridge described it as "a foul and awesome display."[1]

The poet A. E. Houseman once said "Truth is the faintest of our passions."[2] I beg to differ. Sometimes it is the strongest. How many have willingly faced dungeon, fire, and sword for the sake of their convictions? Or consider today's equivalent of the martyr, the whistleblower who sacrifices career, financial security, and often emotional health for the sake of exposing dangerous truths hidden by powerful organizations. Of course, some truths matter more than others, and, as noted above, some truths, like the number of leaves on the tree outside of my office may be utterly trivial and unimportant. Yet, even with the most trivial truth, what we believe or say about it will not be trivial. If, for some reason, someone were to ask me to guess how many leaves were on the tree outside my window, it would be wrong for me to make up an arbitrary number and assert groundlessly that this was the true number. I should have enough respect for truthfulness to admit that I do not know and to suspend belief rather than make an unjustified positive pronouncement, even though the actual number hardly matters.

So, truth matters. It is good not just for what it can do for us, but in itself and for its own sake.

That truth matters for its practical value in getting good things, and avoiding bad ones is even more obvious. Truth is useful, more useful than practically anything else. Often there just is no substitute for truth when it comes to making decisions. To take a relevant and obvious case, either human-caused climate change is occurring or it is not. If it is occurring, then either it will have significant impacts on human life or not. If it is real, as the overwhelming majority of qualified climate scientists say, then no amount of naysaying motivated by politics or profits will make the slightest bit of difference. Nature does not give a damn for your ideology—or your bottom line. If sea waters are going to rise, then corporate shills are going to have no more success in making the tide ebb than did King Canute. Maybe Donald Trump will wake up to climate change when he gets a shark problem in the lobby of Mar-a-Lago.

So, Mother Nature is utterly indifferent to our intentions. Shouldn't we want to know hers? The best bet for knowing what nature does and will do is natural science. In fact, it is the only game in town. Science is fallible, of course, and scientists frequently change their minds. There is seldom 100 percent agreement in any scientific community on any major issue, and scientists generally present their conclusions hedged about with qualifiers, margins of error, and exceptions. The left-wing anti-science propagandists of the '80s and '90s were dead wrong in asserting that science is merely a social construct. Yet there is no question that science has at times been subverted by political and cultural agendas, and even sexism and racism. Check Stephen Jay Gould's classic *The Mismeasure of Man* for an egregious example.[3] When we consider the multiple ways that science can fail, then why should we trust it? Because, as Winston Churchill said of democracy, every alternative is a lot worse.

Further, when science errs, the best corrective is more science. The history of science is not a monotonic ascent from ignorance to knowledge. There have been many dips, slips, and bumps along the way, but the net consequence is that we know vastly more about the universe and how it works than even a few years ago. You and I are not *that* old, and the advances we have seen just in our lifetimes are incredible (e.g., the double-helix structure of DNA was established by Crick and Watson in 1953, just a year after you and I were born). Surely, science has by now established its credentials to the satisfaction of everyone, right?

Wrong. As noted earlier, science has been under ideological attack from the left and the right for the past few decades.

During the "science wars" of the 1980s and '90s the academic left attacked the methods, goals, and credentials of science. Postmodern-ists, poststructuralists, radical feminists, social constructivists, and a few old-fashioned Marxists led the charge. Among the allegations they lodged against science were these: Science is chiefly practiced by and for white males, and works mainly to keep them in positions of privilege and power. Science is an ally of late-capitalist exploiters, and is beholden to big-business interests. Objectivity is what a man calls his subjectivity; that is, the ideal of objectivity enshrined in science is really a self-serving ideology that props up patriarchy. Science is only one way of knowing; there are many other ways that are equally valid. The methods of science are not tools for the discovery of objective reality, but are social constructs established to serve political or cul-tural agendas. There is no objective "out there" reality; rather, "reality" is a construct of our conceptual schemes.

The left-wing science critics were given a stern comeuppance in 1994 when biologist Paul Gross and mathematician Alan Levitt pub-lished their scintillating polemic *Higher Superstition*.[4] Gross and Levitt took up the science critics' claims one by one and showed them to be not merely wrong but fatuous. However, the biggest blow was deliv-ered by physicist Alan Sokal, who in 1996 authored a paper full of intentional gibberish, seasoned with lots of postmodernist and post-structuralist jargon, and submitted it as a serious article to *Social Text*, a leading journal of the academic-left science critics. *Social Text* published the article, and Sokal revealed his hoax. The "Sokal Affair" exhibited the ignorance and lax standards of those who presumed to criticize the work of scientists.[5]

But are not academic brawls the proverbial tempests in teapots? The left-wing science critics may have been muddled and loud, but it is hard to see that they had much of an effect outside of academe. So long as anti-science polemic is restricted to academic journals and university-press books, its capacity to do direct damage to the practice of science is limited. Nevertheless, ideas matter, and they can migrate from the rarefied regions of academic debate to the wider culture, where they can do more damage. As the Voltaire quote at the beginning of this section indicates, there is a discernible trajectory from absurd thoughts to dangerous actions.

But what happens when anti-science is sponsored by big-money interests and big money joins forces with powerful politicians?" Then real trouble brews. Let's take a single case in point. San Antonio congressman Lamar Smith is chair of the House Committee on Science, Space, and Technology. As the *Houston Chronicle* reported on April 9, 2017, Congressman Smith is a leading climate-change "skeptic" (i.e., denier) and he recently held hearings in which a number of climate scientists appeared before his committee.[6] They were not given a friendly reception. Smith uses the same tactics against climate science that creationists have long used against evolutionary science. Smith, of course, is not a scientist; he does no research, but his staff goes through scientific publications by climatologists and looks for points of disagreement. Since scientists always have disagreements, these are easy to find. The points of disagreement are then played up and the wide areas of agreement played down. The impression created is that climate scientists are far less certain of human-caused climate change than, in fact, they are and have far weaker grounds for their conclusions than, in fact, they have. Obfuscation achieved.

Why would Rep. Smith be interested in distorting science and harassing scientists? According to OpenSecrets.org, the number one contributor to Smith's campaign committee is the oil and gas industry, which made contributions of $100,700 during 2015–2016.[7] Is Congressman Smith a bought-and-paid-for lapdog of the oil and gas industry? Well, not necessarily. He could be a sincere crackpot, with reasons of his own to bash climate science. Still, money talks, and when it talks politicians always listen.

Congressman Smith's encounter with climate scientists is just one small battle in a much bigger conflict, one that it would not be hyperbolic to call a "War on Science." Who is waging war on science? Basically two groups: (1) ideologues, generally fundamentalist True Believers— of either the religious or "free market" stripe—who find the results of science uncongenial to their creeds, and (2) large corporations that see their profits threatened by scientific evidence. The standard example of an ideological opponent of science is creationism, which opposes established results in earth science, evolutionary biology, cosmology, and other fields because those results contradict creationists' interpretation of scripture. A typical instance of big-money opposition to science is a polluting industry, such as coal-fired electrical generation, that attempts to sow confusion about climate science because it sees such inquiry as a threat to profits. As mentioned earlier, Big Tobacco led the way by showing how to fund opposition "research" to undermine scientific evidence and sow doubt about legitimate findings.[8] When ideological animus joins forces with big money, then the combination is toxic.

Wait a second, though. How can there be a "War on Science" when STEM fields remain robustly funded and energetically pursued in the United States? If there is a "War on Science," the opposition seems to be losing badly. Why worry about them if they are apparently so ineffective?

Such an argument is specious. If the armies of the night are organized, dedicated, well-funded, well-publicized, and supported by powerful politicians—all of which they are—it would be foolish in the extreme to wait until they have won before science starts to fight back. Further, if the creationists, anti-vaccine activists, climate-change deniers, and such have not yet seriously impeded science, it is not for lack of trying. Here are just a few of their efforts: For more than twenty years, the National Rifle Association has opposed studies of gun violence, including those conducted by the Centers for Disease Control and Prevention.[9] Senator James Inhofe of Oklahoma, seemingly channeling his inner Joe McCarthy, held public hearings where he bullied, badgered, and shamed climate scientists.[10] To indicate the depth of Inhofe's thinking on the subject, on one cold DC day, he brought a snowball onto the Senate floor to refute global warming.[11] Industry-funded "institutes" abuse the Freedom of Information act to make demands for huge amounts of information from climate scientists in an obvious attempt to harass and intimidate researchers.[12] The National Center for Science Education documents the ongoing efforts to water down the teaching of evolutionary science in the public schools.[13]

Donald Trump has ratcheted up the assault on science. An NPR fact check written by Barbara J. King looks at the Trump administration's statements and actions related to the issues of climate change, vaccines, and teaching evolutionary science in public schools, among other issues.[14] Here are some of her findings.

- In 2012, Trump tweeted that global warming was a hoax invented by the Chinese. In 2016, in a campaign speech in North Dakota, he promised to dismantle the Paris Accord on climate change. [N.B., As this is being written Trump has in fact withdrawn the United States from the Paris Accord.]
- Trump's first appointee to head the EPA, Scott Pruitt, is a leading

"skeptic" of human-caused climate change who insists that there is still a viable "debate" about its reality (not according to 97 percent of qualified climate scientists).

- Robert F. Kennedy Jr., a prominent advocate of the view that child-hood vaccines cause autism, was invited to a meeting with Trump, who initially announced that Kennedy would head a Trump-appointed panel to investigate vaccine safety.
- Trump did not mention the teaching of evolution in public schools during his campaign. However, Vice President Mike Pence is on record as saying that the public schools "should teach all the facts about all these controversial issues." But teaching the (nonexistent) "controversy" is a standard creationist ploy to get their content into public school curricula.

Alan Burdick, writing in the *New Yorker*, summarizes Trump's record of hostility to science as well as his own crackpot anti-scientific claims.[15] *This* is making America great again?

The twenty-first century will present many severe challenges to humanity. For one thing, the human population is projected to reach ten billion by 2050. If burgeoning population and climate change create massive famine, there will be a refugee crisis that makes the current one look negligible. And that might just be the tip of the iceberg of looming calamities. You can face danger with eyes open or shut. Open is better. That is why the current regime of untruthfulness, with its concomitant attack on science and rationality, is so deeply disturbing. Truth is hard to get under the best of circumstances. If ideological obsessions and myopic pursuit of profit make truth even harder to get, there will be a terrible price to pay, and young people that we know and love will be the ones who pay it.

WHAT IS THE VALUE OF TRUTH?

PARIS DONEHOO

Your image of the beta fish being watched by a cat and a toddler reminds me of two of my great nieces who were playing in their backyard when their father noticed a rabbit timidly hopping through the grass not far away. The older girl said, "Oh, Daddy, I'm sure he's looking for something to eat, and I wish I had some food I could give him." Her younger sister, however, shouted, "LET'S GET HIM!"

I am certainly not likening the younger girl to a creature with only selfish interests at heart. Far from it. But the story, I think, speaks to your point about the way we process the information that comes to us every day. Do we see only what's utilitarian and pragmatic, or do we have the capacity for seeing something deeper and broader, something that reaches beyond the mundane and borders on the mysterious? When I think back to our days as young "linoleum lizards" romping through forests and yards (our own and those belonging to a few strangers), I marvel at the scenes our imaginations could inhabit. We battled aliens, monsters, and a wide variety of villains, using swords, ray guns, or whatever our minds could dream up. After all these years I still chuckle when I remember episodes of "The Adventures of Captain Zoom and His Sidekick Nicodemus," which we recorded on my primitive reel-to-reel tape recorder.

You are I are Exhibit A of the human capacity for curiosity and wonder, and I would be the last person to argue that those capacities must serve some practical purpose like the cat staring at the beta fish. It seems to me, however, that faith, particularly Christian faith, sees curiosity and wonder serving one larger purpose—not because curiosity and wonder are insufficient qualities within themselves, but because they are gifts from God that can enable us to encounter God. Every summer when I meet my extended family in Florida for a week of vacation, I love to walk on the beach at night and gaze across the waters, listen to the crash of the waves, and feast upon the canopy of stars above me. Each time, I remember the Psalm:

> O Lord, our Sovereign, how majestic is your name in all the earth! You have set your glory above the heavens.... When I look at your heavens, the work of your fingers, the moon and the stars that you have established; what are human beings that you are mindful of them, mortals that you care for them? Yet you have made them a little lower than God, and crowned them with glory and honor (Psalm 8:1, 3–5).

I know, of course, that the stars are luminous spheres of plasma held together by their own gravity, and the waves are caused by the wind whipping across the water, but those scientific facts do not dampen my sense of wonder. For me, therefore, curiosity and wonder are ways of encountering God. That is not to say that scientific inquiry cannot also become an encounter with the Divine. Many scientists and medical professionals have claimed as much. And I am certainly not asserting what some Christians say when standing under the stars at night: "How could anyone see this and not believe in God?" I am simply professing what this experience produces within me. Wonder, for me, leads to an encounter with God.

When teaching confirmation classes on the subject of creation I often bring in books and articles dealing with the commonly accepted scientific theory of a "Big Bang" as the beginning of the universe. We discuss their knowledge and understanding gleaned from schoolwork.

Then I give them copies of James Weldon Johnson's magnificent poem called *The Creation*, which begins:

And God stepped out on space,
And He looked around and said,
"I'm lonely—
I'll make me a world."
And far as the eye of God could see
Darkness covered everything,
Blacker than a hundred midnights
Down in a cypress swamp.
Then God smiled,
And the light broke,
And the darkness rolled up on one side,
And the light stood shining on the other,
And God said, "That's good!"[1]

When the entire poem was read, I would ask, "Which one of these accounts of creation is the right one?" After a few moments of avoiding eye contact, one of them invariably says, "Well, in a way they're both right." It's a teachable moment. It gives me the chance to explore truth that is never one-dimensional. There is no conflict between science and religion as long as you see truth in a multifaceted way. There is truth that can be examined in a test tube or through a telescope, and there is truth that can be encountered through the practices of poetry, music, art, and the human capacity for wonder. For a Christian, this capacity opens the heart to a deep dimension of reality that we define as God. When people of faith ignore this dimension, spiritual practice becomes nothing more than moribund rules, and religion resembles a museum more than a living body.

The above is not meant to divorce religious truth from moral practice. Faith must have norms by which practice is evaluated. As stated above, I believe the ultimate norm for a Christian is the life and teachings of Jesus. Other religions would have a different set of parameters. The point is, I am grateful for the lessons I learned while growing up in a Christian home, and while attending Sunday School and worship services. Though they were, at times, parochial and narrow-minded, overall those experiences still act as brakes on destructive behavior. I do not know if you ever heard this one, but we used to joke that our parents and Sunday School teachers told us not to "smoke, drink, chew, or go with girls who do." Not exactly Reinhold Niebuhr's *Moral Man and Immoral Society*, of course, but it was a start. Whenever someone in my church confessed to feeling guilty about something, I often responded, "Nothing wrong with that. Where would my profession be without guilt?" I am being facetious, obviously, but there is a sliver of seriousness there as well.

Therefore, I cannot separate the practice of truth from moral teaching, but it is much more. Truth is a frame of reference through which all knowledge and experience must pass in order to be interpreted. It is a way of seeing reality. When the life and teachings of Jesus become one's frame of reference, Christian practice results. For example, at various times during the early days of the church's life, various emperors and regional officials would require persons to visit a temple or shrine dedicated to Caesar and proclaim *kaisara kurios* (Caesar is Lord). Most subjects of the empire had no trouble obeying this rule. Religions of the day were polytheistic, and the Roman empire encouraged syncretistic faith, so what was wrong with acknowledging one more god?

Christians, however, saw this requirement through the lens of Jesus, who said, "No one can serve two masters" (Matthew 6:24). Indeed, probably the oldest creed professed by the early church was the simple yet profound statement of "Jesus is Lord." The New Testament epistles affirm the centrality of this claim (see 1 Corinthians 12:13, Romans 10:9–13, and Philippians 2:11). Therefore, most Christians either defied the government's edict, or they went to the temple or shrine and said *Iesous kurios* (Jesus is Lord) or *kristos kurios* (Christ is Lord) instead of *kaisara kurios*. As a result, Christians were branded as traitors and insurrectionists, and many suffered accordingly at the hands of the empire.

Christians did not claim "Jesus is Lord" in order to foment rebellion, but because Jesus was their frame of reference for reality. Whatever command or social standard did not fit within that frame was discarded, even if the consequences were severe. Indeed, early Christians habitually reinterpreted their world in terms of Jesus. John Dominic Crossan points out that every title the early church used to describe Jesus (Lord, Son of God, Savior, etc.), with the exception of Jewish titles (such as Messiah or Son of David), was first used to describe Caesar.[2] Those early Christians were deliberately attempting to re-envision the world through the framework of a Christian worldview. I, for one, devoutly wish the church could return to such a countercultural perspective, but I will say more about that later.

I do not claim, as some of my sisters and brothers do, that this frame of reference is self-evident. It is a choice to see reality through this lens. Evangelist and writer Josh McDowell wrote a very popular book called *Evidence That Demands a Verdict*, which piles layer upon layer of biblical and historical data to prove the deity of Christ and the authenticity of the Bible. Clearly, McDowell thinks anybody with one eye and half sense would become a Christian if he or she simply tallied up the evidence. In my view, such Christian apologetics add nothing substantial to the definition of truth. In fact, they support the current perception of Christians as arrogant, closed-minded, and judgmental.

The practice of truth requires humility, not condescension. What one believes regarding ultimate reality is always a choice. You and I have discussed this often. It is just as arrogant for the atheist to claim he or she knows beyond a shadow of a doubt there is no God as it is for the Christian to claim the opposite. You and I have lived long enough to encounter deep-seated hubris on both sides of the aisle, so to speak, which does nothing more than feed the divisions and mistrust awash in current society. Humility should be the coin of the realm in a post-truth society. The editors of *Christian Century* put it this way:

> Truth telling involves having the humility to be corrected and the humility to join in a shared public world of argument and debate. It also involves a fundamental openness to the world and to other people and a respect for their worth and perspectives. This is why Dietrich Bonhoeffer wrote (in his essay "What Is Meant by 'Telling the Truth'?") that "to speak truthfully, one's gaze and one's thought must be directed toward the way the real exists in God and through God and for God." Rephrased in secular terms: there has to be a shared reality beyond self-interest for the concept of telling the truth to gain traction; otherwise speech is mere self-assertion.[3]

Humility recognizes the value of choice, as well as the reality that our choices are not made within a vacuum. Conclusions about ultimate truth are reached through cultural, emotional, environmental, familial, intellectual, and personal influences, and in a perfect world everyone would at least be aware of these factors, if not studious and reflective of them. I readily admit the impact of my Southern upbringing, family of origin, education, and a host of other puzzle pieces contributing to my choice of the shape of reality. Ultimately, however, it is the community of faith that constructs the frame. The church comes to me with a particular history, tradition, set of norms, and sacred texts, and I lose my integrity when I live in contrast to those values. Indeed, to give lip-service to those values while living an entirely different kind of truth, feeds the perspective—especially prevalent these days among millennials—that Christians have no integrity, harbor barely hidden bigoted opinions, and engage in self-serving politics camouflaged by a religious veneer.

Our post-truth world bears within it a genuine insight: facts do come to us embedded in larger narratives about how the world is and what is worth our attention. Christians don't pretend to operate without a larger narrative. Rather, we claim that the Christian narrative—which is about humans as both precious and flawed, and about the world as God's good and ordered creation, meant for the flourishing of all creatures—is what provides the basis for humility, openness, correction, and argument. That, in turn, is what allows for a community of truth telling.[4]

This mooring within a Christian framework means faith passes the test that so much "spirituality" (to use today's buzz word) fails.

(1) Can you teach it to your children?
(2) Does it carry over into more loving relationships with people not part of your nurturing community?
(3) Will it help you in times of profound crisis?

If your frame of reference cannot answer all three of these questions in the affirmative, then you will get everything you need through regular use of a hot tub more than through the practice of faith. "Much spirituality . . . ," says Lawrence Cunningham, "is highly narcissistic and not easily distinguished from old self-improvement schemes."[5] I encounter such superficiality quite often when I counsel couples prior to their wedding. If they profess to be "spiritual but not religious" (which most of them do) and have no connection to a community of faith (which fewer and fewer of them do), I will ask them if they have given thought to any religious instruction for their children. Invariably the response will be, "Oh, we're just going to let them decide for themselves." They seem to have no concept of the importance of context for making decisions about truth. Without a nest in which to lay the egg, so to speak, a child has no point of reference for any decision, much less one regarding the shape of ultimate reality.

At least you, my old friend, knew what you were rejecting when you walked away from faith, religion, and the church, and for that you have my deepest respect. In my experience, however, most of those who reject the Christian narrative are merely rejecting a straw man they have cobbled together from half-truths, bad examples, popular culture, and personal disappointments.

Far worse, however, are those who continue to claim religious belief while demonstrating nothing that meets the three criteria mentioned above. When any faith becomes unmoored from truth as practice, I observe four devastating consequences. First, the church becomes identified with a particular ideology instead of the practices of Jesus. Too many of those who call themselves Christians are totally indistinguishable from the culture at large. Right-wing Christians can be identified by their staunch support of the military, small government, and patriarchal gender roles. Left-wing Christians can be identified by their embrace of whatever the cause *du jour* might be for the current week. Either way, one can remove the religious language used to support a political view and find nothing outside the arguments promulgated on Fox News or MSNBC.

The early church was not persecuted because they refused to "Put Rome First," but because they lived countercultural lives. As mentioned above, they refused to acknowledge allegiance to anyone but Christ. In addition, they eschewed common practices such as disposing of unwanted children, they cared for Christians and non-Christians during times of calamity and plague, and they rejected the hierarchical standards of the Greco-Roman world. Examine passages in the New Testament such as the letter to Philemon and you will find seeds planted for the abolition of slavery—an institution accepted without question throughout the empire.

What happened? Why did these Jesus followers stop short of complete social transformation? In my view, the church became a prisoner of its own success. As their numbers and influence grew they became more and more assimilated into the dominant culture, and Constantine sealed the deal. When the Roman empire got a "born again" emperor, the church was no longer an *alternative* to the culture. It *embodied* the culture.

And when the church becomes identified with a particular ideological stance, the church always loses. Take, for example, the case of Galileo Galilei who was sentenced to house arrest in 1633 for having the temerity to claim the earth revolved around the sun. Because church and state—or better to say church and culture—were so wedded together, the church became a laughingstock in the days that followed. I have lost count of the number of times I have engaged in conversation with someone wanting to "prove" the falsehood of Christianity who quickly pointed to Galileo's trial. In 1992 Pope John Paul II expressed regret for how the affair was handled, and acknowledged the errors committed by the Catholic Church—a move met by cynical amusement on the part of many, including myself.

History is replete with such assimilation of ideology rebounding on the church. One needs only to think of the "German Christians" who cast their lot with Hitler and have spent the decades since apologizing for it. I have seen photos of church sanctuaries during Hitler's reign with the Christian flag on one side of the altar and the Nazi flag on the other. People are shocked when they see such pictures, but in every church I have served as pastor, and almost every church I have entered, there is a Christian flag on one side of the altar and a US flag on the other. Yet, when I suggest my congregation might remove them both, I am met with lame excuses or downright hostility. Such is the confusion of a church that embraces a certain ideology lock, stock, and barrel.

In the days prior to the 2016 election I saw a photo of a throng of people surging forward to shake hands with, or get a picture of, candidate Donald Trump. At the front of the crowd a woman was holding up a sign that read, "Thank you, Jesus, for President Trump." He had not yet been elected at that point, but I'm sure Galileo turned over in his grave. Evidently, we have learned nothing about the dangers of assimilation.

Second, when Christian faith becomes unmoored from truth as practice it tends to overlook any unchristlike action or attitude as long as it serves an agenda. Any devoted fan of the film *Monty Python and the Holy Grail* will recall the scene in which King Arthur and his knights employ the use of the Holy Hand Grenade of Antioch.[6] After forty years I still find that scene funny, but there is pain in my laughter. I have known far too many good Christian people willing to toss the Holy Hand Grenade of Antioch toward anyone they view as the enemy. Not long after I began working as a Southern Baptist pastor, the denomination descended into what could only be called a Holy War. The Southern Baptist Convention has always been a conservative church, but in the late 1970s a cadre of ultra-rightwing pastors, theologians, and church members flexed their muscles and systematically took over the reins of denominational leadership. I got involved in the efforts of more progressively minded Baptists to stem the tide of this takeover. However, I made a startling discovery: In order to fight them, I had to become like them. Before long I was publicly defending certain practices my compatriots were using in order to oppose my adversaries who were using the same tactics. After several years of this nonsense, I finally recognized the lack of any Christlike behavior in the struggle and pulled back from the fray. As mentioned earlier, I eventually moved my ordination into the United Church of Christ.

The Southern Baptist Takeover (as it came to be called) was crafted by its leaders to position the denomination politically for Republican ideology. And they were successful. During the presidential election of 2004 I happened to turn on a TV documentary called something like "Faith and the Ballot Box." A man stood in the pulpit of a Southern

Baptist Church preaching about the importance of Christian values informing their voting, and he ended his sermon with words to this effect: "And when we get to heaven we want to be able to say, 'Lord, we brought our nation with us.'" I became nauseated, and I could not help but remember all my Baptist forebears who stood for separation of church and state, and suffered mightily for it. But when an agenda becomes more important than acting like Jesus, any action or attitude is sacrificed on the altar of expediency. Can a repeat of the Crusades, or a return to Jim Crow laws be far behind? Fear and hatred of people who are different fuels Trump's travel ban and immigrant policies, yet those actions are endorsed by the very people who claim to be followers of the one who was himself a refugee and an immigrant when he was an infant (Matthew 2:13–15).

Third, when Christian faith becomes unmoored from truth as practice, aggrieved people are created instead of Easter people. In other words, those who call themselves Christians are shaped more by their anger and feelings of disenfranchisement than by the resurrected Christ. For example, there is much talk these days about Christians being persecuted in this country. Speaking to the Faith and Freedom Coalition conference, President Trump declared, "We will always support our evangelical community and defend your right and the right of all Americans to follow and to live by the teachings of their faith. And as you know, we are under siege. You understand that."[7]

Aside from the absurdity of a man who rarely attends church, knows nothing about the Bible, and exhibits no Christlike qualities using the word "we" to include himself in the community of faith, Trump's speech stokes the theory that Christians are increasingly facing mistreatment and discrimination. But are Jesus's followers truly under siege? In some countries, yes, but not in the United States. The hegemony of the Christian church in America is under siege. Even though the United States government has never declared a state religion, as other countries have done, Christianity has been the de facto official faith of this country for many generations.[8] In recent years, however, that supremacy has been challenged by the rise of competing religions brought to these shores from all over the world, the growing acceptance of alternative lifestyles, and the unchristian responses to it all on the part of those who call themselves Christians.

As more and more people turn away from Christian faith—or, at least, what they perceive to be Christian faith—the people left in the church bemoan their loss of societal influence, the days when faith and patriotism were two sides of the same coin. As those practices deteriorate, many of the faithful interpret those losses as attacks on Christian faith and practice when, in truth, they are indications of a society no longer willing to keep the church propped up. As long as the church defined being a Christian and being a good citizen as basically one and the same, the government and the culture were happy to keep stores closed on Sundays, print entire sermons in the newspaper, turn religious observances into school holidays, and have local clergy open football games with prayer. Now that this symbiotic relationship has broken down, many of the faithful claim their faith is under attack, and they scour the countryside for someone to blame—Washington, the educational elite, the "liberal" media, the LGBTQ community, other Christians who do not believe the same way they do, etc.

It is not Christian faith that is under attack. The sense of entitlement the church has enjoyed is under attack. And as the church continues to frame its losses as a deliberate assault, the faithful will become more and more angry. They want the freedom to practice their faith, but they will accept none of the responsibilities that come with such freedom. They want their voices to be heard as they protest laws and practices they do not like, but they do not want to suffer the consequences. Early Christians knew the risks of practicing truth. They knew Jesus had been crucified for living and teaching a countercultural message, and they did not consider themselves above such treatment. Many believers today, however, will follow Jesus as long as he does not lead them to the cross.

The church should be an Easter people, a community living out the implications of Christ's empty tomb. Instead, many communities contain only aggrieved people. And society has noticed. The fourth result of Christian faith unmoored from truth as practice is the rise of the groups called the "nones" and the "dones." The fastest growing religious demographic in the United States is "none." When asked about their religious faith, people reply that they have none. Unfortunately, the millennial generation is solidly in the "none" camp. Within their number, and to a lesser extent other age groups, are those who were raised in the church, or dabbled in it for a while, and now are "done" with it all. Why? They perceive Christians to be hypercritical, anti-gay, sheltered, judgmental, too political, and more interested in saving souls than caring for the whole person.[9] Thus, they have written off the entire church as irrelevant at best, dangerous at worst.

One could make the case, I suppose, that all these matters are merely "in-house" concerns that do not have serious consequences for society at large. I fear such is not the case. In a disturbing article in the *Atlantic* magazine, Peter Beinart claims there is at least an indirect correlation between the decline of religious practice and the increasing brutality of America's partisan politics, as well as the rise of both Donald Trump and the so-called alt-right movement. According to Beinart, Trump did best among those who self-identify as evangelical Christians yet rarely attend church. For example Trump trailed Ted Cruz by fifteen points among Republicans who attended religious services every week, according to a Pew Research Center poll during the presidential campaign, but he led Cruz by twenty-seven points among those who did not. This raises the question as to why these religiously unaffiliated Republicans would buy into Trump's dystopian view of America while their church-going brothers and sisters would not. Beinart is cautious, and rightly so, about claiming a direct line between cause and effect. Yet, he does claim there is evidence that culturally conservative white Americans who are not involved in church are often less successful economically and more likely to experience family breakdown than those who are involved. Is this why they grow more pessimistic, resentful, and develop a dark view of America? Quite possibly. Beinart cites findings by the Public Religion Research Institute claiming that white Republicans who claim to be evangelical Christians yet seldom or never attend worship are nineteen points less likely than white Republicans who attend at least once a week to say that the American dream "still holds true."

But Trump not only gave voice to the despair of non-churchgoing conservatives. They also supported him because he expressed their antipathies and offenses they perceived themselves as having received:

> When conservatives disengage from organized religion . . . they don't become more tolerant. They become intolerant in different ways. . . . When cultural conservatives disengage from organized religion, they tend to redraw the boundaries of identity, de-emphasizing morality and religion and emphasizing race and nation. Trump is both a beneficiary and a driver of that shift.[10]

I will leave an assessment of Beinart's views to those more socio-logically astute than myself. However, I sense he is onto something. The loss of truth as practice has destructive costs for the church of Jesus Christ, and as the church becomes identified with a particular ideology, excuses unchristlike actions and attitudes, and descends into anger and judgmentalism, it drives away those whom God loves, and abandons them to societal forces that can only be described as demonic.

HOW DO WE RESTORE RESPECT FOR TRUTH AND TRUTHFULNESS?

KEITH PARSONS

Once more I want to emphasize how our approaches to truth are different but congruent and complementary. I speak of truth as known and spoken, and you speak of truth as lived. Both are necessary. One must speak truly and live authentically. An authentic life is one lived in conformity with your deepest commitments and values. Further, as you note, to live authentically also means embracing uncertainty, since our deepest commitments involve both choice and trust. As we noted in the introduction, neither theism nor atheism can be established to a certainty or beyond a reasonable doubt. In such a case one must make a choice; it is an informed choice, a rational choice, but still a choice. Further, in making such a choice, each of us must trust our deepest feelings, the ones so deep and so constitutive of our basic identities that they feel to us like instincts.

What applies to religious commitments applies to other deep commitments, like the ones that underlie a commitment to liberalism or conservatism. When the uncertain nature of these commitments is forgotten, and they are elevated into indubitable truths, then the result is intolerance and fanaticism. "It is putting a very high price on one's conjectures to have a man roasted alive because of them," said the philosopher Montaigne.[1] As history too often shows, forgetting that each of us is fallible and so are our worldviews, first leads us to burn books and then to burn people.

I very much appreciated your expansion on my theme of the encounter with truth as an experience of awe and wonder. As you say, that experience is for each of us mediated by what you call our frameworks, and what I prefer to call our worldviews. A worldview (it always sounds more impressive in the German: *Weltanschauung*) is your basic "take" on reality; how at rock bottom you take things to be. Your worldview is theistic and mine is naturalistic. Rock-bottom reality for me is physical reality, the fundamental structure and components of the space/time universe. My experience of awe and wonder is pantheistic in nature, that is, the awe is directed at the universe itself. It is such pantheistic awe that led Einstein to refer to the cosmos as "*Der Herr Gott*," "The Lord God."

When I had the chance to fulfill a lifelong ambition and visit the Galapagos Islands in 2000, I snorkeled in the (remarkably cold) waters around the islands. The islands are volcanic and rise steeply from abyssal depths. This means that just a few meters from the islands, the waters drop off into profound blackness. As I swam I was surrounded by great swarms of tropical fish of every conceivable hue while beams of equatorial sunlight penetrated until they were lost in the abyss. In the beauty of the scene I was overwhelmed with a sense of oneness and solidarity with all of life and, further, with the great cosmos itself, of which I felt a minute but integral part. It was an experience at once both humbling and exalting. I would call it a "Darwinian" moment, an awareness of my connectedness with all living things and with the whole earth and even the universe itself, vast and ancient beyond comprehension. One of the few things I seem to recall from seminary is that Paul Tillich called such experiences an encounter with the "depth dimension." Though you and I interpret those experiences differently, we each have encountered depth, and the experience is of fundamental significance to each of us. It was for each of us an experience of the numinous—being in the presence of the sacred.

With the encounter with awe and wonder comes a concomitant awareness of the pettiness of an ego that needs constant stroking and is sensitive to every perceived slight. I cannot help but wonder if Donald Trump has ever had an experience of depth and wonder. Has he ever had a moment in which he felt himself in the presence of something greater than himself? Trump reminds me of a cartoon I once saw in the *New Yorker*: A tycoon is contemplating the vastness of a starry sky and says to his flunky, "Well, it doesn't make ME feel small!"

Those who are capable of wonder know the value of truth; they feel it in their bones, and are outraged at the liar's willful desecration. They therefore have a visceral recognition that truth is an essential value and truthfulness, genuine respect for truth, is a crucial virtue. As we said earlier, respect for truth means diligence in seeking, upholding, and promoting truth and refusal to lie or to tolerate lying by others. If a society loses its respect for truth and truth-telling, it has lost everything. Every system that has ever oppressed the human spirit has been a system of lies. Tyrants scurry from truth like cockroaches fleeing the kitchen light. The devil was rightly called "the father of lies" because every vice and evil partners with lies. The great systems of totalitarian oppression of the twentieth century—Nazism, Soviet Communism, and Maoism—were erected upon foundations of systematic and pervasive lying.

More basically, the fundamental emotional glue that holds nations together is trust, the belief that your government and fellow citizens can be relied upon to respect certain basic norms of honesty and fairness. If that trust is shattered, and people begin to feel that there is more that divides them than unites them, then national identity is lost and the centrifugal forces that always divide people take over. Dreadful scenarios then can be played out. To see how horrific those scenarios of divisiveness can be, consider the conflicts between Sunnis and Shiites in Iraq, or, closer to home, our own Civil War.

At the most basic level, it is hard to see how there could be *any* sort of organized society without an expectation of sincerity, that is, without the assumption that when others tell you that something is so, you can generally expect that they are telling you what they honestly think is so. How could there be any degree of cooperation or coordination in any enterprise if you could never trust that people mean what they say? Every human relationship other than sheer enmity therefore depends upon an elemental trust. Without such trust, life would not merely revert to a Hobbesian war of all against all. No life would be possible, not even one solitary, poor, nasty, brutish, and short. So, those who attack truth and truthfulness strike at the very foundation of our lives as social beings.

Well, then, we have thoroughly analyzed the problem from our respective viewpoints. What do we do about it? The task is formidable. The forces of falsehood are powerful, well-organized, and well-funded, and have done their job well, effectively spreading untruths and insulating their followers against corrective argument and evidence. In his eye-opening (and hair-raising) book *Lies, Incorporated: The World of Post-Truth Politics*, Ari Rabin-Havt succinctly summarizes the danger of lies and their intractability once entrenched:

> Misinformation is damaging to those who read and absorb it. Once a lie—no matter how outrageous—is part of the consciousness of a particular group, it is nearly impossible to eliminate and like a virus it spreads uncontrollably within the affected communities.[2]

For instance, polls perennially show that millions of Americans do not accept evolution, despite the fact that it is one of the best-confirmed facts of science, and despite the fact that creationist arguments have been debunked thoroughly and repeatedly.[3] The persistence of the rejection of climate science and evolutionary science is a testament to the power of organizations dedicated to the promotion of obfuscation and to the effectiveness of the tactics they employ. Rabin-Havt's book offers many examples of entrenched lies that have survived repeated debunking: The "more guns, less crime" mantra of the NRA; that abortion causes breast cancer; that children from families with same-sex parents do less well than children with opposite-sex parents; that the Affordable Care act created "death panels"; and that voter fraud is rampant.

How do you address lies that have become entrenched? How do you handle willful ignorance? How can you use facts and argument, if facts and argument are intentionally dismissed or ignored? On the other hand, if you cannot use facts and argument, do you descend to the level of subterfuge, disinformation, and emotional appeal that constitute the very distortions that we decry? How do you fight them without joining them? That is the conundrum.

What we are talking about are values, values that you and I share and that we want others to share also. How do you get people to value values? Getting people to accept values is not like getting them to accept the conclusion of an argument. It is not intellectual assent we mainly want but to spark something deep inside and to evoke a passion, a passion for what is right. We want people to *care* about truth and to commit to its defense, not merely to give it shallow approval or lip service. How do you get people to care about the things you think they should care about without resorting to the kinds of tricks we have deplored?

In my philosophy classes I ask questions to make people think about their values. In my introductory class, I have the students read the famous "myth of the cave," from Plato's *Republic*. As I am sure you recall, Plato asks us to imagine a vast underground cavern in which there are prisoners who have been kept there their whole lives and who have experienced nothing but shadows projected on a wall. One prisoner breaks free, and painfully and with great effort makes his way out of the cave and into the wider world. There he discovers that what he has taken for reality during his whole life is nothing but shadow and illusion. He then goes back into the cave to offer the other prisoners a chance to escape their ignorance and know the truth. The film *The Matrix* represents a similar situation, in which the character is offered a choice of taking one pill or another. If he takes one pill, he will live a life of comfortable illusion; if he takes the other, he will know the harsh and disturbing truth.

I ask my class: Would you rather live a life in which you enjoy comfortable illusion, or would you rather know the truth, even though the truth is discomforting? Some opt for one and some opt for the other, and the numbers are fairly evenly split. So I ask defenders of each view to justify their answers. If they choose comfort over truth, I want to know why truth matters so little to them, and whether they do not resent being lied to—which is a form of control—even when it is "for their own good." Those who say they want to know the painful truth are asked why they value truth and why it should mean something to them even if, as in the imagined case, illusion makes you happy and truth is disconcerting. By asking such questions, and pressing for answers, you can get normally unreflective people to pause and ask serious questions such as "Does truth matter?" and "Why does it matter?"

One thing that eventually becomes clear, if you subject people to a bit of intellectual poking and prodding, is that, deep down, they *do* care about truth. You just may have to remind them that they do. (Actually, reminding us of what we already know is precisely what Plato thought he was doing.) For one thing, nobody likes to feel like they have been a stooge or a sucker. Everyone wants people to be truthful *to them*. Donald Trump knows this full well, and he plays it for all it is worth. He *tells* people that they are the victims of systematic lying! Only, he is not the one doing the lying. It's those "enemies of the people," the journalists for the biased liberal news media, those purveyors of "fake news," like the *New York Times* and the *Washington Post*. Trump's followers gobble it up. At one rally, a Trump supporter wore a shirt reading "Rope, tree, journalist. Some assembly required." Really, you have to admire the *chutzpah*. A liar's ultimate con is to get people to believe his lies by playing on their very resentment of lies.

It seems to me that our current crisis is a crisis of trust, the sort of elemental trust that holds societies together. Whom do you trust to tell you the truth? Traditionally, people turned to three sources for guidance: (1) the mainstream media, (2) science, and (3) religion. You and I are old enough to remember that when Walter Cronkite said "And that's the way it is," people believed that was the way it was. When we were kids, science was trusted, and scientists were respected, sometimes almost to an excessive degree. Religious leaders like Pope John XXIII and Billy Graham were seen as standing for a moral authority that was above politics (Graham later squandered much of this image by palling around with Richard Nixon). Now, however, all three—the mainstream media, science, and religion—have all been heavily politicized by partisan rhetoric and ideology. As we have noted, right-wing politicians and pundits demonize the mainstream media and have even succeeded in discrediting science for many of their followers. This is a clever strategy. You discredit the traditional sources of information so that people will turn to you for the truth.

What about religion? My recollection is that when we were young, religion had very little explicitly to say about politics. Religion was about being a decent person, not promoting a political agenda. It seems to me that the politicization of religion really began with the rise of the religious right circa 1980. Jerry Falwell's Moral Majority and their allies were unabashedly partisan, and evangelicals became one of the most reliable voting blocs for Republicans. To be fair, when I went to seminary in the 1970s, at Emory University's famously liberal Candler School of Theology, I met people on the "religious left" who were just as interested in mixing religion and politics as those on the right ("liberation theology"). However, the religious right was much louder, better organized, and better funded than the religious left, and, de facto, became the voice of Protestantism in America. If you mention religion and politics today, the issues that come to mind are abortion and LGBTQ rights, since the religious right rides those hobby horses the hardest. The upshot is that religion is no longer viewed as a moral authority above politics, but as neck-deep in the political muck.

I will leave it to you to say how the religious voice can be reclaimed from the fundamentalists. I will concentrate on how the media and science can regain the trust that they have lost. There is no question that they have lost trust in part because their ideological enemies have defamed them. However, they also have themselves to blame, and they can do things to improve their status.

The media get criticism from all sides. The right condemns the "liberal news media," and much of the impetus for creating Fox News was the perception that conservatives needed a voice in the overwhelmingly liberal media environment. The left notes that mainstream media are owned by a shrinking number of large corporations, and that makes them deeply suspicious. They argue that mass-market news programs in the corporate-owned media are more about generating advertising revenue than reporting the news that really matters. However, I think that the most perceptive critique of the media is not that it is biased to the left or the right but that, on the contrary, it has far too often pursued a bogus conception of fairness. Working on the assumption that there are two sides to every story, news reports scrupulously attempted to present an appearance of neutrality when covering controversies.

But there are *not* two sides to every story. As the saying goes (attributed to Daniel Patrick Moynihan), "Everyone is entitled to his own opinion, but not his own facts."[4] When one side has the facts and the other does not, the disagreement is not a mere difference of opinion. Objectivity is not the same thing as neutrality. Flat-earthers *do not* deserve the same respect due to round-earthers. That the earth is flat is not an "alternative fact" or a difference of opinion. It is wrong. Period. As we noted earlier with creationism, "giving both sides of the controversy" when there is no controversy bestows an undeserved legitimacy on the crackpots.

Journalists should be fearlessly and unabashedly committed to digging up the truth, and when they find that one side has it and another does not, they should drop any pretense of false equivalence between the two. When there is a public dispute, say over climate change, voter fraud, same-sex marriage, or any hot-button issue, and one side makes demonstrably false claims, the media have the responsibility to call them out for their lies, and not hide behind a faux impartiality.

Actually, stung by such criticisms, the media have more recently started doing a somewhat better job of calling out the liars and prevaricators. Fact-check sites have become more common, and they provide a very valuable service. Maybe, in fact, the Trump presidency has restored a sense of mission to many journalists. For instance, many fine pieces of investigative reporting appearing in the *New York Times*, the *Washington Post*, and *New Yorker* magazine have uncovered the complex and sleazy business dealings of the Trump family with Russian oligarchs and other extremely unsavory characters. Rachel Maddow diligently reports these often convoluted connections on her MSNBC program.

Much more could be done. One thing that the mainstream media could do is to proactively expose the *real* purveyors of fake news. There are many organizations, like the Heartland Institute, that present themselves as collections of wonky intellectuals and scholars, but really they are hard-core ideologues assiduously grinding the axes of their corporate funders. The mainstream media should boldly expose the misinformation and disinformation that constantly flows from these organizations.[5] There are also organizations with innocuous sounding names like "Center for Consumer Freedom" and "Center for Accountability in Science" that are really front groups for professional shills, who are paid to lie by business interests.[6]

Why are prominent politicians and their spokespeople so often the featured interviews on news and current events shows, like *Face the Nation* and *Meet the Press*? These are people who have years of experience not giving straight answers, and, short of applying thumbscrews, there is no way to force them to directly address the questions. For years, ABC News White House correspondent Sam Donaldson futilely tried to badger Ronald Reagan into answering his questions, only to have Reagan give a grandfatherly, "Well, Sam . . ." and launch into another irrelevance. It would be far more informative if network news shows would instead interview scholars, scientists, and other legitimate experts on the relevant issues, but network TV is in the ratings business, not the information business, and so will probably always be to some extent complicit in the perpetuation of untruth.

The "March for Science" that occurred nationwide in April 2017 showed that scientists have—finally—gotten a wake-up call. For decades, scientists mostly ignored attacks on science. Scientists are very busy people, and most of their communication has to be with other scientists, not with the public. Therefore, with respect to the promoters of pseudoscience and anti-science, scientists were long content just to let the asses bray. They had real work to do, designing the next experiment or writing up their latest journal article or grant application, and, with some notable exceptions, they saw it as a waste of time to stop and address objections that, for scientists, were nonissues. The problem is that preoccupation is easily taken for arrogance, and if you will not take the field, you lose by default. I think that scientists now realize that part of their job is to communicate what they do, how they do it, and why it is important to the general public. This is why scientists like Neil de Grasse Tyson are important and necessary. Tyson communicates with the public, and he does so effectively.

All too often in the past, when scientists did try to defend science in the public forum, they did so incompetently. In the early days of creationist activism, evolutionary biologists would sometimes take the bait when creationists offered to debate. The debate would usually go like this: The evolutionist would present facts and evidence in the straightforward way appropriate for a scholarly conference or graduate seminar. He was probably expecting the creationist to be a barefoot hayseed alternately strumming a banjo and pounding a Bible, so he never bothered to learn the creationist line. To his chagrin, the creationist was glib, smart, funny, and polished as he rattled off spurious claims far faster than they could be refuted. The result of the debate: Creationism 1, evolution 0.

This is why, like it or not, scientists have to be willing to defend what they do in public, and they have to be able to defend it effectively. Unfortunately, in the past scientists who took on the task of communicating science were all too often dismissed as "popularizers." It should be clear by now that scientists like Tyson, Richard Dawkins, or Brian Greene, who have the skill to explain the power, beauty, and excitement of scientific ideas to laypeople, should be honored, not belittled. Further, it should be obvious by now that scientists no longer have the luxury of taking the public's trust for granted—not when pundits, politicians, and ax-grinders are attacking them daily. Not when dozens of corporate-funded "think" tanks, "institutes," and front groups, staffed by ideologues, shills, and scientific sell-outs, constantly churn out distortion and disinformation. You have to fight back by calling out the ignoramuses and the obscurantists. Name names and do not pull your punches. If you do not speak up, loudly and effectively, the enemies of science will win.

All too often these days, it seems as though Yeats's apocalyptic prophecy in his poem "The Second Coming," is being fulfilled:

Turning and turning in the widening gyre
The falcon cannot hear the falconer;
Things fall apart; the center cannot hold;

Mere anarchy is loosed upon the world,
The blood-dimmed tide is loosed, and everywhere
The ceremony of innocence is drowned;
The best lack all conviction, while the worst
Are full of passionate intensity.

If disaster is to be avoided, then "the best"—the lovers of truth—
had better work up some passion also.

HOW DO WE RESTORE RESPECT FOR TRUTH AND TRUTHFULNESS?

PARIS DONEHOO

I am tempted to bellow a hearty "amen" to your remarks and move on to the next chapter. However, since I am part of a profession that is supposed to have something important to say on every occasion, I will offer some of my own concluding thoughts. Perhaps the reason why you and I respect each other personally and professionally is because we both deal with things that matter. Others may salivate over the latest shenanigans of the Kardashian clan, or call sports radio to pontificate on what the coach in yesterday's game should have done, but you and I are fortunate enough to have careers that handle issues with some weight to them. I do not believe either of us takes such a responsibility lightly.

On the inside of a folder I used to plan my weekly homiletics exercise until retirement I pasted a quote from a college and seminary professor friend of mine who said, "Never preach on anything that doesn't matter." I try to remember that advice every time I engage in the task of researching, writing, and delivering a sermon. After forty years in ministry I continue to be humbled by the call to say a word that might be helpful to someone who is struggling, or might even assist her or him in a change for the better. It is truly an awesome, and dare I even say "sacred," duty. A friend of mine recently sent me a link to a video of a preacher ranting and raving over the horrible sacrilege of "men who sit down to pee." It was not a joke. I suppose I should have chuckled and forgotten about it, but my heart broke at such a gleeful squandering of a holy opportunity. I cannot imagine taking such a petty subject into the pulpit, and I know you cannot imagine taking a similar one into the classroom either.

Jesus derided those who "strain out a gnat but swallow a camel" (Matthew 23:24). Unfortunately, there has been far too much camel swallowing of late. I will be the first to admit that the church of Jesus Christ bears much responsibility for this state of affairs. By conflating jingoism with discipleship, and baptizing patriotism into the fellowship of the one who warned about the danger of serving two masters, we have elevated flag saluting to the level of a sacrament. Back in the 1980s, I heard a speaker at a religious conference relate his experience in a particular church where he was told he could not call himself a Christian if he did not agree with presidential candidate Ronald Reagan's position on the Panama Canal. "When I walked the aisle to join the church of my youth," he said, "the preacher only wanted to know if I believed in Jesus. He never mentioned the Panama Canal."

As I said earlier, the upside to our current crisis of values is its call to each of us to seriously examine where our true commitments and loyalties lie. When I attended Vacation Bible School as a child in my Southern Baptist church, it never occurred to me (or, apparently, to anyone else) to question why our day began with a pledge to the American flag, a pledge to the Christian flag, and a pledge to the Bible. That such a mixed message could be aligned with loyalty to the one called "King of kings and Lord of lords" (Revelation 19:16) is just one example of the church's assimilation into American culture.

I am encouraged, however, by trends, movements, and leaders appearing on the horizon. Preachers and authors like Jim Wallis, Brian McLaren, and Richard Rohr are voicing a more Christocentric message, and are encouraging those who long for something more than consumerism to give faith and the church another look. Perhaps most heartening to me is the emergence of "Red Letter Christians," so called because of their desire to follow the words of Jesus (printed in red in some versions of the Bible) rather than the bastardized faith wreaking so much havoc these days. Sociologist Tony Campolo sums up the movement this way:

> We are evangelicals who are troubled by what is happening to poor people in America; who are disturbed over environmental policies that are contributing to global warming; who are dismayed over the increasing arrogance of power shown in our country's militarism; who are outraged because government funding is being reduced for schools where students, often from impoverished and dysfunctional homes, are testing poorly; who are upset with the fact that of the 22 industrialized nations America is next to last in the proportion of its national budget (less than two-tenths of 1 percent) that is designated to help the poor of third-world countries; and who are broken-hearted over discrimination against women, people of color, and those who suffer because of their sexual orientation.[1]

Granted, the religious sycophants surrounding Trump get the lion's share of media attention, but movements like Red Letter Christianity give me at least a modicum of hope. Yet, there is a theological and historical ambivalence that must be acknowledged here. Jesus said his disciples "do not belong to the world, just as I do not belong to the world" (John 17:16), but he also taught us to pray for God's kingdom to come "*on earth* as it is in heaven" (Matthew 6:10). A disciple of Jesus, therefore, is instructed to cooperate with God in recreating this world while simultaneously holding this world at arm's length. Given the inherent difficulty of such a task, I suppose I should cut some slack to the myriads of good people who shaped my life over the years while often espousing a set of schizophrenic loyalties. In the vast majority of cases, they were simply doing the best they could with the theological tools at hand.

Perhaps that is why current trends disturb me so much. If most people I have known accepted competing loyalties through accidental ignorance, what is to be done about those who, as you say, engage in "willful ignorance"? Where were "Team Trump's evangelical all-stars—pastors and prominent laity who hustle noisily around the Oval Office trying to find an amen corner"[2]—when Anthony Scaramucci unleashed a foul-mouthed tirade that would make a sailor blush? Why did it fall to John Kelly to fire Scaramucci instead of his purport-edly "Christian" boss? How can the Christian Broadcasting Network shamelessly claim there is a "spiritual awakening" underway at the White House because of a Bible study led by Ralph Drollinger to "the most evangelical cabinet in history"?[3] One wonders if they have pon-dered these verses during their Bible study: "Beware of false prophets who come to you in sheep's clothing, but inwardly are ravenous wolves. You will know them by their fruits" (Matthew 7:15–16).

Religious charlatans, of course, are nothing new. They were present at the very beginning of the church (Acts 8:18–19). In my own lifetime I have seen quite a few. The Moral Majority under Jerry Falwell was born while I was a seminary student in the mid-1970s, and I remember the befuddlement of pundits and journalists as they tried to explain the resur-gence of fundamentalist religion they thought had died with the Scopes trial in 1925. During the annual gathering of the Southern Baptist Con-vention in 1985, I sat in on an impromptu press conference with one of the architects of the denomination's fundamentalist takeover, who flatly denied any knowledge of busses full of fundamentalists carted in for only one day with the express purpose of swinging votes. The evidence was in front of the convention hall, and on the convention floor, for all to see.

Donald Trump, therefore, did not create the unholy alliance between evangelicals and Republican politics as much as he cynically exploited it. Now there seems to be nothing he could do to dislodge his religious followers from his base of support. (If the *Access Holly-*

wood video did not send them scrambling to the altar to ask forgiveness, nothing will.) Are these people evil? Perhaps, but I think there is something more frightening afoot—stupidity. By stupidity I do not mean a lack of intellectual ability. Those of us who dislike Trump have too easily dismissed his loyal minions as morons (to quote Secretary of State Rex Tillerson) or worse. No, by stupidity I mean the "willful ignorance" mentioned earlier. Noted German theologian Dietrich Bonhoeffer, who was executed by the Nazis because he would not put Hitler on par with, or above, Jesus Christ, said:

> Stupidity is a more dangerous enemy of the good than malice. One may protest against evil; it can be exposed and, if need be, prevented by use of force. Evil always carries within itself the germ of its own subversion in that it leaves behind in human beings at least a sense of unease. Against stupidity we are defenseless. Neither protests nor the use of force accomplish anything here; reasons fall on deaf ears; facts that contradict one's prejudgment simply need not be believed—in such moments the stupid person even becomes critical—and when facts are irrefutable they are just pushed aside as inconsequential, as incidental. In all this the stupid person, in contrast to the malicious one, is utterly self-satisfied and, being easily irritated, becomes dangerous by going on the attack. For that reason, greater caution is called for than with a malicious one. Never again will we try to persuade the stupid person with reasons, for it is senseless and dangerous.[4]

I hear echoes here of your description of the mistakes scientists have often made when dealing with creationists. By appealing to reasonable arguments, progressively minded Christians have lost as many arguments with toxic Christians as scientists have with creationists. "Do not give what is holy to dogs," Jesus said, "and do not throw your pearls before swine" (Matthew 7:6). It is time for us in the faith community to stop squandering our resources, and our breath, on those who choose stupidity as Bonhoeffer described it. Painful experience has taught me the futility of trying to change the mind of a willfully ignorant or stupid person. As Robert Heinlein is reported to have quipped, "Never attempt to teach a pig to sing; it wastes your time and annoys the pig."

So, if we cannot hope to talk sense into the practitioners of "alternative facts," what can be done? How can we reclaim the religious voice from the clutches of Trumpite faith? First, believe it or not, I want to start with the same "myth of the cave" from Plato's *Republic* that you so eloquently described above. The New Testament writers did not see this world as an illusion, but they did believe the world as they knew it prevented human beings from experiencing the reality of God's grace and love. The story of Jesus's transfiguration (Mark 9:2–8) was designed to teach Christians that this world did not have the last word. God had something better in mind—not merely a heaven of eternal bliss, but a vision for a world where the last are first and the first are last (Mark 10:31), where the poor are lifted up and the hungry are filled (Luke 1:52–53), where peacemakers, the merciful, and the meek are blessed (Matthew 5:5–9).

When early Christians gathered for worship they celebrated this different reality in spite of their current circumstances. They may have been low in the pecking order of Greco-Roman culture, but in worship they saw themselves as "a chosen race, a royal priesthood, a holy nation" (1 Peter 2:9). The world in which they lived may have been filled with pain and sorrow, but in worship they rejoiced in a world where God "will wipe every tear from their eyes," where "death will be no more; mourning and crying and pain will be no more" (Revelation 21:4). They may have felt powerless against the principalities and powers of this world, but in worship even the "gates of Hades" (Matthew 16:18) could not prevail against them. No wonder the writer of Acts describes "something like scales" (9:18) falling from Paul's eyes after his conversion.

One could make the argument that these early Christians were duping themselves, but I contend they were merely practicing what you and I advocate. They made a choice of a worldview, or framework, that guided their lives in positive ways, and reinforced that vision in worship. They had no designs on wielding power or forcing their agenda on those who did not want it, and they certainly did not choose their way of life for personal gain. On the contrary, choosing this way of life often thrust them to the margins of society, made them pariahs to most people, and put them in danger of persecution. Yet their guiding vision of a kingdom where God's will is done "on earth as is it in heaven" so transformed their culture that those who wanted to "make Rome great again" groused, "These people who have been turning the world upside down have come here also. . . . They are all acting contrary to the decrees of the emperor, saying there is another king named Jesus" (Acts 17:6–7). One could substitute the word "president" for "emperor" and it would be just as true today as it was then. Lord only knows what the emperor would have said on Twitter.

Therefore, I think it is time for Christians to rediscover the centrality of worship as a countercultural enterprise. When corporate worship is designed to magnify the God we know in Christ, who upends the principalities and powers of this world, people of faith are not easily suckered by the lies out of Washington or the lies out of Wall Street, Main Street, and Hollywood. In my previous life as a Southern Baptist I became increasingly uneasy about the relentless emphasis on church growth fostered by the denomination and engrained in its spiritual DNA. Everything in worship was supposed to be designed to win converts to Christ. Such might be a laudable goal, but it turns two thousand years of Christian worship on its head, and reduces worship to a means to an end. I wrote my doctoral thesis on the subject of worship, concentrating on ways a Baptist church could focus on God instead of trying to get butts in the pews. An elderly lady in the church I served at the time asked if she could read my thesis. When she finished she said, "I'm seventy years old, and I've been a Baptist all my life, and this is the first time I've ever heard anybody say the purpose of Sunday morning was something other than getting people saved."

Some traditions put time, energy, and money into programs designed to attract people to church so they can come to worship and fill up the sanctuary. The rise of the megachurch has sweetened the pot with entertainment. Most megachurches, in fact, do not even call their meeting space a "sanctuary," preferring instead the word "auditorium," so as to transform worship into a performance for consumers. Of course, there is certainly no excuse for dull, dry worship experiences, but such an emphasis again misses the point. Worship is supposed to call us to see life from God's perspective alone. When the stress is on evangelism, politics, or feeling good, we become prey to the siren call of what sociologist Christian Smith calls "Moralistic Therapeutic Deism":

> Moralistic Therapeutic Deism is a pseudoreligion that jettisons the doctrines of historical biblical Christianity and replaces them with feel-good, vaguely spiritual nostrums. In M.T.D., the highest goal of the religious life is being happy and feeling good about oneself. It's the perfect religion for a self-centered, consumerist culture. But it is not Christianity.[5]

Following Jesus was never supposed to be easy, but we Americans have found a way to do it, and too much of our worship reinforces it. People of faith could find a model in the civil rights movement of the 1950s and 1960s. Most people are familiar with the images of fire hoses tumbling African Americans down the streets of Birmingham, Alabama, or protesters beaten on the Edmund Pettus Bridge in Selma, but how many know what preceded those events? Corporate worship.

Those who wanted to make a difference in the world gathered in African American churches to sing and pray and listen to preaching that pointed every person in the sanctuary toward a reality vastly different from segregated schools, buses, and lunch counters. Fortified with such a vision, they went into the streets to face police dogs and billy clubs. I pray for the day when those of us who have practiced comfortable Christianity for too long can find the same courage through our worship services.

Second, we can reclaim the religious voice in our day through political effort. However, by this I do not mean the kind of political activism found in most churches. In their book *Resident Aliens*, Stanley Hauerwas and William Willimon claim that both conservative and liberal churches are basically accommodationist (in the sense of accommodating themselves to the surrounding culture) in their social ethic. Both wrongly assume that the American church's primary social task is to underwrite American democracy.[6] Such a mistaken assumption is usually voiced as a desire to "make the world a better place," or "bring peace and justice to the nation." However,

> Big words like "peace" and "justice," slogans the church adopts under the presumption that, even if people do not know what "Jesus Christ is Lord" means, they will know what peace and justice means, are words awaiting content. The church really does not know what these words mean apart from the life and death of Jesus of Nazareth. After all, Pilate permitted the killing of Jesus in order to secure both peace and justice (Roman style) in Judea. It is Jesus's story that gives content to our faith, judges any institutional embodiment of our faith, and teaches us to be suspicious of any political slogan that does not need God to make it credible.[7]

Therefore, I want to argue, along with Hauerwas and Willimon, that the political task of the church *is to be the church*. If we could reclaim the radical, countercultural nature of Christian faith, I believe hatemongers posing as people of faith could be exposed for the hypocrites they are. Perhaps there is no more radical instruction than this:

> I appeal to you therefore, brothers and sisters, by the mercies of God, to present your bodies as a living sacrifice, holy and acceptable to God, which is your spiritual worship. Do not be conformed to this world, but be transformed by the renewing of your minds, so that you may discern what is the will of God—what is good and acceptable and perfect (Romans 12:1–2).

What would happen if disciples of Jesus took the risk of living lives and practicing faith that did not "conform" to consumer mentality, militarism, and valuing only beautiful people? What would happen if those same disciples eschewed devotion to the Democratic or Republican Parties, or any "ism" currently available, and instead asked the old question of "What would Jesus do?" The question is dismissed by some as overly simplistic, but it is a better place to start than the wholesale assimilation of American culture (or any other culture) into the church. "The business of the church," says pastor and church consultant Michael Piazza, "is to change people. The business of the corporation is to satisfy them. Churches that get that backward die, and should."[8]

It is helpful at this point to return to Bonhoeffer's discussion of stupidity. I have seen the quote above on Facebook memes, which leaves the impression he is simply condemning stupid people, or, for our purposes, willfully ignorant people. But Bonhoeffer has a more lofty purpose in mind. He desires nothing less than the kind of transformation the apostle Paul discussed in Romans 12:

> Only an act of liberation, not instruction, can overcome stupidity. Here we must come to terms with the fact that in most cases a

genuine internal liberation becomes possible only when external liberation has preceded it. Until then we must abandon all attempts to convince the stupid person. This state of affairs explains why in such circumstances our attempts to know what "the people" really think are in vain and why, under these circumstances, this question is so irrelevant for the person who is thinking and acting responsibly. The word of the Bible that the fear of God is the beginning of wisdom declares that the internal liberation of human beings to live the responsible life before God is the only genuine way to overcome stupidity.[9]

Finally, we can reclaim the religious voice in our day if progressively minded Christians reclaim the Bible as the language of faith. America has largely become a biblically illiterate country. One could excuse it among those who only attend worship on Christmas and/or Easter, but it is inexcusable among those who claim to take their faith seriously. My Southern Baptist training taught me Bible stories and passages, but I had to go elsewhere for nuance, history, and the meaning of myth in those stories. In the United Church of Christ, however, I encountered a tradition that seemed to have given up the Bible for Lent and never took it up again. Most of my parishioners were well-read in a number of fields, but woefully (might I even say "willfully") ignorant of the book they claimed was the basis of their faith. A parishioner actually confessed to me that one reason he and his wife were leaving the church I served was because I wanted everyone to be in Bible study, but he and his wife were "just not into that."

Such sentiments cede the battlefield to the creationists and the "God hates fags" crowd. And on those occasions when they interact with those shouting "Build the wall!" in Jesus's name, they cannot speak in a common language. The biblical story of the Tower of Babel (Genesis 11:1–9) plays out metaphorically—no one can comprehend what others are saying. Quotes from Joseph Campbell or Reinhold

Niebuhr will not be heard by fundamentalists. Only an appeal to scripture will suffice, and, even in that case, minds will not be changed. But others listening to the conversation, who are searching for something to believe in, just might discover that not all Christians check their brains, as well as their hearts, at the sanctuary door.

Progressively minded Christians must get over the fear of sounding like fundamentalists when quoting the Bible. Over the years I have engaged scores of questioning people who were pleasantly surprised to discover there was a different way to look at the Bible than straight-jacket literalism. In fact, literalism is the new kid on the block in biblical interpretation. It arose with Enlightenment thinking and was eventually appropriated by conservative Christianity in the western world. Literalism makes the Bible an idol, and seekers of deeper truth are happy to know they are not required to believe there was a literal ark with a giraffe's head poking out of a porthole bobbing in the waters of a flooded earth. (I have even seen drawings of dinosaurs marching two by two into the ark. Sheesh!)

When Jesus was handed the scroll at the synagogue in Nazareth (Luke 4:16–30) he read these words and claimed to be the fulfillment of them: "The Spirit of the Lord is upon me, because he has anointed me to bring good news to the poor. He has sent me to proclaim release to the captives and recovery of sight to the blind, to let the oppressed go free, to proclaim the year of the Lord's favor." The initial response of the worshippers was positive. "All spoke well of him." If Jesus had launched into a frivolous sermon about patriotism, or remaining true to Grandma's faith, or making Israel great again, the congregation might have dismissed the current rabbi and named Jesus the preaching minister. But Jesus used the occasion to take his hearers to task on their exclusion of foreigners and others who were different from them, and he did it by quoting their own Bible to them. The stories of the widow from Sidon (1 Kings 17:8–16) and Naaman the Syrian (2 Kings 5:1–19) were familiar to everyone, but to hear them used to make hamburger out of the congregation's sacred cows was more than they could bear. No wonder they tried to hurl Jesus off a cliff.

When Attorney General Jeff Sessions almost gleefully announced an end to the Deferred Action for Childhood Arrivals (DACA) program, I wish someone had been there to tell the story of Jesus and his family becoming immigrants and refugees (Matthew 2:13–15). Would Methodist Sessions have tried to hurl that individual off a cliff? When Press Secretary Sean Spicer backed up his boss's claim that his inauguration was seen by "the largest audience to ever witness an inauguration, period, both in person and around the globe," I wish someone had been there to quote Colossians 3:9–10: "Do not lie to one another, seeing that you have stripped off the old self with its practices and have clothed yourselves with the new self." Would Catholic Spicer have tried to hurl that individual off a cliff?

In a climate where the Bible is used as justification for condemning gays, separating children at the border, destroying healthcare, enriching the 1 percent, and gutting programs for the poor, those of us who claim the Bible as our own must learn it, understand it, quote it, apply it, and practice it publicly if the forces of hatred are to be kept at bay. The stakes are too high to relinquish it to those who manipulate it for their own selfish ends.

Many people are familiar with Habitat for Humanity, but few know the name of its founder, Clarence Jordan. Jordan was a Baptist preacher who established Koinonia Farm outside Americus, Georgia, in the late 1940s as an experiment in Christian communal living. From the outset he welcomed anyone who was willing to live and work there, including people of color. In the Jim Crow South such a practice did not endear him to his neighbors.

So imagine Jordan's surprise when he was invited to preach at a church in South Carolina and found the congregation on Sunday morning to be racially integrated—whites and blacks worshipping together. After the service Jordan asked the old hillbilly pastor of the church, "How did this church get this way?"

"What way?" asked the country preacher.

"You know," said Jordan, "integrated. You've got whites and blacks worshipping together. That's unusual in South Carolina. In fact, it's unusual anywhere. How did your church get this way?"

The old hillbilly preacher pushed back in his chair and said, "Well, this church was down to a handful of folks when our last preacher died, and they couldn't get nobody to preach. So, finally, I went to the deacons and said, 'I'll be the preacher,' and they said 'Alright.' The first Sunday as preacher, I just opened the Bible to Galatians 3, put my finger down, and read, 'As many of you has been baptized into Jesus has put on Jesus, and there is no longer any Jews or Greeks, slaves or free, males or females, because you is all one in Jesus.' Then I closed the Bible and said, 'If you one with Jesus, you one with all kind of folks. And if you ain't, you ain't. So there shouldn't be no race divisions among us.'"

Jordan asked, "Then what happened?"

"Well, after the service the deacons took me into the back room and told me they didn't want to hear that kind of preaching no more."

"What did you do then?"

"I fired them deacons."

"How come they didn't fire you?"

"Because they never hired me."

"And then what happened?"

"I kept right on preaching that way until I preached that church down to four people. And I found out that revival sometimes don't mean bringin' people in but gettin' people out what don't love Jesus. Those of us who were left decided that all that racist garbage we'd been taught since we was knee-high to a grasshopper was just nonsense. When a body has really been converted and filled with Jesus, all of that baloney is just washed away. So after that we only let people into the church if they were really Christians. And the church started growing and kept on growing."

That night, Clarence Jordan was driven to his hotel by a sophisticated young professor of English literature from the University of South Carolina. He told Jordan that he drove seventy miles each way to attend that church. Jordan asked, "Why? There are plenty of other churches closer. Besides you're a student of the English language and that old hillbilly preacher can't utter one sentence without a grammatical error. Why would you travel all this distance just to hear him?"

And with level gaze the professor replied, "I go to that church because that man preaches the gospel!"[10]

And that's the truth.

CONCLUDING THOUGHTS ON TRUTH

KEITH PARSONS

Wow! If I stuck it to the hypocrites and ideologues the way you do, I would be dismissed as a "dirty atheist." You, with your Christian bona fides shining through, cannot be dismissed. Reading your last essay was like reading an Old Testament prophet rebuking the religious elites and establishment of that day, blasting the idolaters and calling out the self-servers who mask ambition behind a veneer of piety. David Hume said that when he heard that a man was very religious, he immediately concluded that he was a rascal. It was those idolaters and lip-servers he was thinking about. We need a lot fewer Christians like that and a lot more like you.

I asked you to explain how Christianity could reclaim its voice from fundamentalism, and your answer was to be *more* Christian and *more* biblical, and to reclaim a countercultural Christianity that opposes the gods of this world rather than providing theological cover for them. Like David Hume, I am an unbeliever, and we tend to see more easily the bad things about religion. We see the frauds and the hucksters, the dogmatists and the fanatics, and the pious liars and the smug hypocrites. We must remind ourselves that Christianity, at its best, is a counterculture that stands erect and delivers a stern prophetic "No!" to the headlong, and often heedless, pursuit of the supreme values of this world—profit, pleasure, and power. Christianity at its best, right back to its Founder, challenges all that is superficial, selfish, and smug, and redirects us toward that which really matters, such as love, justice, and compassion.

And, as we have argued abundantly here, truth matters too— crucially and indispensably. If truth ceases to matter, then, very soon, nothing else will either, except for power. All evils in their infancy are cradled in lies. The Holocaust began with lies. Just as new evils are born in lies, so ancient evils prop themselves with a crutch of lies. The institution of slavery, tottering in its nineteenth-century senescence, was propped up with the lies of its dead-end defenders. Each ugly little bigot and every foaming fanatic is a fluent and practiced liar. Truth, on the other hand, is dreaded by tyrants, and that is why speaking truth to power is so important. Today's big-money special interests pay truth a backhanded compliment by their extensive and expensive efforts to distort and obscure it. Every corporate-funded "think" tank that churns out lies inadvertently reveals the elemental, visceral terror that the truth inspires in their paymasters.

What we are now seeing at the highest levels of power in our country is the complete devaluation of truth. A Niagara of lies gushes daily from the White House, in the form of 3:00 a.m. tweets, press conferences that are exercises in obfuscation, and pronouncements by the supposedly "serious" and "responsible" cabinet members. The Republican "establishment," though frequently a target of abuse by Trump loyalists, obeys a strict rule of silence, refusing to challenge even the most outrageous statements. As of this writing, the only exceptions are a few lame duck or out-of-office Republicans who have faced their last primaries. Democrats speak out, but they are easily dismissed.

What we need is for the most influential conservatives to do as William F. Buckley did when, in the pages of *National Review*, he excoriated the John Birch Society and its founder Robert Welch as extremists whose paranoia and detachment from reality (Welch regarded Ike Eisenhower as an agent of communism) endangered the conservative movement. Today, Bircher-level extremism is no longer fringe, but is mainstream doctrine in the GOP, as shown, among many other indicators, by the unabashed repudiation of science by the highest officials. We earlier noted Charles P. Pierce's observation that when extremists are mainstreamed, irrationality is normalized and stupidity is elevated to the level of a virtue.

The surest symptom of willful stupidity is an absolute imperviousness to the truth. When I first started to blog I was astonished at the number of correspondents who positively refused to be swayed by any amount of evidence or rational argument. At first, I made the mistake of trying to reason with those who made outrageous claims, but I quickly found that every attempt to explain, clarify, or support was met with increasingly shrill and abusive rhetoric. I soon discerned that the aim of these interlocutors was not to engage in rational debate, but to insult, and, if possible, to provoke an emotional response from me. Making you angry or upset is precisely the aim of the internet troll, and I eventually learned to starve them by ignoring them, and by blocking them if they were persistent. The ultimate social media troll now occupies the White House, and his verbal emissions cannot be blocked.

In this dire situation, both secular and religious people must unite to affirm that truth is a crucial value and truthfulness is a supremely important virtue. We must speak the truth as we honestly perceive it, and we must speak our truth to power. Obscurantists will surely attack us with their weapons of ridicule, misrepresentation, and calumny, but we must not be deterred. We also must not descend to their level of scurrility and hatefulness (see the next section on civility). To reject our current culture of lies and steadfastly seek and speak the truth is the noblest form of dissent.

CONCLUDING THOUGHTS ON TRUTH

PARIS DONEHOO

Perhaps the word you and I have been dancing around throughout this chapter is the one attributed to comedian Stephen Colbert: "Truthiness." He used it in the premier episode of his satirical show *The Colbert Report* because "truth" did not convey the absurdity he was trying to convey. "We're not talking about truth," he said. "We're talking about something that seems like truth—the truth we want to exist."[1] In character that night as Dr. Stephen T. Colbert, he scoffed, "Now I'm sure some of the 'word police,' the 'wordinistas' over at Webster's are gonna say, 'Hey, that's not a word.' Well, anybody who knows me knows I'm no fan of dictionaries or reference books. They're elitist. Constantly telling us what is or isn't true. Or what did or didn't happen."[2]

It was funny that night. It's not funny anymore. When Kellyanne Conway castigated the media for not covering a massacre in Bowling Green, Kentucky, she was resorting to "truthiness." Conway needed facts to demonstrate Trump's travel ban was not anti-Muslim, so she concocted one. Two Iraqi refugees had masterminded the "Bowling Green Massacre," and "most people don't know that because it didn't get covered." Media outlets all over the country immediately exposed the facts. The "massacre" was not covered by the media because it never happened. Two Iraqi citizens living in Bowling Green *were* arrested in 2011 and sent to federal prison for attempting to send weapons and money to al-Qaeda in Iraq, but there was never any violence, much less a massacre. And the story *was* covered by more than ninety newspapers, not even counting TV news coverage.[3]

Comedians everywhere had a field day with Conway's gaffe, and wags all over the nation had fun with it. Musician Dave Stinton posted a YouTube video singing a plaintive song called "That Day in Bowling Green."[4] Someone even fabricated a website for the "Bowling Green Massacre Victims Fund." Yet Conway was never censured by Trump, nor was there a cry from his loyal supporters to fire her for playing fast and loose with facts. No, as of this writing she is still serving as counselor to the president. Ergo, truthiness reigns supreme.

Truthiness has weaseled its way into religion as well. At public events where I meet someone for the first time, and he or she discovers I am a minister, I am usually given one of two responses. Either the person (a) launches into an apologetic or angry explanation for why he or she does not attend church, or (b) dismisses the particularity of my faith with this bromide: "Well, aren't we all worshipping the same God?" In my younger days I might politely agree and excuse myself for a second helping at the punch bowl. After forty years of suffering through such vacuous comments, however, now I am more likely to say something like, "If you're worshipping the God of the Ku Klux Klan, then, no, we're not worshipping the same God. If you're worshipping the God who tells you to picket the funerals of dead soldiers because Americans don't hate gays enough, then, no, we're not worshipping the same God. If you're worshipping the God who asks nothing from you but lip service, then, no, we're not worshipping the same God."

The adherent of truthiness affirms "we are all worshipping the same God" because it is convenient and does not require us to examine our commitments and our practices. Truthiness would have Christians believe:

1. *America is God's nation.* I saw a Facebook post from someone defending brutal attacks on Barak Obama because, he claimed, "God gave Israel to the Jews, and he gave America to the Christians." I wonder what he would say to Jesus, who countered, "My kingdom is not from this world" (John 18:36)?

2. *We need to go back to the old-time religion.* If by "old-time religion" one means an uncompromising commitment to the Bible and the model of the early church, I would agree. What is usually meant by "old-time religion," however, is regression to whatever era better suited the one decrying the present day. I confess to wistful feelings for a simpler time as well, but I lean on the words of Hebrews 13:8: "Jesus Christ is the same yesterday and today and forever."

3. *God is a God of love, yes, but . . .* I have heard this sentiment expressed verbatim or suggested in other words. Some believers think God's love must have limits. After all, don't we mere mortals struggle to love unconditionally? This theology, however, gives us an easy "out." As long as God's love has the word "but" as an addendum, one can excuse any lie, any harm, any oppression as a necessary exception to God's love. Never mind 1 John 4:8: "Whoever does not love does not know God, for God is love." There is no "but" at the end of that sentence.

Truthiness in science is manifested, as you so ably describe, in climate-change denial, and creation "science." Truthiness in the media is manifested in Breitbart News and others of its ilk. But truthiness in faith is particularly disturbing to me because the church should serve as a counterbalance to the three idolatries above. Far too many congregations, however, act as if they are the religious wings of the Republican or Democratic parties, or they are more interested in feeling good than in practicing discipleship, or they merely hide their collective heads in the sand, hoping for better days ahead. In other words, they are trying to be anything except the church.

Many theologians and historians believe the western church is currently experiencing a reformation which, in the long run, will prove to be just as far-reaching as the sixteenth-century Protestant Reformation. Looking back over my four decades in ministry, I am inclined to agree. The only question is whether the reforms will strengthen the church or undermine it. The future hangs on whether or not people of faith follow the Truth who "became flesh and lived among us" (John 1:14), or succumb to the lure, and the expediency, of truthiness.

NO CIVILIZATION WITHOUT CIVILITY

WHAT IS CIVILITY?

PARIS DONEHOO

It is not without a sense of irony that you and I move now to the subject of civility. Both of us have made rather uncharitable statements in the last chapter about Trump and his minions. To some our words will be called uncivil, and our arguments here will be dismissed as hypocritical. I suppose, therefore, that you and I could rely on the time-honored Southern tradition of blunting the edge of our words by simply attaching the suffix "Bless his/her heart" to every poisonous observation—i.e., "He's so stupid he couldn't pour water out of a boot with the instructions printed on the heel, bless his heart," or "She's so ugly she would make a freight train take a dirt road, bless her heart."

Another option would be the tradition of just avoiding unpleasant discussions altogether. My late mother-in-law used to sweep difficult discussions under the rug with the words, "We don't talk about unpleasantries." Although I did not hear those words until I was a young adult, I certainly practiced them for too many years. Only in the care of several excellent professional counselors was I able to untangle the web of denial through which I subsumed a seething anger beneath a veneer of amiability.

Such personal deceit is particularly destructive within church life. Persons bring into the sanctuary, as they should, their personal fears and annoyances, but, instead of dealing with them honestly, they often push them down in order to maintain friendly relationships. Sooner or later, however, those subterranean demons must surface, and they often are transferred to petty issues like carpet color or changes to the bylaws. In my Baptist days, a fellow clergyperson joked about congregations that argue and split into two churches instead of one with the new entity calling itself something like "Harmony Baptist Church." My Dad, with tongue firmly planted in cheek, often said, "Church splits are mighty good for the pew business," as he presided over our family's church furniture manufacturing establishment.

Neither option promoted or preserved civility during our childhoods, and they are particularly anemic now. You and I lived through the tumultuous days of the 1960s, when our parents were shocked at the vitriol generated by the civil rights movement and the Vietnam War. Over the years, however, I have watched as honest discussion deteriorated into angry debate, and angry debate degenerated into shrieking dispute. The goal, it seems, is not a mutual exchange of ideas, or even winning an argument, but demonization of the one with a different opinion. A political cartoon I saw aptly sums up our current situation. It depicts an open casket with the words "Civil Discourse" printed on the top with two women gazing down at the deceased. One woman says, "He looks so natural," and the other woman counters, "No he doesn't."[1]

Is our situation worse than the antebellum days when Congressman Preston Brooks attacked Senator Charles Sumner with a cane in the Senate chamber?[2] Perhaps not, but such is not the point. You and I do not live in nineteenth-century America. We live in twenty-first-century America, and we must decide what civility means, and practice it, if our society is to avoid another tragedy on par with the Civil War.

So, from my religious framework, how should I define civility? As always, I begin with Jesus. Some of his most famous sayings from the Sermon on the Mount and elsewhere deal with the gracious treatment of others:

"Blessed are the peacemakers, for they will be called children of
  God" (Matthew 5:9).
"I say to you that if you are angry with a brother or sister, you will
  be liable to judgment" (Matthew 5:22).
"Let your word be 'Yes, Yes' or 'No, No'; anything more than this
  comes from the evil one" (Matthew 5:37).
"Do not resist an evildoer. But if anyone strikes you on the right
  cheek, turn the other also" (Matthew 5:39).
"Love your enemies and pray for those who persecute you"
  (Matthew 5:44).
"Do not judge, so that you may not be judged. . . . Why do you see
  the speck in your neighbor's eye, but do not notice the log in
  your own eye?" (Matthew 7:1, 3).
"Then Peter came and said to him, 'Lord, if another member of the
  church sins against me, how often should I forgive? As many as
  seven times?' Jesus said to him, 'Not seven times, but, I tell you,
  seventy-seven times'" (Matthew 18:21–22).

The epistles of the New Testament seek to follow Jesus's example.
The apostle Paul scolded the Christians in Corinth for settling disputes in court instead of resolving disagreements within the assembly
of believers (1 Corinthians 6:1–6). The methodology should be love,
said Paul, with the goal of spiritual maturity: "Speaking the truth in
love, we must grow up in every way into him who is the head, into
Christ" (Ephesians 4:15). The writer of 2 Timothy counsels, "The
Lord's servant must not be quarrelsome but kindly to everyone, an apt
teacher, patient, correcting opponents with gentleness" (2:24–25).[3]
And you do not have to be a biblical scholar to surmise there must
have been a problem with uncivil talk and behavior within the faith
community addressed by the book of James:

"If you have bitter envy and selfish ambition in your hearts, do not be boastful and false to the truth. . . . For where there is envy and selfish ambition, there will also be disorder and wickedness of every kind" (James 3:14, 16).

"Do not speak evil against one another, brothers and sisters" (James 4:11).

"With [the tongue] we bless the Lord and Father, and with it we curse those who are made in the likeness of God. From the same mouth come blessing and cursing. My brothers and sisters, this ought not to be so" (James 3:9–10).

Clearly, the impetus of Christian faith is toward gentle speech and action. Even when disagreements arise, as they always will, the pattern of Jesus is to seek the wellbeing of the other person with respect and care.

At this point, however, honesty demands I acknowledge many apparently uncivil statements from Jesus. Along with soothing words about forgiveness and kindness, Jesus spoke his mind on many occasions, using phrases that would have horrified my matronly Southern mother if they had fallen from my lips:

"Woe to you, scribes and Pharisees, hypocrites! For you are like whitewashed tombs, which on the outside look beautiful, but inside they are full of the bones of the dead and of all kinds of filth" (Matthew 23:27).

"You brood of vipers! How can you speak good things, when you are evil?" (Matthew 12:34).

"You are from your father the devil, and you choose to do your father's desires" (John 8:44).

"You faithless generation, how much longer must I be among you? How much longer must I put up with you?" (Mark 9:19).

But Jesus did not limit himself to caustic remarks. All four gospel writers record one overt, ferocious act. Luke describes it this way: "Then he entered the temple and began to drive out those who were selling things there; and he said, 'It is written, "My house shall be a house of prayer"; but you have made it a den of robbers'" (19:45–46).

The authors of the epistles also engaged in speech that was less than benevolent. Paul was so incensed at those who taught that gentiles had to become Jews (and thus observe Mosaic law—even circumcision) before becoming Christians that he snarled, "I wish those who unsettle you would castrate themselves!" (Galatians 5:12). Elsewhere, he claimed, "Such boasters are false apostles, deceitful workers, disguising themselves as apostles of Christ. And no wonder! Even Satan disguises himself as an angel of light. So it is not strange if his ministers also disguise themselves as ministers of righteousness" (2 Corinthians 11:13–15).

So I appear to be on the horns of a dilemma. To be faithful to my religious tradition I can either follow the advice of my mother (and probably yours too), who said, "If you can't say anything nice, don't say anything at all," or I can rail against hypocrisy and injustice abroad in the land, but I cannot do both. Fortunately, as he often did, Jesus modeled a third option. He was willing to suffer—and ultimately did suffer—because of, and even on behalf of, the very people with whom he disagreed. During his abuse by Jewish and Roman authorities during his trial, he never lashed out at those who mocked him and struck him (Matthew 27, Mark 15, Luke 22, and John 19). Dying on a Roman cross, he gazed upon the very people he had denounced as "whitewashed tombs" and prayed, "Father, forgive them; for they do not know what they are doing" (Luke 23:34). Although he once denounced Peter himself as "Satan," and later heard his disciple deny he even knew him (Mark 14:66–72), the message proclaimed at the empty tomb was to "Go, tell his disciples *and Peter* that he is going ahead of you to Galilee" (Mark 16:7). In other words, though Jesus had criticized Peter, and been betrayed by him, Peter did not need to fear retaliation. When Jesus taught forgiveness, he practiced what he preached.

Therefore, as with truth, civility is a practice. "Speaking the truth in love" is not merely finishing an insult with "Bless his heart," but practicing sacrificial love toward those with whom we disagree, even those who seek to harm us. It means recognizing that even persons who disgust me, such as the Charlottesville Nazis, are human beings created and loved by God, and, thus, deserving of my respect. That image of God may be difficult to recognize, and loving them might mean holding my nose as I interact with them, but I have Jesus's example to follow. I am under no illusion as to the difficulty of this task, and Lord knows I fail often, but I cannot claim to be a follower of Jesus and practice anything less.

The problem with so much modern discourse is its lack of love for the other person or group. Our interactions are born in grievance and fueled by anger, if not outright hatred. James rightly saw such interaction as antithetical to the gospel and the character of Jesus, when he wrote in his epistle, "Your anger does not produce God's righteousness" (1:20). It may be a Herculean task to love one's enemies, but our current atmosphere of poisonous invective does not solve the problems besetting the nation, nor does it bridge the chasms of mistrust between us.

Defending her boss's crude attack on yet another critical journalist, White House press secretary Sarah Huckabee Sanders claimed Trump had every right to "hit back harder," rationalizing, "I don't think you can expect someone to be personally attacked day after day, minute by minute, and sit back."[4] I am glad Jesus did not practice such incivility. One would think that Sanders would know better since her father, Mike Huckabee, is an ordained Baptist minister. One would think her Sunday School class would have learned Jesus's instruction to "turn the other cheek" when attacked. Perhaps she was absent that day, bless her heart.

WHAT IS CIVILITY?

KEITH PARSONS

> *Act in such a way that you treat humanity, whether in*
> *your own person or in the person of another, always at*
> *the same time as an end and never simply as a means.*
> —Immanuel Kant, *Groundwork of the*
> *Metaphysic of Morals*

I had to laugh about those who say the nastiest things and conclude with "bless her heart." On several occasions I have spoken in favor of atheism before audiences of conservative religious people. When I do, some seemingly concerned person will arise to assure me in sanctimonious tones that he or she is praying for me. I tend to roll my eyes because I imagine what they are praying is something like this: "Dear Lord, please smite Dr. Parsons with all the plagues of Egypt. In thy mercy. Amen." Self-righteous people have ways of disguising their nastiness from themselves. Unfortunately for them, their tricks do not fool anybody else.

So, are we hypocrites because we say some seemingly uncivil things about Mr. Trump? The problem is that truth sometimes conflicts with civility. There are some truths that just cannot be said nicely. If Donald Trump is a lying, bullying bigot (Bless his heart!), pointing out that he is can only be said harshly. I try to address the truth versus civility conundrum below. Let me begin by saying what I think that civility is.

Civility means treating people with what is called "common decency," but which is all too uncommon and getting rarer. There used to be this thing called "manners." Hard as it is to believe today, these were actually taught to children. Sorry. I am sounding like the elderly curmudgeon that I am. The manners you and I were taught as kids meant more than not talking with your mouth full of food or using your indoor voice when inside. Being mannerly meant simply being aware that you are not the only person on the planet and that others have as much of a right to be here as you do. How you act around other people matters because their feelings matter and their feelings matter because people matter, even strangers. Therefore, when you are around other people you cannot indulge every impulse but need to exercise a degree of self-control.

I said above that civility matters because people matter, but why do people matter? Why does it matter how you treat people? As Kant famously put it in the above quote, you should treat people as ends in themselves, and not merely as means.[1] In other words, don't use or abuse people, but treat them as having inherent dignity. What is that dignity? It is the inestimable worth of rational beings, those who alone can respect moral goodness for its own sake. For Kant, the purest good is a good will, the will to do the right thing just because it *is* the right thing—out of pure respect for the moral law, Kant says. Humans have the capacity to choose the good simply because of its goodness, and this makes them worthy of the deepest respect.

In practice, what does showing such respect require? Basically, it means treating people as they show by their choices that they deserve to be treated. And what do people deserve? Well, departing a bit from Kant's script and giving my own view, I would say that, first, it means that every human being, bar none, has certain natural, inherent rights, where a right is a claim that someone can make that we have a moral duty to respect. Another great philosopher, John Locke, says that all human beings have a right to life, liberty, and property. We have a moral responsibility not to arbitrarily deprive someone of those things. This is why, for instance, the indefinite detention of human beings who have been convicted of no crime is a gross violation of their rights.

However, there are circumstances in which individuals may be deprived of life, liberty, or property, and it is no abuse of that person's rights when they are. Persons may be legitimately deprived of life, liberty, or property when they have chosen to do bad things, such as violating the rights of others. When we justly punish a criminal, Kant says, we are respecting his dignity, not violating it. Punishment can be an act of civility. We respect someone's worth and dignity by respecting their choices, and when they choose to do the wrong thing, we respect their choices by treating them as they deserve.

How you deserve to be treated is determined by how you choose to treat others. If you treat others with respect, then you retain your natural, inherent right to be treated with the same respect. However, if you trample on the rights of others, you thereby surrender your own claim to such rights. For instance, if you choose to steal or destroy someone's property, you thereby repudiate your own right not to have your own property taken, or your own liberty curtailed. What you choose for others, you, in effect, choose for yourself, and you cannot object when others, in the form of duly constituted authority, then treat you in the manner you have chosen.

Most of us, fortunately, are not in the business of punishing malefactors. What, then does civility require of us in our daily, mundane interactions? How, specifically, does it apply in our discourse with those with whom we disagree? Regarding the things that matter to us most, such as politics and religion, there are always going to be those with whom we have deep, intractable disagreements. These disagreements are deep in the sense that our positions are not merely collections of propositions to which we give intellectual assent. Rather, they are indicative of our basic moral and cognitive commitments. More things divide liberals from conservatives than the truth values that they assign to given propositions. There is some very interesting research that indicates that liberal or conservative convictions are rooted in fundamental features of personality and perception.[2]

When you are very different from someone, even concerning trivial matters of taste, there is a temptation to think that something is wrong with that other person. Sports rivalries sometimes turn bitter, and fans of the opposing teams view each other with deep suspicion if not dislike. I have heard that marriages in the state of Alabama have broken up over conflicting loyalties to the University of Alabama Crimson Tide and the Auburn University Tigers. So, when deep disagreements are about things that really matter, like politics and religion, there is a strong temptation to think that the other party must be somehow morally or intellectually flawed. Those bleeding-heart, crybaby, snowflake liberals. Those callous, clueless, crackpot conservatives.

How, then, do we listen to our better angels and treat civilly those with whom we have deep disagreements? Primarily, in addressing our interlocutors, our default assumption should be that we are talking to a rational being of good will, and not an evil idiot. One of the things I really dislike about some of the so-called "new atheists" of the past couple of decades is that they often seem to take for granted that religious believers are either knaves or fools. As I made clear in the introduction, I am a defender of "old atheism," which assumes that the existence of God is an issue about which reasonable people may be expected to disagree. True, there are irrational and fanatical theists—and atheists. However, there is no reason to assume that belief or nonbelief must be due to stupidity or moral turpitude, though I have often heard polemicists on both sides assert so.

So when you confront someone with whom you strongly disagree, civility requires that your default assumption is that he or she is a reasonable person amenable to rational persuasion. You respectfully address arguments and evidence toward that person and refrain from condescending, dismissive, or insulting remarks or implications. Sometimes you will get an equally reasonable and civil response, and then you can have a true debate, where important ideas get the attention they deserve and the ad hominem abuse is skipped. Sometimes, though, your effort to be reasonable is rebuffed and you get arrogance or hostility in return. What do you do then? I would say that you might note that you were offering to have a civil and rational discussion, and once more extend an invitation to have such a conversation. If again rebuffed, just break off the discussion. No need to get into a shouting match. Look for intelligent discussion elsewhere.

Sometimes, though, isn't incivility justified? Are not some people truly ridiculous or contemptible, and therefore worthy of being treated with ridicule or contempt? What about individuals of sordid character and extremist convictions, like Judge Roy Moore, recently defeated Senate candidate from Alabama? Are there not times that ridicule, in the form of mockery or satire, can be of great social benefit, exposing the nakedness of emperors, the duplicity of hypocrites, and the emptiness of self-serving bombast?

Yes indeed. I think one particularly memorable case was a highlight of the 2008 presidential election. For reasons that will probably never be fully fathomed, the usually judicious John McCain selected the astonishingly vacuous Sarah Palin as his running mate. Americans were faced with the prospect of the woefully unqualified Ms. Palin being but a heartbeat away from the most powerful office in the world. But the times call forth champions, and so comedian Tina Fey stepped into the breach. Her wickedly spot-on satire of Palin ("And now let me entertain you with some fancy pageant walking!") conveyed the disturbing truth far more effectively than any number of earnest editorials or grave commentaries. As H. L. Mencken put it, "One horse laugh is worth ten thousand syllogisms."[3] That is why the pompous, the sancti-monious, and the pretentious fear laughter more than anything. Surely, though, you are not respecting someone when you subject them to satire; satire is ridicule, and it is downright uncivil to ridicule someone.

So there is an undeniable tension here. You and I are defending both truth and civility, but sometimes the one conflicts with the other. Some people really are crackpots, fanatics, bigots, and liars; I did not hesitate to call them out as such in the previous section, and I will not in the remainder of the book. I think that such characterizations were eminently justified, despite their harshness. When, then, is bluntness to the point of incivility, or even ridicule, a justified response? How do we justify it without opening the door to every kind of incivility? If I claim to be justified in employing impolite discourse at times, cannot anyone, by that same measure, stake the same claim?

Jerks often excuse their insolence by saying that they "are only being honest." Honesty, however, does not justify gratuitous rudeness. Even when important issues are at stake, diplomacy (which is a laudable kind of hypocrisy) is still usually preferable to bluntness. Sometimes at meetings you might hear a colleague say something that you consider fatuous, but, out of respect, you refrain from saying just how silly it sounds to you. So, on many, indeed most, occasions, civility should be maintained even if it means refraining from speaking the blunt truth. Instead of saying to your colleague, "That is probably the dumbest idea I have ever heard!" say something like, "I see your point, but I am not sure that your suggestion would work in the present circumstance."

Sometimes, though, the situation is urgent and requires bluntness, or something even stronger. When something is not only wrong, but dangerously wrong, threatening seriously harmful consequences for many people, then you have to fight it with the most effective tools available, even at the expense of civility. The duty to be civil is a prima facie duty, but like all prima facie duties it can be overridden if the circumstances are dire enough. For instance, if mockery might help keep a dangerous demagogue from occupying high office, you might have to violate the rules of civility.

On the other hand, might not people, by their own incivility, abjure their own right to be treated with respect? Just as a burglar by his thievish actions surrenders his right not to be imprisoned, so those who traduce and revile others implicitly give permission to critics to speak harshly of them. No fair dishing out the vitriol and not being willing to get it back. It has always amused me, by the way, that the religious right has often denounced its targets—e.g., liberals, atheists, gay-rights advocates, evolutionists, and feminists—with rancor and contempt. Yet then, when somebody gives them back a little taste of their own rhetorical medicine, they shamelessly play the victim card as they whimper, cringe, and whine about the "persecution" of "good Christians" like them. Further, if anybody has ever deserved to be mocked, ridiculed, or put down it is Donald Trump, whose whole campaign was based on calumny, crude abuse, and even incitements to violence. He has no right to object when, say, Alec Baldwin mocks him effectively and hilariously.

Still, we might fear that by justifying ridicule and mockery in any instance, we are justifying them in every instance. Can we give clear guidelines specifying when such tools are legitimate and when they are not? I think so:

1) *Ridicule only the powerful, never the powerless.* After the 2016 election, when we heard that Trump had won due to the support of rural whites, some wanted to mock these Trump supporters as "rubes," "rednecks," or "hillbillies." Don't. It is shameful to blame the victim by mocking the marginalized, the oppressed, or the disadvantaged. There is a disgraceful scene in Bill Maher's film *Religulous* where Maher taunts and

ridicules worshippers at a truck stop chapel. The burly truckers responded with true Christian charity by allowing Maher to leave with all of his teeth still in his jaws. I read about some frat boys who thought it would be funny to stage a "ghetto party" where they put on black face and mimicked what they took to be the dress and mannerisms of inner-city African Americans. I would love to see those pampered and privileged guys try to negotiate the minefield that is inner-city poverty in this country. That would really be funny.

2) *Ridicule people for the bad, stupid, or dangerous things they have done, not for what they cannot help.* In medieval times it was considered good fun to laugh at a disabled person. Now we rightly abhor such behavior and are, or should be, deeply offended when we see a candidate for the presidency engaging in it. In other words, don't dehumanize people; rather, mock them for their all-too-human sins.

3) *Don't base mockery on offensive stereotypes such as those about race, ethnicity, gender, or sexual orientation.* Remember the old Ed Sullivan Show that was on every Sunday night when we were kids? One of Ed's most popular acts was comedian Bill Dana, who would portray José Jimenez, a dimwitted, buffoonish Mexican character who spoke in highly accented and broken English. Mexican-Americans were understandably offended by the invidious stereotype. Avoiding such characterizations is not just "political correctness," but shows decency toward innocent persons who have been harmed by such negative images.

4) *Observe limits of taste and decency even when you ridicule.* Not long ago a so-called comedian was roundly and rightly criticized for an image in which she displayed what appeared to be the severed head of Donald Trump. This was tasteless, inde-

cent, and inexcusable. For a comedian, it also has the disadvantage of not being funny. Satire is effective when it underlines and emphasizes the actual foibles of its targets. Palin's silliness and shallowness, and Trump's bluster and boorishness, so beautifully skewered by Fey's and Baldwin's impersonations, are what made those skits so funny and effective.

In short, public debate and discourse is often rough and raucous. Anyone who enters the public arena to do battle should not expect much deference or gentleness. I would say that vigorous and even boisterous disagreement is a sign of a healthy democratic process. In a society like North Korea, anyone who lampoons the Dear Leader will have a short and abruptly ended career. But standards of decency and civility should impose limits on even the most wide-open, free-speech-respecting society, and when those limits are too frequently flouted, especially by those in high positions, serious trouble starts to brew.

HAS CIVILITY BROKEN DOWN IN OUR DAY?

PARIS DONEHOO

I love the statement "Civility matters because people matter." Those words border on being Christlike. Jesus talked about treating other people with love and respect because to do so was the same as treating him with love and respect. More on that, however, in a later section. Perhaps "Thou art not far from the kingdom of God" (Mark 12:34, KJV).

I am glad you raised the subject of humor in civility. There is an old saying claiming the devil can do anything except laugh. I cannot help remembering those words whenever some petulant politician or self-righteous Christian pokes fun at the opposition but seethes with rage when humor is made at his or her expense. I am certainly not demonizing them, as many are wont to do these days, but I find it hard to trust anyone without the capacity to guffaw at his own foibles, or chuckle along with her challenger. Trump's angry tweets disturb me, not only for their crude content, but for his inability to laugh *with* those who are laughing *at* him. One need only look to Trump's speech at the 2016 Al Smith Charity Dinner—where politicians are expected to be self-deprecating—to see a man who not only feels no need to ask for God's forgiveness, but who cannot entertain any humor at his own expense.

By contrast, look to the 1960s, when *The Smothers Brothers Comedy Hour* often ran afoul of censors, politicians, and leading figures of the day, including President Lyndon Johnson. On their last show, however, Tom and Dick Smothers read a portion of a letter they had received from LBJ himself: "It is part of the price of leadership of this great and free nation to be the target of clever satirists. You have given the gift of laughter to our people. May we never grow so somber or self-important that we fail to appreciate the humor in our lives."[1]

I contend the loss of our ability to laugh at ourselves is Exhibit A in the breakdown of civility in our day. The writer of Ecclesiastes says there is "a time to weep, and a time to laugh; a time to mourn, and a time to dance" (3:4), but we have lost any sense of balance. Instead of a "both/and" society we have become an "either/or" society. Our local clergy association decided to devote a meeting to telling funny stories about our various ministries, but then came the horrendous carnage at a church in Southerland Springs, Texas. One of our number said, "I know we were planning to share funny stories at our next meeting, but given what happened last week, I don't think it's appropriate. Now is not the time to laugh."

On one level I sympathize. The horror of the massacre is beyond comprehension, and utterly heartbreaking, and I believe we should weep over Southerland Springs just as Jesus wept over the city of Jerusalem (Luke 19:41). But is life one-dimensional? Is there no response to such a monstrous evil other than dissolving into despair or becoming consumed with rage? Both responses are widely practiced, but neither is helpful. It is as if the seriousness of our era precludes laughter. When all of life is filtered through a dark cloud, then none of life is allowed to be joyful.

In my work as a pastor I counseled countless individuals who had lost a spouse or a child or someone else close to them, who felt guilty if they laughed or enjoyed themselves in any way. They felt it was somehow disloyal to their lost loved one if they moved on with their lives instead of dropping anchor in grief. Perhaps the ennui of our present time is rooted in something similar. Because so much is serious business we cannot allow laughter to permeate our belief system without letting "our side" down somehow.

Proverbs 17:22 says, "A cheerful heart is a good medicine, but a downcast spirit dries up the bones." I look around these days and I see a lot of downcast spirits and dried up bones. When *everything* is believed to be critical, cheerful hearts fall by the wayside. I have been told that Osama bin Laden's goal on 9/11 was not the destruction of America. He knew a handful of planes flown by amateur pilots would not bring the mighty United States to its knees. His goal was to sow seeds of suspicion, fear, and anger among the populace so that citizens would turn on each other. If such was his goal, he was more than successful. The antecedents of mistrust were certainly present prior to 9/11, but they have taken root in our collective psyche and produced an incredibly paranoid citizenry. And paranoid people cannot laugh with others or at themselves. During my regular dental checkup, the hygienist saw a TV report on the massive fires in southern California during the final weeks of 2017, and she informed me the conflagrations were set by terrorists. I thought she was joking until I noticed the deeply serious look on her face. Since she had a metal hook in my mouth at the time I decided discretion was the better part of valor.

One need look no further than the explosion (pardon the pun) of gun sales in this country over the last few years to realize just how fearful our society has become. On *The Late Show with David Letterman* I saw Letterman display a magazine ad featuring a beautiful landscape with a photo of an assault rifle placed in the foreground, and the copy read, "Peace of mind at 1200 yards." I wonder how many owners of such "peace of mind" have ever encountered the words of Jesus in John 14:27: "Peace I leave with you; my peace I give to you. I do not give to you as the world gives. Do not let your hearts be troubled, and do not let them be afraid." If they know those words, they certainly are not taking them along with them to the gun shop.

But it gets worse. During the consumer culture holy days of 2017— otherwise known as Christmas—Walmart sold Christmas tree lights made to look like red and green shotgun shells. Online shoppers could buy Christmas ornaments made from real bullet casings. On Amazon a shopper in the holiday spirit could buy a T-shirt emblazoned with the image of a pistol and the words, "If Jesus had a gun, he'd be alive today," or another one bragging, "Guns don't kill people. I kill people." You could buy a garden gnome brandishing an AK-47 and gaze at it in your yard while drinking from a gun-shaped coffee mug that makes it look as if you are holding a gun to your head every time you take a sip.[2]

Keith, both of our fathers were avid hunters. In fact, hunting was what bonded their friendship, and you and I tagged along with them on many a quail hunt. Neither of them, however, treated guns in such a cavalier fashion. They taught us a healthy respect for them, and they never used them fearfully. I once asked my Dad why he did not own a pistol, and he replied, "Because the only use I can think of for a pistol is to kill a man, and I don't need to do that." I believe your Dad and mine would have been shocked and offended by today's smug and vulgar gun culture.

Sociologist Philip Gorski says the subtext of our uncivil society is a basic misunderstanding of the kind of freedom that a republic promises—and demands. Many Americans conceive of freedom too narrowly, as mere *absence of restraint* or, more narrowly still, as the absence of *governmental* restraint. But freedom is more complex. Among other things, it means being the master of one's passions. People who cannot order and govern their own desires are not in control of themselves. They are dominated—tyrannized—by their own passions:

> There is no way around it: civic virtue is morally demanding. It involves self-discipline and self-sacrifice. The American founders rightly worried that the republican vision might be too demanding for the citizens of the young nation. "What sort of government shall we have?" Benjamin Franklin was reportedly asked at the Constitutional Convention. "A republic—if you can keep it!" he warned.[3]

One of the great attractions of libertarian liberty, says Gorski, is that it is morally undemanding. It requires little more than belligerence and bluster: "Mind your own business!" "Get off my lawn!" "It's a free country!" "I know my rights!" Libertarian liberty is a lazy person's freedom. But, then again, many people are lazy, and choose viciousness instead of civility.[4]

Thus, when the *Washington Post* reported the allegations about Senate candidate Roy Moore's sexual harassment of underage women, Moore was quick to couch the allegations as a "spiritual battle," and told his supporters, "I believe you and I have a duty to stand up and fight back against the forces of evil waging an all-out war on our conservative values."[5] His supporters took their defense of him to even more ludicrous extremes. Alabama State Auditor Jim Ziegler had the audacity to claim that Moore had merely followed biblical precedent. "Take Joseph and Mary," he said. "Mary was a teenager and Joseph was an adult carpenter. They became the parents of Jesus."

Ziegler's reasoning is absurd historically as well as biblically. First-century life expectancy was approximately forty years, so marriages took place at ages that would be considered very young by twenty-first-century standards. Plus, the scant records of Jesus's birth in the New Testament (it is mentioned only in the Gospels of Matthew and Luke and nowhere else) give no hint as to the ages of Joseph and Mary. We can only surmise their ages given the cultural practices of the time. The idea that Joseph was much older than Mary comes from the need for some within the church to support the doctrine of Mary's perpetual virginity. If Mary remained a virgin throughout her life, then passages like Mark 6:3, Matthew 13:55, John 7:3, Acts 1:14, and 1 Corinthians 9:5, which mention Jesus's brothers and sisters, are rather inconvenient, so a legend was concocted claiming Joseph was an elderly widower with children from a previous marriage. If Ziegler had bothered to do a little biblical and historical spadework he would have seen the fallacy of his own argument. But, as Gorski says, libertarian liberty is a lazy person's freedom.

When the United Nations voted 128 to 9 to condemn Trump's recognition of Jerusalem as the capital of Israel, the president characteristically went on the attack. "We're watching those votes," he sneered. "Let them vote against us. We'll save a lot. We don't care," implying a not so veiled threat to cut off foreign aid to countries who dared to disagree with Trump's America. UN ambassador Nikki Haley was more specific. "The United States will remember this day," she said to the delegates, "in which it was singled out for attack in this assembly. We will remember it when we are called upon to once again make the world's largest contribution" to the UN and when other member nations ask Washington "to pay even more and to use our influence for their benefit."[6]

Translation: "If you don't play by our rules, we'll take our toys and go home!" I was not surprised to hear such petulance on the playground at Knollwood Elementary School in Decatur, Georgia, but I never thought I would hear it spewed from the mouth of the president of the United States and echoed by his ambassador to the UN. It is one thing to object to a different opinion, but something else entirely when the objector turns to bullying. Civil societies must act civilly to each other or civility is dead.

Not surprisingly, this breakdown in civility is reflected all across America. One need only perform a random check of Facebook posts and Twitter feeds to see a society as divided, if not more so, than it was prior to the Civil War. A few days prior to this writing, a member of our local school board made some remarks about Jews and Muslims that many of us in the clergy found offensive. A well-worded, non-incendiary statement was drafted to express a counter viewpoint and was signed by many religious leaders (myself included) representing a variety of faith communities in town. The statement was read at the next meeting of the school board. Within a few days, hateful phone calls were received by the president of our clergy association and the author of the statement. Many of the rest of us (myself included), received anonymous mailings of a pamphlet called *Decoding the Mark of the Beast*. The message was hard to miss: "You are in league with the Antichrist, Buster!" Ergo, nations who disagree with Trump are threatened with a severing of funds, and clergy who disagree with a school board member are threatened with eternal damnation. Either case is unworthy of a civil society. I am not accusing the school board member of engineering these attacks. There is no evidence for that. Obviously, however, others were watching.

I must conclude with a cautionary note to myself as well as others who are disturbed by these trends. We cannot restore civility by resorting to uncivil speech and actions ourselves. Calling out the president and his henchmen for their unchristlike statements is fair game. Poking fun at them for the farcicality of their policies and behaviors is needed in a civil society. But painting fellow citizens who support him with words like "stupid" or "imbecile" merely fuels the demise of civility. I count as friends and former parishioners some who voted for Trump, and some who still support him, and they are good people, and intelligent people. I can disagree, and do so vehemently, with their perspectives, but I must avoid self-righteously reducing their personhood to nothing more than their opinions.

I was sickened when Trump publicly mocked a reporter with a physical disability. I need to guard against sinking to such a low myself. Moreover, I must constantly remind myself of the verse I quoted in the previous section: "Your anger does not produce God's righteousness" (James 1:20).

HAS CIVILITY BROKEN DOWN IN OUR DAY?

KEITH PARSONS

> *But somehow a movement based on ideas had devolved into a new tribalism that valued neither principle nor truth: A Brave New Age that replaced Edmund Burke and William F. Buckley Jr. with Ann Coulter and Milo Yiannopoulos. Moral reasoning was supplanted by polls; ideas were elbowed aside by charlatans and media clowns; while ratings spikes were proof that one was not "out of touch." The gleeful rejection of established norms of civility, tradition, and basic decency played well in an era of reality television, but was the antithesis of what conservatism had once represented.*
> —Charlie Sykes, *How the Right Lost Its Mind*, p. xiv

What you say about guns is profound and disturbing. As you note, you and I grew up with guns. In my house they were in the closets, under the beds, and I knew exactly where Dad kept a loaded pistol in his bedroom drawer. We took the presence of guns for granted. Yet what we see now is something different. It is some sort of weird gun fetish. Maybe it is the kind of the idolatry you spoke of earlier. When we are so paralyzed that the massacre of dozens in mass shootings, and even the mass murder of small children at Sandy Hook, cannot motivate our lawmakers to offer more than "thoughts and prayers," then we are in the grip of some obsessive fear, something we fear more than mass shootings.

Of course, politicians are afraid of the National Rifle Association, but those who vote for them are afraid of something else. As you say, we are terribly afraid of each other, so we are arming to the teeth. Why would fear go up as crime rates are dropping nationwide? Fear and hatred are two sides of the same coin, and unquestionably hatred is being whipped up by demagogues like Donald Trump who demonize Muslims and immigrants and scream that liberals are taking away our guns. Yet the current rancor has deeper causes, which I try to explicate below.

So, has civility broken down in our day? Of course it has. How, though, do you argue this other than anecdotally? It would be all too easy to go into curmudgeon mode and relate story after story to justify a foregone conclusion. For instance, surely, anyone our age has overheard teenage girls at the mall using language that, fifty years ago, would have made a sailor blush. Ever had someone race to get ahead of you in the grocery store checkout line? Ever had some jackass nearly cause an accident because he was too busy with his phone to drive? Sure you have.

Sure such things have happened to you, but are there any objective measures of incivility? Are there any quantified, statistical measures showing that incidents of incivility have multiplied in our public spaces? It may only appear to have done so because the ubiquity of cameras these days makes it so much more likely that jerky behavior will get widespread exposure. So on every evening's news we see incidents of road rage, and every comment section of every post on the internet has someone calling another a "moron" or "loser" or worse.

Each of us has had encounters with significant rudeness. Perhaps one reason for the pervasive nastiness is that, to use a gun metaphor, so many people now seem to go about with a hair trigger. They are waiting, perhaps hoping to be offended, eager for an occasion to fulminate.

A couple of years ago I published a piece on *Huffington Post* titled "Message to My Freshman Students."[1] It got over a thousand comments, some of which were supportive and some critical. Intelligent criticism is always welcome, of course. Some responses were bitterly rancorous and hostile. My article argued for the mild conclusion that freshmen should take more responsibility for their own education. I also pointed out that K–12 teachers were held responsible if students did not learn enough, generally as judged by standardized tests. In higher education, however, professors lead the proverbial horse to water, but the responsibility for learning falls wholly on the student. Some readers were *deeply, deeply* offended, calling me "arrogant," "condescending," and worse. Judging by the tone of some of the responses, you would think that I had suggested that freshman students be filleted, pan fried, and served up with truffles.

So, yes, it is very easy to get the impression that Americans are now a ruder and cruder lot than they were a generation or two ago. Is there any way to support this claim other than by compiling such anecdotes? What can serve as an objective measure of rudeness? I am fairly confident that some academic has developed the appropriate methodology and published the results in a peer-reviewed journal. For our purposes here, I propose a simpler but, I think, still reliable measure: See how people vote. If people vote for a spectacularly rude boor, then either (a) they approve of such behavior, or (b) they are not much bothered by it, at least not enough not to vote for the boor.

During his 2015–2016 campaign for president, Donald Trump consistently evinced behavior that was egregiously rude, uncivil, inflammatory, vicious, vulgar, and offensive. Yet sixty-three million Americans voted for him. Far from taking offense at his ugly oafishness, his supporters only rallied more strongly to him, seeming positively to relish Trump's bad boy persona. One can only conclude that, for them, Trump represented the ideal expressed in the title of the notorious 2 Live Crew album: *Nasty as They Wanna Be.*

But was Trump really any nastier than, say, the famously crude Lyndon Johnson? Johnson won by a landslide in 1964 after a campaign that ran ads implying that his opponent, Barry Goldwater, was a loose cannon who would get us into nuclear war. No contest. Trump's campaign was orders of magnitude nastier than Johnson's or any other in our lifetimes. Let's review some of its low points.[2]

In the Republican primary, Trump posted pictures intended to show that Ted Cruz's wife is less attractive than his wife, Melania. Besides making this invidious comparison, Trump indicated that he still thinks that appearance is the most important thing about a prominent woman. He, liar supreme, called Cruz "Lyin' Ted" and implied—no kidding—that Cruz's father was somehow involved with the JFK assassination. (Trump's comments often mix rudeness with nuttiness.) He referred to another primary opponent, Marco Rubio, as "Little Marco," and, in one incident future historians would have a hard time believing if it weren't on video, he defended the size of his penis when he thought that Rubio was questioning his manhood.

During his first televised debate, host Megyn Kelly asked him questions about his attitudes toward women, as when he called women he disliked "fat pigs" and "disgusting animals." Trump, offended that Kelly would have the rudeness to quote his words back to him, later illustrated his misogynistic attitudes with his infamous tweet alluding to her menstrual cycle. Equally infamous was the incident in which, furious that disabled reporter Serge Kovaleski had questioned one of his claims, Trump ridiculed the reporter, who suffers from a congenital condition that affects his joints. Trump mocked the reporter's condition by making spasmodic motions and distorting his voice. He later denied that he was mocking Kovaleski, but when you view the video of the incident, it is clear that this was precisely what he was doing. They say that Caesar Augustus would laugh at a hunchback. Donald Trump is not nearly so uncouth; he would only do so if the hunchback had criticized him.

"Politics ain't beanbag," as they say. You don't step into the ring without expecting to get punched. When you run for public office, you know that every aspect of your character and public record will be examined in the harshest light. You don't expect fairness, and if your opponent thinks that he can win by taking the low road, that is what he will do. Even judged by the lax standard of campaign rhetoric, Trump set new lows. He insulted a Gold Star family because they dared to criticize his bigoted attitude toward Muslims. He belittled the heroism of Senator John McCain, who spent years as a POW in North Vietnam, saying that he preferred those who didn't get captured. (Trump did not serve in Vietnam—or anywhere.) He consistently referred to his Democratic opponent as "Crooked Hillary," and led crowds in chants of "Lock her up!" He encouraged violence against demonstrators who protested at his rallies, some of whom were in fact physically assaulted. Locking up political opponents and calling for violence against protesters is something they do in Turkey or Russia, and not acceptable (until now) in the United States.

Since taking office, Trump's behavior has not gotten more presidential. Every criticism elicits angry 3:00 a.m. tweets filled with crude insults and personal disparagement. Female critics are especially badly treated. Trump said of *Morning Joe* commentator Mika Brzezinski that she is "crazy," has a "low IQ," and was "bleeding badly from a face lift" at a social gathering. Once again, Trump showed that, in his view, a woman's worst failing is to fall below his standard of female appearance.

So, again, those who voted for Trump either approve of his over-the-top boorishness or do not think that it is a very big deal. Maybe the reply is that when you cast a vote for someone, you do not thereby express a blanket approval of that person. Voting often means that you hold your nose and vote for the candidate that you think will do less damage. So casting a vote for Trump need not indicate any degree of tacit approval of his ugly attitudes and behavior. However, there have to be limits. There have to be things that candidates can say or do that simply disqualify them from consideration. If a candidate can say things that are bigoted (e.g., that Mexican immigrants are criminals), sexist ("Grab 'em by the [bleep]"), hateful (like making fun of a disability), dangerous (reporters are "enemies of the people"), and crazy (take your pick), and you still vote for him, then this inevitably says something about *you*. Either you endorse such statements, or they don't bother you that much. (They should.)

Those of us who did not vote for Mr. Trump have to face the fact that sixty-three million of our fellow citizens regard his grotesque incivility as, at worst, a venial and forgivable failing, a peccadillo perhaps, or a minor stain. Yet when the occupier of the highest national office consistently acts like a teenager having a tantrum, such behavior is normalized and mainstreamed. Manners matter. Rudeness is violence in the embryo stage. Those who have no compunction about being rude today will have fewer inhibitions about being violent tomorrow. So it really matters how we interact with each other, and those in the highest and most visible positions of public authority have a responsibility to maintain standards of civil and decent discourse.

If Trump were a complete anomaly, a phenomenon that could not have been anticipated, the political equivalent of the asteroid that wiped out the dinosaurs, then perhaps we should not be so alarmed. We could then see the Trump presidency as a bizarre aberration, an extreme outlier, like a thousand-year flood, that does not indicate an overall change of climate, and after which we can expect a return to normality. However, what we have seen in this country, for at least the last twenty-five years, is a profoundly deepening rancorousness and divisiveness in politics. Long gone are the days when even a Democrat could like Ike. Progressives disagreed with Reagan and George H. W. Bush, but few found them personally detestable.

That all changed with the election of Bill Clinton, whom Republicans vociferously hated and tried to remove from office. In turn, progressives vehemently and stridently despised George W. Bush and his whole administration. With the election of Barack Obama, the rancor reached an even higher pitch, unquestionably due, in part, to racism. I remember one "tea party" type carrying a sign reading "The zoo has an African lion. The White House has a lyin' African." The whole "birther" nonsense was obviously driven by racism. Now we have Trump, and the divide between his supporters and despisers is a Grand Canyon–like gap.

What we have seen in this country, then, is an excrescence of viciousness and vehemence in political feeling, as shown by the glaring heat of political rhetoric. Why? At the expense of being labeled an amateur and armchair sociologist (which I most certainly would be), let me suggest some possible reasons. We have already mentioned that the media and the internet endlessly repeat and magnify the inflammatory rhetoric and partisan fury. But where does the fury come from?

One obvious venue where the rhetoric has burned white hot is on AM radio, where Rush Limbaugh and his many clones dominate the talk shows. The success of Limbaugh was due to the fact that he discovered, and unleashed, the thermonuclear heat of white male anger. Since colonial times, white males had been the privileged class, enjoying innumerable unearned benefits and advantages over minorities and women. Then, in the 1960s, the civil rights and feminist movements began to chip away at the bastions of white male privilege, eroding the edifice bit by bit. By the early '90s, when Limbaugh became a prominent figure on the right, many white males, especially those of the working and lower-middle classes, had come to feel that they were the victims of discrimination. As they saw it, they were busting their humps in tough jobs while their meager salaries were heavily taxed to pay for welfare for minorities. As one bitter bumper sticker had it, "Work harder. Millions on welfare depend on you." Affirmative Action rules promoted women and minority members over white men, who, rightly or not, regarded themselves as more qualified.

Unquestionably, though, white male anger largely had an economic cause. For about thirty years after the Second World War, a man with only a high-school education could get a high-paying manufacturing job, for instance with General Motors or General Electric. Such jobs brought many millions of working people into the middle class. Later, as these jobs began to dry up (due to automation and outsourcing), a furious backlash grew among working men. That backlash took the form of a deep resentment, the feeling that all of society now existed to serve the interests of everybody except white male working stiffs, who were made the victims of "reverse discrimination" and caricatured in the media as clueless, bigoted "Archie Bunker types."

Few people took note of that swelling resentment, but Limbaugh did, and he told those disaffected white men exactly what they wanted to hear: Feminists are "feminazis," humorless, man-hating harridans who are the "political correctness" thought police. Minorities are now a bunch of crybabies who play the victim to excuse their own shift-lessness, constantly whining about racial oppression that no longer exists. Illegal Mexican immigrants are flooding the country bringing crime and taking jobs from American working people. Liberal politicians bribe their constituents with government giveaways and entitlements, funded by taxes on hardworking white men. Liberal academics are effete intellectual elites who amuse themselves by sitting around the faculty club, sipping Chablis, and making fun of Real Americans and real American values. Bureaucrats seek to justify their existence and expand their power by generating a byzantine regulatory regimen that oppresses small business owners and discourages entrepreneurs. It was a potent message, and it was heard and absorbed by millions, and not just by men. To the chagrin of feminists, many women have stayed firmly to the right, often taking the lead in the "culture wars" battles against abortion and same-sex marriage. Very many angry white men are joined in anger by their wives.

So I think that much of the heat of current political discourse comes from unleashed white male anger and the manipulation of that anger into support for a faux-populist right-wing extremism. White working-class men should be angry, but their anger has been exploited and directed at the wrong targets—feminists, minorities, and liberals—rather than the real architects of their misery—the real elites, the "pigs at the trough," as Arianna Huffington calls them.[3] These are people like the CEOs who, already obscenely wealthy, made themselves obscenely wealthier at the expense of workers in office cubicles and on factory floors whose pensions and 401(k)s disappeared. Working men are indeed getting stiffed, but not by the groups blamed by Rush Limbaugh.

Another problem is that, in many areas of the country, due to gerrymandering, the winner of the Republican primary is the de facto winner of the general election. Here in Texas, as of this writing, no Democrat has won a statewide office since 1994. The voters who show up to vote in Republican primaries tend to be the angriest and most extreme members of the electorate. The result is pressure on candidates to move ever further right, since an incumbent's greatest fear is to face an even more conservative opponent in the primary. This means that rhetoric gets more and more extreme as candidates must appeal to the angriest and most fanatical voters. With anger and extremist ideology fueling political rhetoric, it is small wonder that it has grown more inflammatory and abusive. Liberals, for their part, often respond in kind, dismissing conservatives as fascists, ignoramuses, and idiots. (If they are so dumb, how come they keep winning and Democrats keep losing?)

So we live in a dangerous time, when millions frankly detest millions of their fellow citizens. Speaking personally, I am not immune to the rancor, and it would be hypocritical for me to mount a high horse and assume sanctimonious tones of superiority. I hate that farrago of religious fundamentalism, free-market fundamentalism, gun fetishism, conspiracy theories, nativism, assorted phobias (homo-, xeno-, and Islamo-, among others), anti-science irrationality, and sheer tinfoil-hat-wearing lunacy that currently passes for "conservatism" in this country. (William F. Buckley Jr. is probably spinning in his grave, not to mention Edmund Burke.) I regard as detestable the media purveyors of this poisonous pastiche (it is too incoherent even to constitute an ideology). I also loathe the billionaires, like the Koch Brothers, who, not content to wallow in their own lucre, spend many millions to promote cruel policies that would deprive the widow of her mite. I despise the politicians who are the lapdogs of the Kochs and their ilk, and who throw millions off Medicaid to make a political point.

I am not just mad about one thing, but lots of things, and so, I think, is everybody. During past times of polarization, the divisions usually centered on one issue, an issue with many ramifications, to be sure, but still you could say pretty straightforwardly what was tearing people apart. In the Civil War, though North and South had many differences, slavery was the biggest wedge issue. During the Vietnam War, though many matters of lifestyle and outlook divided the "hardhats" from the "hippies," the war itself was the focus. Now there is no one focus. Many, many things divide us. It is not just abortion or gun rights or immigration, but these things and many more. Perhaps this is why the current conflicts have been called a "culture war." A culture is a whole complex of beliefs, practices, and traditions, and when cultures clash, the conflict is particularly intractable. When you dislike pretty much everything about someone—their beliefs, their tastes, their morals, and their whole worldview—then you are going to have a hard time being civil to them.

Like Limbaugh, the Republican Party took sides in the culture wars and launched its boat onto the rising tide of white anger. For a long while, the GOP had the best of both worlds. It could depend on the votes of angry white working people to stay in office, while all along fulfilling their true mission—namely, serving the interests of the rich and the large corporations. When running for office, Republicans would say all the right things about abortion, gun control, immigration, "family values," and the other wedge issues that were red meat for their angry white base. Once elected, Republicans got down to their real business of making the rich richer.

Eventually, though, the base grew tired of being taken for chumps by the GOP establishment and began to demand more than lip service for their votes. This led to the origin of "tea party" populism and to the success of Donald Trump. Donald Trump therefore is the big fat chicken coming home to roost for the GOP. After years of using code words and dog whistles to rile up the base on issues like gay rights and immigration, they opened the door for a man who shouts his bigotry from the rooftops and doesn't bother to dissemble or sugar coat. When Trump first announced his candidacy in 2015 with a denunciation of Mexican immigrants as criminals and rapists, his poll numbers shot to the top and, except for a brief period when he fell behind Ben Carson, his numbers stayed there through the primaries. The GOP made its Faustian bargain, and Trump is what they got, and a nation that has forgotten civility is what we all got.

WHY IS CIVILITY SO IMPORTANT?

PARIS DONEHOO

You may be an amateur sociologist, but I think your analysis is correct, particularly when it comes to the rise of angry white men due to their economic and social decline. A concomitant phenomenon (I speak as an amateur sociologist of religion), is the loss of the Christian church's hegemony in American society—specifically, protestant Christian supremacy. I don't know about your experience, but when we were kids in the cultural bubble of Decatur, Georgia, I did not even know any Catholics. I met my first one when I got to high school, and was shocked to discover he did not have horns and a tail. My friendship with him was my first step into the world of ecumenism. Everybody else in my world was either Baptist, Methodist, or Presbyterian, with an occasional Pentecostal thrown into the mix from time to time. To be fair, they did not all attend church regularly, but they all identified themselves as some flavor of Christian. I knew about Buddhists, Hindus, and Muslims (whom we mistakenly called "Mohammedans") only through the efforts of missionaries who crossed the pulpit of my home church to tell tales of their efforts to convert such "pagans." On a macro level, protestant religious leaders enjoyed ready access to the White House, and resolutions passed at denominational meetings could actually influence public policy.

All that began to change in the tumultuous 1960s. Though I would not notice it until much later, the churches that were full to overflowing began to lose membership. There were many contributing factors, too numerous to define here, but those who stayed in the pews began to panic at the trend. Many a pastor lost his job because he could not "grow the church." If it was not the pastor's fault then someone, or something, else must be to blame.

Enter Jerry Falwell and the Moral Majority. Falwell and others did not engineer the American church's decline, but they capitalized on it. The church was flagging, they claimed, because America was falling prey to an evil cabal of atheists, intellectual elites, pluralistic theologians, feminists, homosexuals, abortion rights activists, and liberal politicians. Ronald Reagan saw his opportunity and took it. Government is the problem, he claimed. If we could unravel government oversight of business, dismantle the welfare state, and get tough with the godless communists around the world, America would return to its former greatness. (Trump may have coined the phrase "Make America Great Again," but he did not invent its sentiment.) Ministers who had decried social action sermons by pastors who supported civil rights and attacked the Vietnam War, now publicly took up Reagan's call to arms. Some of them, like W. A. Criswell of Dallas First Baptist Church, openly endorsed him. By the end of George H. W. Bush's term, Patrick Buchanan would sum up the situation this way: "There is a religious war going on in our country for the soul of America. It is a cultural war, as critical to the kind of nation we will one day be as was the Cold War itself."[1] The change that had been sweeping the country since the sixties, he declared, "is not the kind of change America wants. It is not the kind of change America needs. And it is not the kind of change we can tolerate in a nation that we still call God's country."

The Southern Baptist Convention in which I had been raised, educated, and ordained, spent the late 1970s and all of the 1980s embroiled in a fight to wrest control of the seminaries from "liberal professors," and the denominational leadership from pastors "who don't believe the Bible," much of it spawned by ultra-conservatives like Judge Paul Pressler and Paige Patterson. (You may think the term "ultra-conservative Southern Baptist" is redundant, but at that time it was not.) Like Reagan had done on the campaign trail, and Jerry Falwell had done on TV, this new breed of religious leaders was smart enough to know how to take advantage of the fear stemming from the changes upsetting religious life in America.

Though I was never high in the pecking order of the denominational machinery, I eventually became a target. I had been outspoken in my disapproval of the convention's tilt to the extreme right, and soon I was painted as one of those reprehensible pastors who were out to ruin the faith of good Christians. A lady in my church struck up a conversation with another woman at the beauty salon, and when her new acquaintance discovered which church she attended, the woman stiffened, scowled, and snarled, "You know your pastor doesn't believe the Bible, don't you?" The word was out. The fundamentalists won the day, Paige Patterson became president of the seminary I had attended—until he was fired in the wake of the #MeToo movement[2]—and I moved my ordination into the United Church of Christ.

So why is civility important? My experience teaches me its importance because without it we lose our ability to speak to one another, trust one another, and learn from one another. The late theologian Carlyle Marney said, "One of the great adventures of life for every human being is to learn to put adjectives and nouns in their proper places."[3] The nouns, for Marney, were words like person, human being, and creation of God. They say something essential about someone, something without which he or she ceases to exist. By contrast, the adjectives were words like male, female, tall, short, fat, skinny, black, white, gay, straight, Christian, Muslim, conservative, liberal, Republican, Democrat, and a host of others—significant words, to be sure, but mere descriptors, nonetheless. When our social interaction elevates adjectives to the place of nouns it becomes easy to objectify, and ultimately demonize, those with whom we disagree. The personhood of the individual is lost. He or she is reduced to a stand-in for the group that makes us uncomfortable. We do not see a human being; we see a race. We do not see a creation in the image of God; we see a religion. We do not see a soul into whom God breathed the breath of life (Genesis 2:7); we see political party. Adjectives are important, but they are not ultimate reality. Civility is constructed on nouns, not adjectives. Unfortunately, our current culture is predicated upon adjectives instead of nouns. The descriptors seem to be all that matter anymore.

I could give numerous examples of how destructive it can be to forget the nouns, but let me deal with one of the most egregious. In rejecting a bipartisan deal on immigration reform, President Trump questioned why the United States would accept more immigrants from Haiti and "shithole" countries in Africa instead of from nations like Norway.[4] (Silly me; I had no idea Norwegians were clamoring to reach our shores.) Why would Trump prefer Norwegian immigrants over Haitian and African immigrants?

One answer would be that the former group is white and the latter group is black. If such is the reason, then Trump is elevating the adjectives in the immigration debate to the place of nouns, and forgotten (if he ever knew) the book of Genesis's assertion that of all humankind is created in the image of God (1:27). Moreover, if any Haitians and Africans are Christian (and many of them are), what is to be done with Galatians 3:28: "There is no longer Jew or Greek, there is no longer slave or free, there is no longer male and female; for all of you are one in Christ Jesus"?

So, is Trump a racist? He claimed to reporters, "I am the least racist person you have ever interviewed. That I can tell you."[5] Perhaps. I cannot look into any person's heart, but Jesus said, "You will know them by their fruits" (Matthew 7:16), and I see the "fruit" of racism in his remarks. An African American ministerial colleague said it more colorfully: "If it walks like a duck, and waddles like a duck, and quacks like a duck, it's a duck!" I shudder to think that we are returning to the kind of blatant racism you and I breathed as children in the deep South, when words like "black" and "white" were elevated to the status of nouns.

If Trump is not a racist, as he claims, there is yet another reason why he prefers Norwegian immigrants to Haitian or African immigrants. He says he wants to replace so-called "chain migration" with "merit-based migration." Chain migration is immigration whereby a person or family comes to the United States from a particular country (like Haiti or an African nation) then sponsors others, usually family members, from the same locale to join them here. By contrast, merit-based migration is founded on an analysis of whatever skills are deemed necessary in the current American economy, and immigrants are allowed into the country only if they meet the stated criteria.

Therefore, if race is not an issue for Trump, then immigrants from "shithole" countries are undesirable because they will not significantly contribute to the American economy. Only immigrants who can improve the lives of those of us who are already in the country are allowed to live and work among us. Once again, such a practice puts adjectives in place of nouns. Words like poor, rich, skilled, and unskilled become more important than words like person or human being.

If merit-based migration had been the law of the land during the 1950s, I would have never met my wife, Penny. Her uncle, Sylvestro Bonadonna, had been born in the United States to Italian immigrants, thus making him a citizen. As a child, he returned to Italy with his parents, and then came back to America as an adult. After the Second World War, when Italy was so devastated it could have been described as a "shithole" country, he sponsored his younger brother, Placido, to join him in the States. Placido sent for his wife, seven-year-old daughter, and six-month-old Providenza from Ventimiglia, Sicily. Little Providenza was given the nickname of Penny, the name she still uses today. Her parents were poor and unskilled, but they found jobs in factories and soon became US citizens, whereupon they began to "chain migrate" family members from Sicily to these shores. From the efforts of impoverished, barely educated immigrants, who would never meet merit-based standards today, America now enjoys the contributions of:

An orthopedic surgeon
A pediatric dentist
An elementary school principal
An occupational therapist
A lawyer
A computer specialist
A high school guidance counselor
The owner of an insurance agency
Real estate agents
Accountants
Numerous independent businesspersons

If Trump and his minions had been running the show in 1954, not only would I have been deprived of a wonderful wife, but this country would have been deprived of the gifts of Penny's family. The adjectives used to describe them obscured their value. Thank God, those adjectives were not the last word on the subject.

To my knowledge, Jesus never weighed in on the immigration debate, but he had plenty to say about what should be valued within human interaction. "When you give a banquet," he said, "invite the poor, the crippled, the lame, and the blind. And you will be blessed, *because they cannot repay you*, for you will be repaid at the resurrection of the righteous" (Luke 14:13–14, emphasis mine). Clearly, Jesus did not take skills or economic status into account when he assessed a person's value. Anyone who could call the poor "blessed" (Matthew 5:3; Luke 6:20) was looking at life through an entirely different lens.

My niece Melissa got the nouns and adjectives in their proper places when she posted a photo on Facebook of a child in Africa, named Moses, whom she sponsors through Compassion International. She wrote:

> Moses shares my birthday, and my faith in Christ, but we have nothing else in common. I guess he does live in a pretty undesirable place, but that was out of his control. I was born in the US and that makes me pretty lucky or blessed (however you choose to see it). My heart breaks for immigrants who are so desperate to find a new life and home in a place that is not ravaged by war, disease and poverty. In my opinion, the purpose of immigration is not to recruit ideal candidates for a perfect nation but to provide hope, opportunity and a second chance.[6]

There can be no civil society if the place of nouns and adjectives is reversed. Years ago, I stopped at a gas station, and the attendant struck up a conversation with me. I was enjoying our interaction until he referred to a prominent African American leader as a "banana eater." I quickly paid for the fuel and left the premises. His boorishness is etched in my memory because it stood in contrast to the more genteel language to which I had grown accustomed. Moving in church circles as I had for many years, I encountered numerous people who held opinions different from my own, but they were rarely expressed in such crass language. When Barak Obama was elected president, however, I was shocked at the latent hatred and rudeness that suddenly crawled out from the shadows. Rep. Joe Wilson (R-SC) yelled "you lie!" as Obama addressed a joint session of Congress. Arizona governor Jan Brewer stuck a finger in the president's face during a heated discussion about immigration on an airport tarmac in Phoenix. House speaker

John Boehner invited the Israeli prime minister to address Congress about the dangers of dealing with Iran without informing the White House. Often I heard the N-word applied to the commander in chief, sometimes in public, often in private conversation.

But I knew our society had turned an appalling corner when Carl Paladino, co-chair of Donald Trump's New York state presidential campaign, sneered, "I'd like [Michelle Obama] to return to being a male let loose in Zimbabwe" to live "in a cave with Maxie, the gorilla." Then he had the gall to claim his words were "not racist."[7] The sentiments of the guy at the gas station were now reigning supreme in public discourse. Civility either had been redefined or abandoned altogether.

I must, of course, apply the same standards to myself. The common good is not served when I, and others of my ilk, sink to the same verbal and attitudinal low that eviscerated Obama. As much as I enjoy calling Trump the "Orange Wonder" or the "Commander in Tweets," nothing is gained by resorting to snarky labels. As much as I dislike the opinions of Trump supporters, I must remember to see them too as nouns, not adjectives. I need to write Paul's words from *The Message* paraphrase of Colossians 4:6 on the tablets of my heart: "Be gracious in your speech. The goal is to bring out the best in others in a conversation, not put them down, not cut them out."[8] Nothing is gained if I merely parrot the same incivility I see in others. Incivility is compounded, not decreased. Democracy dies when we lose the ability to talk to each other, and opt instead for talking past one another. Jesus said, "Blessed are the peacemakers" (Matthew 5:9), not "Blessed are those who post slurs and insults on Facebook."

In the novel *The Great Divorce*, C. S. Lewis imagines hell, not as fiery inferno, but as a town made up of concentric circles of empty homes. Everyone lives at the outer edge of town because no one can get along with his or her neighbor:

As soon as anyone arrives he settles in some street. Before he's been there twenty-four hours he quarrels with his neighbor. Before the week is over he's quarreled so badly that he decides to move. Very likely he finds the next street empty because all the people there have quarreled with *their* neighbors—and moved. If so he settles in. If by any chance the street is full, he goes further. But even if he stays, it makes no odds. He's sure to have another quarrel pretty soon and then he'll move on again. Finally he'll move right out to the edge of the town and build a new house.[9]

Does life imitate art? There are indications that more and more Americans are choosing to live in communities where their neighbors think and believe much like they do. Rather than interact with persons who hold differing views, they prefer the echo chamber of like-minded neighbors. Rather than learning to interact with others in civil ways, we take the easy route of isolation and incivility. And, according to Lewis, incivility is the definition of hell.

Can we learn to talk with one another? We must. It is no longer an option, not just for our next-door neighbor, but also for the person with whom we disagree the most. Real-live conversation is a crucial avenue for dealing with people we consider truly contemptible. "You can't reason with Hitler," goes the old adage. I agree wholeheartedly. Perhaps, however, you could actually talk to him, or someone like him. The writer of 2 Timothy said, "The Lord's servant must not be quarrelsome, but kindly to everyone, an apt teacher, patient, correcting opponents with gentleness. God may perhaps grant that they will repent and come to know the truth, and that they may escape from the snare of the devil, having been held captive by him to do his will" (2:24–26). It takes time, and there is no guarantee of success, but talking with one another should be a civil society's first option, and it is the most Christlike action for a follower of Jesus.

I know this sounds incredibly naive, but I have seen it work. As a pastor, I had to deal with all kinds of people, some of whom were downright unreasonable. When I forgot the proper place of nouns and adjectives, and reacted with unreasonableness on my part, I simply made matters worse. When I took a deep breath, and tried to listen more than speak, I could sometimes defuse the situation.

A minister friend of mine named Gary demonstrated the value of this approach in dealing with one of the most contemptible groups I know—the Ku Klux Klan. During the early 1980s, Gary was a pastor in the small town of Millville, Pennsylvania. One evening in the fall of 1982 the Ku Klux Klan made an appearance in town. In full regalia, members of the Klan's regional klavern stood at the four corners of the town square handing out flyers promoting their racist ideology. The good people of Millville feared what might happen next.

At the next meeting of the local ministerium, of which Gary was the president, the antics of the Klan were the hot topic of the day. Because they were of one mind on the subject, they decided to publicly oppose the KKK lest their silence be construed as tolerance for such a malicious agenda. They composed an open letter to the Klan stating both rejection of their beliefs as well as a desire to meet their representatives. The letter was published in a local newspaper.

Not long after the letter was printed, Gary received a phone call from the local Klan leader accepting the ministerium's invitation for a meeting. They agreed to a date and location. Soon after the arrangements were made, a lieutenant from the state police called Gary and said, "We read your letter. I need to meet with you before you have any more contact with the Klan." He visited Gary at home and warned, "Please don't underestimate these people. They're dangerous and violent. They want to pick a fight." He then went on to describe how the Klan had recently manipulated pastors in Skokie, Illinois, into meeting with them and made sure the media took photographs of clergy shaking hands with Klansmen. When those photos hit the newspapers, the Klansmen were able to claim they were supported by local pastors. "Please, Pastor, don't meet with them," begged the state policeman. "We have the situation well in hand. Besides, we have people on the inside of the klavern, and if you pastors get involved it could jeopardize our efforts at neutralizing them."

Gary thanked the lieutenant for his candor and called an emergency meeting of the ministerium. The lieutenant was invited to the meeting. Not only did he show up, but the state police sergeant also attended, along with a cadre of pastors from a neighboring locality. The police and the visiting pastors vehemently objected to the proposed meeting with the Klan, and even scolded the ministerium for acting independently to communicate with the klavern. "What makes you think you bring any expertise to the table?" they admonished. "This will not end well. Please rescind your invitation."

When their guests had departed, the pastors of the ministerium conferred and discussed what to do. They decided it came down to this: If the danger of meeting with the Klan should not be underestimated, then neither should the danger of breaking one's word to an enemy be underestimated. It was a matter of integrity, they said. The meeting with the Klan would proceed.

On the appointed evening, three pastors met with three Klansmen. Each pastor tightly clutched a Bible in his right hand to insure there would be no photos of clergy shaking hands with Klansmen. When the meeting began, the Klansmen tried to provoke an argument in favor of their racist views, while the pastors based their position in scripture, pointing out the copious passages repudiating the KKK's bigotry and intolerance.

Over the following three hours, however, the tenor of the conversation shifted. Instead of spewing the party line, the Klansmen began to reveal the personal, not ideological, reasons for their anger and hatred. Two of them shared incredibly painful events from their childhoods and the lifelong suspicion of being consistently misunderstood. They acknowledged feelings of alienation, and the sense that they never really belonged to any group or to society at large. Tears streamed down their faces. Even though Gary and the other pastors could never excuse the venom that infected their souls, they began to see these Klansmen as human beings with wounds much like their own, and, in a way, they felt sorry for them.

And when the meeting was over, the leader of the klavern said, "You know, no one has ever taken the trouble to listen to us. If you don't want the Klan in your town, we will never be back." And they were as good as their word.[10]

Can this scenario be replicated everywhere? Of course not. But when name-calling and demonizing on one side is met with name-calling and demonizing on the other side, nothing changes. Martin Luther King Jr. said, "Darkness cannot drive out darkness; only light can do that. Hate cannot drive out hate; only love can do that."

What happens, however, when you cannot engage a person as a noun instead of an adjective? What happens when the shameful individual refuses to talk, or refuses to be trustworthy in his or her language? New York senator Charles Schumer likened talking with Trump to "negotiating with Jell-O."[11] Clearly, in such a scenario, civil conversation is not an option, at least not initially. If the perpetrator of injustice will not interact with integrity, should not I, as a Christian, be willing to blast injustice in all its forms? Yes, but not by playing by the demagogue's rules.

One of Jesus's most famous sayings is found in Matthew 5:39–41: "Do not resist an evildoer. But if anyone strikes you on the right cheek, turn the other also; and if anyone wants to sue you and take your coat, give your cloak as well; and if anyone forces you to go one mile, go also the second mile." These words would appear to be incredibly useless when facing a person bent on monstrous injustice. They sound passive and submissive. However, nothing could be further from the truth. In the Greco-Roman world of Jesus's day, only the right hand was used to strike another person because the left hand was used for "unseemly" purposes (think toilet activities). Therefore, to strike someone on the right cheek meant a backhanded blow with the right hand—precisely the way a person in a position of power would strike a peasant. To offer one's left cheek for another wallop required an openhanded blow with the right hand that would only be used by someone striking another person of equal status. Therefore, "turning the other cheek" meant the striker had to treat the peasant as an equal, or he must walk away, leaving the peasant to have the last word. The injustice is resisted without the humiliated one sinking to the level of the oppressor.

Likewise, the phrase "going the second mile" has been often misconstrued. Roman law permitted soldiers to force civilians to carry their gear for one mile, but because soldiers often abused the privilege, Roman law stringently prohibited more than one mile. To voluntarily carry a soldier's gear a second mile, as Jesus instructs, puts the soldier in a difficult situation. Either the soldier will appear to be flouting the law, and thus risking punishment, or he has to wrestle his gear from the civilian, again treating him as an equal.

Finally, under civil law, a coat could be confiscated for nonpayment of debt, but a poor person used the coat as a blanket at night. The only other garment typically worn by a peasant was an inner garment, a "cloak." Jesus says to voluntarily give up the cloak as well. In other words, to strip naked, thereby demonstrating to everyone what the system is doing to the poor. Moreover, in the Jewish culture of the day, nakedness shamed the person who observed it.[12]

In context, therefore, the phrase "Do not resist an evildoer" could more accurately be translated, "Do not retaliate revengefully by evil means." Rather than violently resisting or passively accepting the degrading words and actions of hate-mongers, bullies, bigots, and demagogues, Jesus advocates a third way. When honest conversation cannot broker mutual dialogue, Jesus would have us actively defy those who would "call evil good and good evil, who put darkness for light and light for darkness" (Isaiah 5:20) by loving them enough to stand in their way without sinking to the use of their tactics. Civility is right behavior just as much as truth is right behavior. "The good person," said Jesus, "out of the good treasure of the heart, produces good, and the evil person out of evil treasure produces evil; for it is out of the abundance of the heart that the mouth speaks" (Luke 6:45).

It should be apparent that this was precisely the approach of Mahatma Gandhi and Martin Luther King Jr. They fought to expose oppression, hypocrisy, and degradation without resorting to violence or invective. Perhaps nothing personifies this better than the words of Mother Pollard. Pollard was an African American woman living in Montgomery, Alabama, during the famous Montgomery bus boycott of 1955–1956. Though she was elderly (some reports claim she was approximately seventy-two years old), Mother Pollard joined in the boycott, refusing to ride the buses nor accept rides to any destination. When someone (possibly a journalist) asked her why she was, at her age, voluntarily suffering for what she believed to be a just cause, she replied, "It used to be my soul was weary and my feet were rested; now my feet is tired, but my soul is rested."[13]

In the face of those who would exploit the shrieking divisions between us, I pray for souls—including my own—that are rested.

WHY IS CIVILITY SO IMPORTANT?

KEITH PARSONS

I said earlier that civility matters because people matter. Individuals matter because rational beings bear an inherent worth and dignity. Yet we exist not just as individuals but as members of groups—families, communities, nations, and the human family itself. We are, by nature, social beings adapted by evolution to live in interaction with our fellow human beings. In prehistory, we interacted with small groups of seldom more than one hundred individuals. Now we live in a hyperconnected world that makes the seven billion (and counting) human beings our neighbors. For the foreseeable future we will have only this one planet to share, so we have no choice but to get along with our neighbors, whether they are next door or in Botswana. If we want to get along with our neighbors, civility is necessary.

Speaking of Botswana, as you note, there was a huge brouhaha over remarks credibly attributed to Donald Trump characterizing African nations as "shithole countries." We really do have to thank Trump for helping us to write this book. He makes sure that we never run short of fresh material!

Let's take his disgusting remark as a paradigm of incivility. What is the real harm of such a remark, especially if made by the president of the United States? Well, as you say, there is the obvious racial undertone. By contrast to his vulgar characterization of African countries, Trump spoke highly of Norway and wished that we could get more immigrants from there. (Lotsa luck with that! By many measures

Norwegians have it better than we do.) Trump's implied contrast was plain: Norway = white = good vs. Africa = black = bad. If the president says things that sound racist, then this inevitably reflects badly on the whole country. Image matters. It matters whether America is seen as saying "Give me your tired, your poor, your huddled masses yearning to breathe free" or "If you are white, you are right. If you are black, get your ass back to your shithole."

One reason that image matters is that we need people from those countries that Trump scorns. I loved your list of all the professionals and stellar achievers from your wife's family, the descendants of a group of poor, unskilled Italian immigrants who came to the United States in the early fifties. That story has been repeated many, many times here in Houston. Houston is now the most diverse city in the country. We have people from everywhere, including lots and lots from the supposed shitholes. These hardworking immigrants from all over, with their many rich cultural traditions, are making Houston into a showcase for the cultural and economic (and culinary!) benefits of diversity.

Trump, who must have formed his image of Africa from watching old Tarzan movies, also supposedly said that Nigerians would never want to go "back to their huts" after seeing the United States. The *Houston Chronicle* recently reported that Nigerian immigrants here have the highest average level of education of any immigrant group.[1] If highly capable, educated, and industrious people are made to feel unwanted by ignorant and deplorable remarks (and policies), they might take their talents and skills elsewhere. This is not making America great again, unless "great" is defined as poorer and dumber.

Actually, things are now much worse. In our current situation, incivility could get us killed. Two man/child leaders of nuclear powers taunt and dare each other like kids on a playground. When Trump and North Korea's Kim Jong Un engage in trash talk, the consequences could be cataclysmic.[2] We might find ourselves in the absolutely absurd situation where playground posturing escalates into nuclear war. Teddy Roosevelt was right when he said that you need to speak softly but carry a big stick. When the stick is nuclear weapons, you need to speak very carefully indeed.

Having recently published a book on the history of nuclear weapons and nuclear testing, let me pause to make an aside here. Paris, you and I were ten years old when the Cuban Missile Crisis occurred. Sober historians call it the most dangerous event in history, and they are right. Tens or hundreds of millions of people could have been killed. You and I are damned lucky to be here. The intermediate range Soviet missiles in Cuba could easily have hit Atlanta with a three-megaton warhead. We would have been toast. Of course, the American response would have obliterated the Soviet Union, not that it would have mattered to the scattered radioactive ashes that would have been left of you, me, and our families.

Remember duck-and-cover drills, sirens tested every Wednesday at noon, and TV public service announcements telling us to get busy on our fallout shelters? I worry that people today, including our leaders, have forgotten just what thermonuclear weapons mean. I like the suggestion made by Harold Agnew, one of the leading physicists who helped develop the hydrogen bomb in the fifties. Shortly before his death a few years ago, Agnew was interviewed by PBS.[3] He suggested that every generation or so, world leaders should be gathered in some remote area for a demonstration. Strip them down to their underwear, he said, and place them about thirty miles from ground zero. Set off a multimegaton blast. Let them put on welder's goggles and stare into that light, "brighter than a thousand suns;" let them feel the oven-like heat that builds and builds and will not shut off; make them endure the shock wave that hits like an earthquake; make them hear the roar that resounds seemingly forever; let them see the blinded and burned birds blasted from the sky. Perhaps that will educate them, mused Agnew. With Donald Trump I am not so sure that even this would work.

The point is that the world has always been a dangerous place, but nuclear weapons in the wrong hands make it exponentially more dangerous. When opposing sides possess ultimate weapons, civility becomes literally a matter of life and death. The leaders of nuclear armed nations cannot be overgrown children prone to the exchange of taunts and dares. Yet that is what we have.

To get to the heart of the problem, and to understand why civility is so important, we have to first understand the nature of violence in its worst manifestations. So, let's consider the causes of genocide and what they imply about the importance of civility.

The most infamous of the genocides of the twentieth century was, of course, the Holocaust perpetrated by the Nazis. The Jews in Germany were an extremely well-assimilated group. Many had become Christians and had married gentiles. Jews fought alongside other Germans in the First World War, sometimes winning the highest decorations for bravery. Jews were prominent in all fields of the arts, sciences, and medicine, making important contributions throughout society. Most famously, Albert Einstein was Professor of Physics at the University of Berlin. Many victims of the Holocaust said, "I thought I was a German."

Fifty years after the Holocaust, in the mid-nineties, genocidal violence erupted once again into the world's consciousness. (It had never really gone away.) In the former Yugoslavia and in Rwanda, ethnic animosities flared into wholesale massacre, with neighbors turning on their neighbors and committing the grossest atrocities against them.

What happens? How do people turn on their friends and neighbors and commit the worst acts of violence against them? In chapter five of his book *The Brain: The Story of You*, neuroscientist David Eagleman explains the process.[4] Essential to human success has been the formation of social groups in which the individual members of the group work not just for their own benefit, but cooperate for the benefit of the group as a whole. The problem is that for every in-group there is at least one out-group, those classified as "others," the ones not like us.

Eagleman performed experiments showing that our empathetic reactions decline markedly with respect to persons perceived as belonging to out-groups. When this tendency to feel less empathy for those not on our team is combined with the dehumanization of the out-group, violence, even genocide, becomes possible. There is a region of the brain called the medial prefrontal cortex that is active when we are interacting with people or thinking about them. This region becomes inactive when we are thinking about objects rather than persons. To think of someone as an object rather than a person is to dehumanize that individual. When we are exposed to propaganda or other cultural influences that stigmatize out-groups, our brains can be manipulated into shutting down its empathetic responses toward those "others" and we start to think of them not as persons but as things. We are beginning to understand the neurological basis of genocide.

Such dehumanization happened notoriously in Nazi Germany, when all the skills of modern propagandists were employed to defame the Jews, and to depict them, literally, as vermin. What occurred in Germany in the 1930s has happened elsewhere many times. For instance, as shown in the movie *Hotel Rwanda*, radio broadcasts by one Rwandan tribal group referred to members of the rival tribe as "cockroaches." You step on cockroaches. When our brains can be tricked into viewing others not as persons but as things or even as vermin, the normal moral categories and rules that we apply to human beings no longer apply. This is why even "good" people can stand by passively when terrible things are being done.

I once saw a photo taken in a Midwestern town in the 1930s. Men, women, and children of all ages were chatting and laughing, mingling in the most carefree way. It looked like the whole town had turned out for a holiday in the park. But in the middle of that happy crowd were two African Americans who had been lynched and were hanging from a tree. That picture made my blood run cold, and it should. It shows how easily we can forget the humanity of others when we relegate them to a despised out-group with no moral status. When you deprive someone of a moral status, you give yourself permission to do anything to them, from lynching to genocide.

I do not think that it is alarmist or hyperbolic to say that our country today is characterized by strong identification of people with in-groups and the concomitant stigmatization and even demonization of out-groups. We are polarized, as the title of this book indicates. There has always been a left/right divide in this country, as in the politics of every country, but the divide is now a yawning chasm, and those on one side frankly despise those on the other. People blame Congress for its hyperpartisanship and dysfunction, but the divisions between lawmakers merely reflect the divisions between their constituents. You and I have both admitted that we ourselves were not always above the rancor. Let me elaborate.

I am a liberal and an atheist living in Texas, so, naturally, there are times I am going to feel out of place. However, I had never felt such a sense of alienation from my own country, not even at the height of the Vietnam War, as I did in 2004 when the voters selected George W. Bush for a second term. To me it was simply inconceivable that an administration that had exploited the tragedy of 9/11 to mislead us into an unnecessary war and the quagmire of the subsequent insurgency could get the support of a plurality of the voters.

Were these voters just idiots, willing to believe any nonsense the Bush administration spouted? Did they believe the lies about "weapons of mass destruction"? What about waterboarding, torture at CIA "black sites," "extraordinary renditions," Gitmo, and the horrors of Abu Ghraib? Did they care that the Bush/Cheney war of choice had killed many more Americans than 9/11? Where was their outrage? I had to conclude that many millions of my fellow Americans were either idiots or evil, or maybe both. But, of course, except for Congress (ahem), relatively few of our fellow citizens are either evil or idiots, and it was wrong of me to think of them in such terms of blanket derision. When you start thinking of people as evil idiots, you give yourself permission to stop thinking of them as people.

At rock bottom, then, civility is most crucially important because treating people civilly reminds us that they are *people.* The practice of civility stands against the forces of dehumanization and so against the forces that divide societies and make neighbors into enemies. At any given time the social fabric is pulled in opposing directions. There are both centripetal and centrifugal forces, forces that pull society toward a common center and away from that center. When the centrifugal forces are strong, as they are now, people forget the ties of history, culture, tradition, or even of common humanity. Acts of common decency and civility restore the balance and remind us that disagreements can be deep but that what we share is deeper still.

Civility therefore is more than politeness. It is more than manners. Good manners are an expression of civility, but at a deeper level civility is the practice of acknowledging the inherent worth and dignity of another. It is the opposite of dehumanization, of thinking of someone as a thing and not a person. Civility is therefore like the canary in the coalmine. When civil discourse dies, and people address each other only in the tones of mutual contempt, then bad things, really bad things, are on the horizon.

Recall again the period before the Civil War, when North and South addressed each other in the most censorious tones of moral condemnation. Or consider the Reformation, when Protestants and Catholics regarded each other as minions of Satan. Protestant woodcuts regularly depicted the pope as the Antichrist, and Catholic propaganda returned the favor, showing Luther in league with the devil. Small wonder Europe was convulsed with religious wars and persecution for the next century.

When you undermine civility, as Donald Trump so egregiously does, this is not just an offense against decorum or propriety. It is not merely the lack of the sort of gravitas we normally expect of a president. It is not, as some of his supporters seem to think, just a matter of style. It is an attack on the very substance of society, the fundamental traits of comity, decency, and mutual respect that keep us from each other's throats. It is no accident that "civility" and "civilization" derive from the same Latin root. The latter is impossible without the former. No civilization without civility.

A president, as the most public person on earth, inevitably sets a highly visible example. The standard Donald Trump's behavior sets is this: Have no internal filter; say anything that pops into your head. Anything. Never take the high road. Rather, abuse your critics in the most offensive way, freely disparaging their ethnicity, gender, appearance, or disability. Openly display your prejudices and praise other bigots. Respond furiously to every perceived slight or provocation. Pick fights, even over the most trivial matters. Freely lie about people and make groundless accusations to discredit them. Openly attempt to intimidate critics into silence. Enjoy bullying and belittling others. Never apologize or admit error. Never display modesty or humility; rather, indulge in the most blatant and exaggerated braggadocio. Lie about your abilities and accomplishments. Boast about the supposed size of your genitals. Boast even about harassing and abusing women. Employ vulgar and scatological language, not merely in private, but openly and publicly. Demand unquestioning loyalty and unqualified admiration from everyone around you.

Seriously, does anyone want the most visible person in the country setting such an example for their children? Would anyone tolerate their fifteen-year-old acting that way? Would anyone want their children to live in a world where Donald Trump's standard of behavior was the norm?

HOW DO WE RESTORE CIVILITY?

PARIS DONEHOO

Some of my childhood memories have been lost in the mists of time, but I do remember "duck and cover" drills. I recall practicing survival skills during a nuclear attack, which required us to file calmly into the school hallway and crouch against the wall. As added insurance, we were to grab a coat on the way out the door (it did not matter who it belonged to) and use it to shield our heads from flying glass and other debris. Aside from the futility of such a practice, it never occurred to me to wonder what we should do if the dirty Commies attacked Decatur, Georgia, during the school months of September through November, or March through May, when it was too warm to wear coats.

But I digress. Nuclear war, or any other kind of war, is not a laughing matter, but the breakdown in civility is framing it as something worse—acceptable. As you say, violence becomes the default setting in human relationships when we cease defining the "other" as human. War and genocide are the logical ends of a society that has adopted the motto of "shoot first and ask questions later." A few months before my retirement, I attended a workshop led by our local police department on tactics for dealing with an active shooter in a public space. In this case, the public space was a church. I never dreamed I would see the day when the church I served would affix stickers to exterior doors depicting a handgun in a red circle with a slash through it, and openly discuss whether we should lock our doors after worship began on Sunday mornings. I refused to consider the latter suggestion, but I was

191

fully aware that the presence of two multicolored benches emblazoned with the words "All Are Welcome Here" outside our building made us a target. As I write these words, the news is full of reports about the senseless murder of eleven worshippers at the Tree of Life Synagogue in Pittsburgh.[1] I fear we no longer have the luxury of keeping our distance from such atrocities by labeling them aberrations and the perpetrators as "crazy." We must confront the complicity of our leaders, and our own complicity, in the disintegration of civility.

If incivility is feeding this hatred and paranoia, what is to be done? When the president of the United States labels Democrats "treasonous" and "un-American" because they would not stand and applaud his State of the Union speech,[2] how can civility be restored? What hope is there when the resident of the White House engages in taunts and tirades our mothers would not have tolerated in our five-year-old mouths?

I must begin by admitting there has never been a "golden age of civility" to which we can return. As much as we Southerners liked to think ourselves genteel and civilized during our childhood days, the very air we breathed was laced with racism. Though none of the adults in my life would ever have approved of deliberate disrespect for an African American, much less acts of violence against them, our language seethed with paternalism and barely disguised condescension. A friend of mine once noted that a black dentist had opened up an office in the building where his father worked, and sneered, "Can you imagine him putting his fingers in your mouth?" Just a few miles up the road from my home was Forsyth County, Georgia, where African Americans had been driven out in the early days of the twentieth century, and eighty years later every black person knew he or she dared not be found within the county lines after dark.

You and I heard our parents, aunts, uncles, and various other adults cuss the "guv-mint" and decry LBJ and liberal congressmen as tools of the communists. Our home state voted overwhelmingly for George

Wallace in 1968 because of his segregationist views. Therefore, neither of us can campaign to "Make America Civil Again!" as if we simply lost our way from some halcyon past. The difference now is the level of coarse and crass language spewing from our leaders' mouths, and the childish behavior that passes for statesmanship. It could be argued that certain unwritten rules governed not only politicians, but society as a whole. Everybody knew you were not supposed to discuss politics or religion in polite company, and most people expected a level of propriety in social discourse, particularly among those fortunate enough to be in leadership positions. President Jimmy Carter scandalized the nation in 1979 when he was asked about the possibility of Ted Kennedy running against him, and he replied, "I'll kick his ass." A similar comment by Trump today would barely register on social media, and likely would not even be mentioned on the evening news. What is shocking does not shock us anymore, nor does the outrageous fill us with outrage.

In the context of a discussion about taking oaths, Jesus said, "Let your word be 'Yes, Yes' or 'No, No.' Anything more than this comes from the evil one" (Matthew 5:37). In other words, a person of integrity does not need a lot of peripheral language to convince others of his or her sincerity. A simple "yes" or "no" should be sufficient. Posturing, name-calling, deflecting, and outright falsehoods are not needed if one demonstrates reliability in daily action. Obviously, Trump must fill the air with verbiage about how wonderful he is, how ill-treated he is by the "fake news" media, and the size of the crowd he is addressing, in order to hide the emptiness of his argument. In addition, over time such excess verbosity anesthetizes us. Like drinking from a fire hose, we simply become numb to it all.

Therefore, those of us who find the present uncivil situation intolerable must resolve not to add to the current hostility, if possible. Like you, Keith, I am not proud of some of my attitudes and words toward those with whom I vehemently disagree. I was appalled at the vitriol unleashed on Bill Clinton, long before the Monica Lewinsky scandal, by Republicans and their supporters, but during the George W. Bush years I struggled against my propensity to be just as censorious. I have laughed at many Facebook posts about Trump that, on reflection, were nothing short of vicious. I have painted all Trump supporters with the same brush, claiming they have no more brains than a doorknob (bless their hearts). I have not been civil, nor, and more important to me, I have not been Christlike. I am convicted by these words from the letter of James: "With [the tongue] we bless the Lord and Father, and with it we curse those who are made in the likeness of God. From the same mouth come blessing and cursing. My brothers and sisters, this ought not to be so" (James 3:9–10). Such behavior is hypocritical for anyone—on either side of the aisle—who claims to be a follower of Jesus, and it merely serves to ratchet up the histrionics in our current society.

One way to restore civility—as simplistic as it sounds—is to be civil toward each other. Does that mean keeping my mouth shut in the face of injustice? No, it does not. I can identify evil without lowering myself to the practice of evil. The apostle Paul said, "If it is possible, *so far as it depends on you*, live peaceably with all" (Romans 12:18, emphasis mine). I learned long ago I cannot control the actions of others. Like you, Keith, I am fortunate to be in a profession where I can wield a great deal of influence within a particular group of people, but they are autonomous human beings who make their own choices regardless of what I say or do. I have no authority to force them to be civil. I can, however, practice civility toward them. That is my choice. Disagree? Yes. Offer my perceptions clearly and forcefully? Yes. But attack, demonize, ridicule, lie, deliberately obfuscate truth, or condemn? Absolutely not. As Paul said, as far it depends on me, I must choose to model a different approach.

Of course, even *civil* discourse often has negative fallout, especially in today's hypersensitive climate. Unlike some pastors, I rarely thundered blatantly political sermons from my pulpits, although everyone knew where I stood politically. There were always people who disagreed with my take on issues, and the activities my congregation sponsored or supported. Sooner or later they would complain that the church had become "too political," and I had become "too political," and they walked out the sanctuary door never to be seen there again. I grieved those losses because most of them were truly good people. I realized, however, that civility is a contract between two parties, and if one party chooses to end the relationship, there is little I can do about it. Living "peaceably with all" does not depend exclusively on me. My heart breaks when I realize how many ruptures in the body of Christ I have seen, principally in the last few years as we have lost the capacity to dialogue with one another. And yet, I am not ashamed of the public positions I have taken on immigrant rights, the rights of people of color, women's rights, LGBTQ rights, interfaith dialogue, peace issues, and other concerns. If Jesus had shied away from identifying the chasms between the values of the current culture and the values of the Kingdom of God, he would have been a regular speaker at Rotary meetings instead of ending up on a cross. One of the most stirring preachers I have ever heard— African American pastor William Jones—once said, "The greatest sin of the church is she withholds the Gospel from herself."[3]

Reflecting on the shooting of Congresswoman Gabrielle Giffords, and the tragic killing and wounding of nineteen of her constituents, Jim Wallis, founder and editor of *Sojourners* magazine, and Chuck Colson, founder of Prison Fellowship, said, "We should not lose this moment for moral reflection and renewal."[4] Perhaps that is a crucial element of civility we have been missing. Whenever we are faced with a national trauma, especially the fiendish manifestations of public violence, Americans seem to retreat to their corners and begin shouting solutions. We are a nation of "fixers" and we long to fix the problem. Perhaps we should take more time to ask what these excruciating ordeals say about us as a nation. Adherents of both the right and the left know the problems are multilayered, yet we persist in jumping immediately to assigning blame and advocating a solution rather than entering into dialogue with one another. Jesus said, "Whoever wishes to be great among you must be your servant" (Matthew 20:26). Sadly, we do not see a competent example of such behavior from our national leaders, from the White House on down.

If the church could disengage itself from its licentious dalliance with the surrounding culture, it could become the role model this country needs. "The faith community," say Wallis and Colson, "should lead by example and model the behavior that is informed by our biblical teachings—behavior that is also essential to the survival of democracy."[5] The book of James gives us a roadmap: "Let everyone be quick to listen, slow to speak, slow to anger" (1:19). Our current culture practices just the opposite. We are slow to listen, quick to speak, and even more quick to get angry.

What would happen if every person who claims to be a follower of Jesus were to interact with others using James's words as a guideline? A few colossal arguments within congregations I have served would have taken on a decidedly more Christlike tone. Some locally contentious civic issues could have been resolved with less lingering animosity. If troubled people felt heard, perhaps we could reduce the horrific incidents of random violence plaguing us. If all sides of a public debate could listen before launching into a tirade, we might actually improve the common good. If politicians were willing to at least entertain the notion that their opinions might be wrong, or partially so, we might break the gridlock we see in government. Most of us are quick to blame our elected officials for the paralyzing logjams stifling progress, but they are mere reflections of society as a whole. Congress is divided because America is divided. Government cannot function because the rest of cannot "be quick to listen, slow to speak, and slow to anger."

Notice James did not forbid anger altogether. Anger is a natural human emotion, and, like fire, it can be helpful as well as destructive. Jesus became angry on numerous occasions. His anger, however, was never directed at those who simply had the effrontery to disagree with him. His anger was directed at those who used their power to perpetuate injustice to the poor, the powerless, and the marginalized.

Finally, there is one more practice that people of faith can insert into our current morass. We can pray for each other, for our leaders, and for those with whom we vehemently disagree. Jesus could not have said it any more plainly: "You have heard that it was said, 'You shall love your neighbor and hate your enemy.' But I say to you, love your enemies and pray for those who persecute you, so that you may be children of your Father in heaven" (Matthew 5:43–45). The writer of the first letter to Timothy is even more specific: "I urge that supplications, prayers, intercessions, and thanksgivings be made for everyone, for kings and all who are in high positions, so that we may lead a quiet and peaceable life in all godliness and dignity. This is right and is acceptable in the sight of God our Savior" (1 Timothy 2:1–3).

During the most recent season of Lent, my Lenten discipline (or maybe I should call it penance) was to pray for President Trump every day until Easter. I must confess it might have been one of the most difficult tasks I have ever undertaken. It would have been much easier to fall back on tried and true practices of giving up candy or swearing, but I have discovered it is more beneficial for me to add something to my life during Lent instead of taking something away. Ergo, I prayed for the president each day. Every fiber of my being wanted to pray, "Lord, may Trump meet with an unfortunate accident," or "Please, God, show him what a doofus he is." But that would have been dishonest. If I truly believe Trump too is created in the image of God, then I must believe he is loved by God just as much as I am loved by God. Consequently, though the forty days of Lent have come and gone, I continue to pray for President Trump.

What do I hope will result from my prayers? Aside from my conviction that we eviscerate prayer by concentrating too often on results, I choose to believe any heart can be changed, even those whose hearts appear to be cold. On the other hand, I often find that the best outcome of my prayers is a softening of my own heart. If my prayers for Trump generate more civility in my own behavior, maybe others around me will be more civil as well. Like a teacher who gains control over her students by speaking softly rather than shouting, I might be able to get the attention of an opponent and actually have a positive interaction. As long as I do not stoop to using prayer as a weapon against the ungodly, something good could occur. At least it's a better option than yelling at the TV screen every time the news comes on.

HOW DO WE RESTORE CIVILITY?

KEITH PARSONS

You put your finger on it when you said earlier that in thinking about people we have to distinguish the nouns from the adjectives. In other words, we have to think of people as people first and not in terms of the various labels or categories we use to classify them. When I was a kid I noticed that members of my extended family would say in praise of a black entertainer like Nat "King" Cole that he was a great "colored" singer. Why not just a great singer? Why did they have to specify that he was a "colored" singer? Even newspaper accounts would identify black leaders or achievers as "Negro," even when their race had nothing to do with the story.

Why? Because when prejudice is pervasive and systematic, it makes us think of people *primarily* in terms of a classification. Even when no abusive epithets are used, we are made to think of some people *primarily* in terms of labels—"black," "Jewish," "gay," Muslim," "Mexican," etc. When we think of people in terms of a label rather than as individuals, then we do exactly what Martin Luther King Jr. famously warned us not to do—we judge by the color of the skin (or something equally irrelevant) and not by the content of the character.

Let me hasten to add that sometimes we *do* have to mention the labels. Conservatives often charge liberals with playing the game of "identity politics" that puts all the emphasis upon labels. For instance, the Black Lives Matter movement was criticized for its focus on black lives. On the contrary, should we not affirm that ALL lives matter?

However, when the issue is one of apparent prejudice against a particular group, you cannot protest the treatment of that group without naming the group. If inordinately large numbers of unarmed black people are being killed by police, you cannot address the problem without mentioning that the ones being killed are black. In this case, to protest against the use of a term of identity becomes a backhanded way of denying the problem.

When we think of people as people first, treating them civilly becomes easier, and, as we said earlier, treating them civilly reminds us of their humanity, thus creating a virtuous feedback loop. So, how do we prompt people not to conflate the nouns with the adjectives when thinking of others? You teach the Gospel; I teach Aristotle. For me, Aristotle's *Nicomachean Ethics* is the book that comes closest to being my Bible.[1] I am not an Aristotelian fundamentalist. Aristotle was wrong about many things (unsurprising for someone writing over 2,300 years ago). He defended slavery (for "barbarians" only) and was a dreadful elitist who scorned hoi polloi as mere seekers of bodily pleasure. Yet in all essentials about what really matters and why it matters, I think he was right.

Aristotle taught that the only way to achieve fulfillment as a human being is to act virtuously toward your fellow humans. For Aristotle, virtue was not what they told me it was in Sunday School. Virtue is not something we do, not because we want to do it, but because we have to do it to keep God from getting mad at us. For Aristotle, virtue is excellence. A virtuous person has achieved excellence as a human being by developing states of character that permit that person to interact in the best and most fulfilling ways with other humans. Other things being equal, a person who displays such virtues as justice, generosity, courage, and self-control will get along with others far better than one who is unfair, selfish, cowardly, or volatile. Virtuous people can cooperate with others to achieve the maximum benefit for all involved, and will therefore enjoy stable and nurturing relationships, good friends, and good will. Those who lack virtue, on the other hand, will live tempestuous and unsatisfying lives. They may purchase trophy wives, but they will not know true affection; they might have flatterers and toadies, but no real friends; they might have power and be feared, but people will secretly despise and ridicule them; they might be rich, but they will never have enough; they might die unrepentant, but often they die alone.

One of the virtues that Aristotle considers is self-control, which in Greek is called by the lovely word *Sōphrosýnē*. Self-control is the virtue of learning how not to let your emotions run away with you, but to use them rationally. Consider anger. As you mentioned, anger can be a very destructive force, but sometimes it is good. There are things we should be angry about, such as injustice, willful stupidity, bigotry, greed, and fanaticism. There are times and places where anger is the very motive that we need. Sometimes we only get things done when we reach the point when we say, "Alright. That's it. Enough is enough." Sometimes we even need to get angry with loved ones. I heard a story about a woman who gave her husband a nicely wrapped birthday present. When he unwrapped it, he was puzzled to find that the present was a doormat. His wife told him, "I am giving you your own doormat because I refuse to be your doormat any longer." Sometimes we have to get mad enough at being treated as a doormat to finally decide not to take it any longer.

There is, then, nothing wrong with anger per se. It is a necessary emotion, and often a very useful one. However, as you note, like fire, which is useful when controlled and dangerous when it is not, anger must be constrained. Perhaps the worst advice ever given by the pop psychologists was to advise people to go ahead and vent their anger. Let it out, they said, or you will boil over like an overheated teakettle. Nonsense. People are not teakettles. You will not literally boil over if you exercise self-control.

Aristotle said that your anger is well-controlled when your anger meets the following conditions:

1) You are angry for the right reason.
2) You are angry at the right person or persons.
3) You are angry to the right degree.
4) You are angry at the right time and place.
5) You show your anger in the right way.[2]

By contrast, those who lack self-control will get mad for silly or inappropriate reasons, as when Trump was furious when the press said truthfully that his inauguration crowd was smaller than Obama's. Those who lack control will get angry at the wrong persons, blaming those who are not responsible. They will also become inordinately angry over a relatively minor provocation, as do those who display "road rage" by becoming homicidally angry when they think someone has cut them off in traffic. The volatile will also become angry at the wrong times and places, blowing up at Thanksgiving dinners, for instance. Finally, the intemperate will show anger in ways that just make things worse, say by blustering, pounding the table, and shouting insults rather than in constructive ways, say by channeling anger into the energy to get something done.

How do you learn self-control? It is not easy, as I can testify, as one who naturally has a tendency toward a sharp temper, and who does not suffer fools gladly. With the help of my wife, Carol, I have learned to not retaliate or get into an exchange of gestures with those who do rude things to me on the road. (Not giving in to road rage is prudent, too, because here in Texas many drivers are heavily armed.) Also, I sometimes have to count to ten, or even a hundred, when the "powers that be" at my university make a decision I consider to be stupid and harmful. I have a sign over my desk that says, in Old English script:

"𝕭e thou not an asshole. 𝕿hink before thou speakest!"

This reminds me to consider my words before firing off an inflammatory missive that will just make things worse.

Learning to control and use our anger in rational and helpful ways rather than blowing up is a big key to becoming more civil. People sure can be vexing, no question about it. When you have stated, and restated, your position with eloquence, clarity, and logic, and someone continues to disagree, this is vexing. This is the point where internet exchanges quickly dissolve into foaming tirades and vicious calumny. Even scientists and philosophers can lose their cool and give in to scorn. I went to a scientific conference some years back and learned that one eminent scientist had been invited but declined to attend because he refused to share the stage with another scientist who would be there. Indeed, the history of science has many famous spats. The same applies *a fortiori* to philosophy. I have read in the pages of the *New York Review of Books* one very distinguished philosopher saying that his view was dismissed as "pathological" by another equally distinguished philosopher. He then assured the reader that this assessment was fully reciprocated.

As Aristotle noted, it is easy to get mad; anybody can do that. It is hard to get mad in constructive ways, but if we do achieve that discipline, we will realize that fulminations, though perhaps temporarily satisfying, generally accomplish nothing. A couple of years ago I finally decided never to raise my voice in anger at others, because every time I had done so, I soon regretted it. Too bad it took me sixty-plus years to learn this. On the other hand, if, despite vexation, you can remain civil in your tones and words, then your anger might actually do some good. You might actually get someone to listen.

There is in Aristotle a deeper basis for civility—namely, that at rock bottom all human beings need the same things to flourish, and so the same basic things are valuable for all human beings. However irreconcilable someone's values might appear to you, you can know that, deep down, the same things must be important to each of you, and that gives a basis for dialogue rather than dismissal. At bottom, Aristotle notes, no one chronically ill or in straits of dire poverty can be doing well. Therefore, mental and physical health are important for everyone, as well as at least a modicum of prosperity.

Further, humans are rational animals, obviously not in the sense that we always or even usually act rationally. Rather, we are rational in that we have a capacity to learn to think logically and decide wisely. As rational creatures we therefore need to develop our minds and put them to good use. Not everyone needs to be a philosopher, mathematician, or a scientist, but the saying "a mind is a terrible thing to waste" applies to everyone. With minds, as with muscles, you either use it or lose it.

Nobody (well . . . hardly anybody) makes a conscious choice to be stupid. You get stupid by being lazy and letting others do your thinking for you. The world is full of people who want to do your thinking for you, not just pundits and politicians, but advertisers and ideologues of all stripes—everyone who has a vested interest in getting you to think their way. Chiefly, they want you to make decisions (how you vote, what you buy, what causes you support) based on their agendas, not yours. So, being rational means learning to think for yourself, that is to think critically, and to make sound decisions based on *your* beliefs, values, and desires, not on someone else's.

Also, as social creatures we need each other; we need interaction with family, friends, associates, and larger and more inclusive communities. Hermits are rare, and the forced deprivation of interpersonal contact, as in solitary confinement, can have dire effects, even psychosis. Since we need each other, we have to get along. Any social unit, from a family to a nation-state, just IS a cooperative enterprise whereby individuals come together to seek a common good. As social creatures, therefore, we can flourish only if we are good at getting along with the others, that is, if we are capable of cooperating with others to pursue our mutual benefit.

The upshot—and this is the crucial point for our discussion here—is that at rock bottom, at the level of our humanity, human well-being is the same for everybody because we are all rational and social animals. In polarized times, it seems as though those on the other side hardly resemble us at all. When I compare what seems reasonable and right to me with how it seems to many of my Texas neighbors, it feels like we are on different planets. Their values and even their perceptions seem so vastly different from mine. We have basic and seemingly irreconcilable differences on issues like abortion, gun control, public education, healthcare, LGBTQ rights, and practically every other issue. Our positions are diametrically opposed, and if we do try to talk, it seems that we just talk past each other, and the exchange only exacerbates hostility and suspicion. Our views appear simply incommensurable. That is, there is no possible common ground on which we could both stand that would permit us even to understand each other, much less even reach agreement.

If Aristotle is right, though, deep down we have the same needs, and what is valuable for one holds for the other also. As human organisms, our basic values simply cannot be *fundamentally* opposed. Everyone needs mental and physical health. Dire poverty is bad for everyone. As rational creatures, we cannot flourish in conditions that stunt our minds or impair our abilities to make rational decisions. As social creatures, all people need to be free to participate fully in social life at every level—to form bonds of family and friendship, to engage in the life of the community, and to enjoy the full rights and responsibilities of citizenship. No one may be automatically or arbitrarily excluded or marginalized.

In summary, all human beings, as human, have the same basic needs and therefore at rock-bottom share the same basic values—even if they sometimes have to be forcefully reminded of what is really valuable. Despite appearances, then, our differences are not incommensurable. If we are willing to work hard enough (a very big "if"), we can uncover the common ground that multiple layers of suspicion and distrust have buried. The story you told of the ministers and the Klansmen brings out this point beautifully. I am not saying that doctrinal differences are merely superficial and do not "really" matter. I am saying that those differences do not have to make us dismiss each other as evil or idiots. In other words, by perceiving our common humanity we can still be civil to one another.

CONCLUDING THOUGHTS ON CIVILITY

PARIS DONEHOO

One of my bittersweet tasks as a Christian pastor has been to stand in front of a congregation I dearly loved and call them to follow a way of life that I myself find difficult to follow. Over the years I have learned to be honest with them about my own struggles, and many of them say my honesty has been helpful in their attempts to live Christlike lives. Throughout the writing of this section I have found myself with the same conflicted feelings. I have been railing against the loss of civility while often contributing to its downward spiral. I have made suggestions for civil speech and action while the daily news leaves me so angry I could go bear hunting with a switch and lash out with every derogatory name I can conjure. Like the apostle Paul, "I can will what is right, but I cannot do it" (Romans 7:18).

But I must try, as all of us must try. Reciprocal hatred spells the end of a democratic society. As Martin Luther King Jr. wisely said, "If we do an eye for an eye and a tooth for a tooth, we will be a blind and toothless nation." My mother, and many other adults in my childhood years, used to quote the old adage, "Sticks and stones may break my bones, but words will never hurt me." They meant well, of course, but it is not true. Words can hurt me, you, and everyone else, and I have the hours spent in a therapist's office to prove it.

Some years ago, famed journalist David Brinkley published a collection of essays under the title *Everyone Is Entitled to My Opinion*. When I heard that Brinkley was coming to a local bookstore I bought a copy and gave it to my dad. Because the two of us had so often sparred with each other over our often radically divergent opinions, I thought the gift was fitting and humorous. I would not find it so funny today, not because I could not joke with my dad (God rest his soul), but because the title of Brinkley's book has become the benchmark of public and private discourse. If everyone is a truth merely unto himself or herself, how far away is society as a whole from the story I read in this morning's newspaper about a man who shot a woman in the leg because she was not moving fast enough at a drive-through window at a Steak 'n Shake restaurant?

The church could be a powerful leader in countering these trends. It pains me to admit, however, that the unholy alliance between church and culture, as well as church and politics, is feeding, not starving, the beast. You mentioned a prominent scientist who refused to appear on a program because of another scientist who would be presenting. I know of pastors who refused to participate in denominational events when they found out I would be taking part. The first year our church hosted what has become an annual Community Christmas Carol Singalong, a local newspaper printed an article about it. In the online version of the article, several people castigated us for committing the mortal sin of singing a verse of *Silent Night* in Spanish. I fail to see how such attitudes create a civil society.

Mark Twain understood the consequences of incivility between people of faith. In *Letters from the Earth*, he described an experiment he conducted in which he caught a cat and a dog and put them in a cage, and in an hour had taught them to be friends. In another hour he had taught both of them to be friends with a rabbit. In two days he added a fox, a goose, a squirrel, and some doves. Finally, a monkey. They all lived together in peace, even affectionately. Twain continued:

> Next, in another cage I confined an Irish Catholic from Tipperary, and as soon as he seemed tame I added a Scotch Presbyterian from Aberdeen. Next a Turk from Constantinople; a Greek Christian

from Crete; an Armenian; a Methodist from the wilds of Arkansas; a Buddhist from China; a Brahman from Benares. Finally, a Salvation Army Colonel from Wapping. Then I stayed away for two whole days. When I came back to note results, the cage of Higher Animals was all right, but in the other there was but a chaos of gory odds and ends of turbans and fezzes and plaids and bones and flesh—not a specimen left alive. These Reasoning Animals had disagreed on a theological detail and carried the matter to a Higher Court.[1]

In his usual sardonic way, Twain describes the bitter tragedy of human beings, all created in the image of God, elevating adjectives to the place of nouns.

The church I served prior to retirement took a different approach. In the fall of 2017 we adopted a theme of "Live Love, Stop Hate" and looked for ways to promote concrete efforts in that direction. We designed yard signs with those words printed prominently along with a quote from 1 Corinthians 13:8: "Love never fails."[2] We asked parishioners to display them in their yards, at their places of business, or anywhere else they could. Within a few days other congregations in town and in neighboring hamlets were asking for signs. People unconnected to our church, and some unconnected to any church, called or stopped by for signs. Obviously, we had struck a nerve. Over and over persons expressed their distaste for the vitriol spewing from all levels of government, and society in general, and thanked us for giving them a chance to uphold a positive message.

We printed more signs. We printed bumper stickers and soon saw them around town. In conjunction with another church we had the signs translated into Spanish, and soon saw them cropping up in our city, which is approximately 50 percent Hispanic. One of the most moving experiences I have ever had was the night of our city's annual Interfaith Thanksgiving Service when the congregation ended worship at a local synagogue and marched across the street for fellowship at a

Lutheran church, flanked on both sides by local clergy from various faiths holding our "Live Love, Stop Hate" signs. And all this took place just a couple of weeks after the horrific shooting at Sutherland Springs Baptist Church in Texas.

From these efforts came a series of seminars we called the "Live Love Symposium" in which we presented a variety of programs on subjects like immigration, civil rights, anti-Semitism, bullying, interfaith dialogue, transgender issues, and refugee resettlement. The programs were attended by people from all over the community. Our entire Christmas Eve offering was given to two local agencies—one to sponsor parenting classes for immigrants, and another to teach English as a second language. The ideas that continue to be spawned from these efforts is nothing less than inspiring.

I share these events, not to toot my church's own horn (well, maybe a little), but to show what can happen when people—particularly people of faith—avoid the temptation to reduce personal interaction to the lowest common denominator. It also demonstrates the impact ordinary people can have on the tenor of society. Democratic governments can outlaw hate speech and set up mechanisms for discovering persons likely to act on their hate (systems that failed miserably in the case of the massacre at Stoneman Douglas High School in Florida), but democratic governments cannot force us to be civil to one another, much less love each other. Only we the people can accomplish that. As both of us have said repeatedly, there is no excuse for silence in the face of injustice, or acquiescence in the face of oppression. But the example of Jesus is clear. "Whoever wishes to be great among you," he said, "must be your servant, and whoever wishes to be first among you must be your slave; just as the Son of Man came not to be served but to serve, and to give his life a ransom for many" (Matthew 20:26–28). No government can mandate love when everyone around you descends into hate. No set of laws can require forgiveness when everyone else is unforgiving. Love and forgiveness come from within us after having been taught them in our homes, instilled within us in our communities, and modeled for us in our leaders. Each of us, individually and collectively, have the power to create a society where decisions are made without rancor, and ideas are expressed without fear of reprisal.

In commenting on the violent demonstrations in Charlottesville, Virginia, in August of 2017, Rick Bragg, a native of Alabama, captured my feelings precisely:

> I recognize evil when I see it, and stupidity, and banality. I hear that many of the people who marched in Charlottesville were Southern men, but I didn't know them. I saw men in custom molded neo Nazi helmets and designer flak jackets and hundred-dollar aviator glasses. It used to be that all they needed to dress up to hate was a good white sale. Southerners should be angry to be dragged down among them, by even the vaguest association. We can say that's not happening, but it is.[3]

Being civil to such uncivil bigots, much less loving them, may be one of the most difficult tasks I ever undertake. I am convinced, however, that it is worth the effort. The other path is far too frightening to consider. For me, my starting point is the Galilean peasant who never claimed that following him would be easy, and who boldly tells me to love my enemies.

Bragg did not grow up in church like I did. When he did go, however, he says he remembers men with clip-on ties standing before their congregations telling them to love one another. "Those men of God," he says, "could have preached politics, could have used their modest pulpits to stroke the resentments of the place and time like a mean cat. But they chose to do otherwise. They did not give in to expediency, to opportunism. They preached, instead, about loving your brother and your sister. They asked us to be generous if we could, to help the sick and poor. They also preached on hell, of course."

So how does that relate to the venom spewed from self-righteous "patriots" that day in Charlottesville?

> I did not grow up gentle, or much enlightened. I grew up in an everyday racism; the Confederate flag license plates that rode on the front bumpers of our pickups hurt others like a thumb in the eye. It took me a while to get it, but it came to me, even as a boy. I do not need a statue or flag to know that I am Southern. I can taste it in the food, feel it in my heart, and hear it in the language of my kin. It may be that I only remember this through the eyes of a boy, but I believe I heard the best of who we are in those sermons in that little bitty church.[4]

Pass the sweet tea, please.

CONCLUDING THOUGHTS ON CIVILITY

KEITH PARSONS

What might incivility cost us? It might cost us everything. As I said earlier, rudeness is violence in the embryo stage. If mutual contempt becomes the "new normal"—and I think that to a large extent it has—then I fear that the violence we have already seen on the fringes will be mainstreamed. In Charlottesville, Virginia, in August 2017, a white supremacist rally was met by crowds of counterprotesters. A young woman was killed when one of the white supremacists drove his car into a group of counterprotesters. On February 1, 2017, right-wing provocateur Milo Yiannopoulos was scheduled to speak at UC Berkeley. A group of masked left-wing thugs created such an atmosphere of violence and intimidation that the Berkeley police shut down the event. (It is just too delicious a piece of irony to reflect that in the 1960s Berkeley was the home of the Free Speech Movement.) How much more do we have to hate each other before violence at demonstrations becomes routine? What comes after that?

It does not have to be like this, and my memory is that it *was* not always like this. What has changed? Psychology professor Alison Gopnik, writing in the *Atlantic*, indicates that what we need to relearn more than anything is how to disagree without contempt:

> Marriage counselors say that relationships can weather anger, misunderstanding, jealousy, fundamentally different values—even the occasional bout of hatred. But they can't survive contempt, which

has become the signature political emotion of our times. Trying to make a state more like a community doesn't mean making it homogeneous or even more harmonious. Instead, the problem . . . is how to establish a background of trust and commitment that allows conflict without contempt.[1]

Healthy families argue, sometimes boisterously, but ties that bind are stronger than the divisions, and disagreement does not lead to disdain. We need to be able once again to hear the voices of those who disagree with us without grinding our teeth and contemptuously snorting "liberal moron" or "right-wing idiot." Contempt is the toxin poisoning our political milieu.

Nevertheless, there are people—powerful and dangerous people— who are truly contemptible, and contemptible people deserve contempt. How do we regard the truly contemptible?

Consider the corrupt ideologue Scott Pruitt, the former head of the Environmental "Protection" Agency under Trump. To list here everything that Pruitt did to the detriment of the environment and human health would take the rest of my space. The *Washington Post* reports that pollution is estimated to kill nine million people worldwide every year.[2] Yet, as Pruitt saw it, it was literally his divine mission to help the polluters and exploiters of the environment. According to an article in the March and April 2018 issue of *Mother Jones*, Pruitt is a devoted follower of a particularly conservative branch of the Southern Baptists that interprets the book of Genesis as commanding us not to serve the earth, but to use it "for the glory of God."[3] For Pruitt, this religious imperative translates into a noxious ideology that is anti-science and anti-environment and obedient to the fossil-fuel polluters.

I regard both the man and his doctrine with the contempt that I think they richly deserve.

I am afraid, then, Paris, that I have not and will not achieve the state to which you so admirably aspire, namely being able to follow

Jesus's command to love one's enemies, even those worthy of contempt. There are some people that I genuinely and wholeheartedly despise, and I think for good reason. I guess an approximation of Aristotelian virtue is the best I will hope to achieve. As a good Aristotelian, I want to despise only at the right time and place, for the right reason, toward the right person, in the right degree, etc. How, then, do I keep from hating too broadly when confronted by the likes of Scott Pruitt and other multifarious provocations?

There is plenty for someone like me to hate. There are atheist bloggers who diligently report the multiple stupid, ugly, bigoted, and vicious things said and done *every day* in the name of religion, often by conservative Christians. I think these bloggers do a great service and I applaud their diligence. I often append my own acerbic comments. How, though, do we call out the bigots, hypocrites, fanatics, and idiots, without falling into the trap of thinking that *all* conservative Christians are bigots, hypocrites, fanatics, and idiots? I have to remember—and remind myself over and over (and over) again—that true zealots like Pruitt are relatively rare, and that other bloggers could list the many great and wonderful things done in the name of religion every day.

The vast majority of my fellow citizens, including most of the ones who voted for Trump, are just folks. I have known and loved many such folks. Indeed, if I despise people because they are conservative Republicans or evangelical Christians, then I would have to loathe most of my extended family, and I am really quite fond of them. Yet the fact that fundamentally decent people supported the egregiously indecent Trump still needs to be explained.

Most people are not really doctrinaire at all. Indeed, most people are not reflective. They are not dumb; they just have neither the time nor the inclination to think out positions in detail as you and I do. When they vote, they vote for the one that seems to hear their pain and frustration. Trump seemed to hear; Hillary Clinton most definitely did not. Yes, I do think that Trump's character should have mattered more to these people, and I think that even decent people have become alarmingly tolerant of indecency. Yet I do not think that most Trump supporters were "deplorables," as Clinton termed them.

It is also important to remind yourself often that there are thoughtful and intelligent people on the other side of the political divide. I recently got a flier from a group calling itself "Conservative Republicans of Harris County" that included a helpful list of what "conservative Republicans" support versus what "liberals" advocate. Here is a sample: Conservatives are for traditional family values; marriage between one man and one woman. Liberals are for same-sex marriage. Conservatives are for the sanctity of human life. Liberals are for abortion on demand. Conservatives are for securing our borders. Liberals are for open borders. Conservatives support law enforcement officers. Liberals are for the rights of criminals over law enforcement. Conservatives support the rights of citizens to own guns. Liberals are for gun control. Conservatives support free enterprise. Liberals support entitlement programs. And so on.

As I said earlier, I truly hate the witch's brew of extremism, bigotry, and sheer craziness that currently passes for "conservatism" in this country. If tarring with a broad brush is the name of the game, I could do the same thing with a bigger brush and blacker tar. But suppose we tried something different. Instead of promulgating simplistic and invidious stereotypes, let's try to find out what the other guy is really saying.

Of course, there will always be plenty on the other side who do fit your worst stereotypes. There really are snowflakes who obsess over "microaggressions" and "trigger warnings" and whine for "safe spaces" at their universities where their ears will not be sullied by contrary opinions. There really are truck drivin', immigrant hatin', gun totin' bubbas with Confederate flag decals and "Come and take it" stickers on their pickups. Yet there are also plenty of intelligent, decent, and reasonable people on the other side. Liberals should read David Brooks, George Will, Charles Sykes, Ross Douthat, and Jennifer Rubin. Conservatives should read tough-minded, no-nonsense liberals like Paul Krugman, Robert Reich, George Lakoff, Ruth Marcus, and David Corn.

So, step one in being civil is just to stop screaming and listen; really listen. Instead of devoting all your energy to castigating the worst people on the other side, try to find the most reasonable and intelligent opponents. You do not have to agree with what you hear, of course, but at least give them the courtesy of criticizing what they actually say rather than attacking a straw man. Reserve your contempt for the few who are genuinely contemptible. Remember that the vast majority are not evil or idiots but are fellow mortals groping in the darkness and blundering their way through this vale of tears—just like you.

SECTION III
E PLURIBUS UNUM : COMMUNITY IN DIVERSITY

WHAT IS COMMUNITY IN A PLURALISTIC SOCIETY?

KEITH PARSONS

Let's start at the obvious place, the motto printed on every dollar bill: *E pluribus unum*—out of many, one. This was the original motto of the United States, not "In God we trust," and it referred to the formation of one nation out of the separate states. However, the history of this country has involved a much more comprehensive forging of one out of many. It has been the forging into unity of people literally from everywhere. And what is this unity that was forged from so many distinct and diverse individuals? It is the nation we call "the United States of America," of course, but the unity we speak of is more than just becoming a taxpayer or being eligible to vote. It is a sense of belonging and identity, of being an integral part of something that is also an integral part of you, and of commitment to a core set of distinctive values. Indeed, the essential definition of "American" is one who is committed to American values. We call this unity we speak of "community in diversity." To know what it is we must understand it in the context of history and see it in contrast with its opposite.

Throughout history, what sorts of things have united people into a shared national identity? For some peoples, it has been a mystical attachment to land, like Mother Russia. More ominously, it has sometimes been race or "blood." Sometimes a shared religion gives a sense of identity, as in Pakistan or Iran. All nations forge identity through a shared history, especially a history of struggle against a common enemy. You and I both heard from our parents and others of their generation how the Second World War united the country with itself and its allies in a campaign that, literally, delivered the world from evil.

A few other countries have a different kind of story to tell, one of unity arising from plurality. In the first book of his history, Livy tells of the early days of Rome when it was a small settlement adjoining the malarial swamps of the Tiber River, surrounded by larger, wealthier, more powerful, and intermittently hostile neighbors. The first thing Rome had to do was to have a sufficiently large population, so King Romulus invited anyone and everyone to come to Rome, slave or free—anyone destitute or displaced or seeking a new start. No questions asked. Keep your nose clean, be willing to work—and fight when necessary—and you could be a Roman. So men from all around who needed refuge or a clean slate came to Rome. By such means Rome grew quickly and started to challenge its neighbors, and, truly, the rest is history.

The founders of the United States, as classically educated gentlemen of the day, were certainly familiar with the story of Rome's beginnings. Perhaps it gave them a thought, the most audacious thought ever in the history of nations—namely, that a people could find their unity in an idea—not geography, not blood, not religion, but an idea. All sorts of people from all sorts of backgrounds and with diverse beliefs could forge an identity based on this idea. The idea was that the very things that divided the people of other nations could be the greatest strength of the United States.

At that time, the most divisive thing was religion. Intellectuals of the Enlightenment, like the founders, were vividly and painfully aware of the religious wars and persecutions that had soaked Europe in blood during the two previous centuries. From 1618 to 1648, Catholics and Protestants slaughtered each other with holy fervor in the Thirty Years'

War. Large districts were left essentially depopulated. The rancor continued unabated, even after the dazed survivors declared the Peace of Westphalia. As recently as 1780, the anti-Catholic Gordon riots had engulfed London.

What, though, if a nation assured every religion a right to worship unmolested and without persecution or harassment? Freedom of conscience to worship—or to refrain from worshipping—as seemed best to each person, would be guaranteed. All that would be asked in return was the willingness to allow *all* others the same freedom, and even to stand up for their religious freedom just as you would your own. Religious tolerance was formally enshrined in the First Amendment to the Constitution, which guarantees that, "Congress shall make no law respecting an establishment of religion or prohibiting the free exercise thereof." In short, the best guarantee of *your* freedom of conscience is the vigorous defense of *everyone's* freedom of conscience.

This was and is a radical idea. It still has not penetrated in many places around the country. In the year 2000 I attended a graduation event at a *public* high school near Marietta, Georgia. The occasion began with a fervent, specifically Christian prayer, "in Jesus's name." The principal addressed the crowd, congratulating them on attending to support a family member because, after all, family was the second most important thing in life after accepting Jesus Christ as your savior. (I am not making up any of this.) The principal also offered each graduate a copy of the Ten Commandments with his or her diploma. The "service"—I can only call it that—ended with another fervent prayer in Jesus's name. I was amazed that there was no altar call.

Now to take a public event of supposedly secular purpose, one that occurs in a space paid for by the public, and is officiated by persons on the public payroll, and is attended by people of all sorts of backgrounds and faiths, and turn it into a revival meeting, is clearly an aggressive display by the majority religion. It appropriates a time and place that is supposed to be for all and makes it into an in-your-face way of marking territory and putting others in their place. Looking at the names of the graduates, I saw many that indicated Jewish, Hindu, Buddhist, or Muslim backgrounds. The message to these people was clear: "Shut up. Stay in your place. This here's Jesus Country!" True, this is not as bad as the dungeon, fire, and sword of past centuries, but it is bad enough.

Despite the fact that some folks in Georgia, Mississippi, Texas, and other locales may not have gotten the message, America stands for freedom of (or from) religion. As a graduate student at the University of Pittsburgh, I would sometimes walk around the neighborhood. I would pass the orthodox Jewish community center where I would see the men dancing joyously in a big circle. I would pass the big Catholic Church and the Greek Orthodox and Baptist houses of worship, all thriving peacefully within a few blocks of each other. I would think how great this was, and how rare in the context of global history. Just think: No massacres, no burnings at the stake, no sectarian riots, no suicide bombers, and no foaming incitements or rabble rousing from pulpits. It is truly a great achievement, and should rank with anything ever accomplished by our, or any, society.[1]

What applies to religion also works with everything else that has divided people over the eons, like ethnicity, race, national origin, gender, or sexual orientation. Our nation has been slower in learning the lesson with some of these distinctions than with others. You and I have seen big changes in our lifetimes. We were children during the height of the civil rights movement. I remember vividly such incidents as the bombing of the church in Birmingham that murdered four little girls in September 1963, and the murder by the Klan, with the connivance of local "law enforcement," of the three civil rights workers in Neshoba County, Mississippi, in June 1964.

More recently, we have seen big changes in the status of LGBTQ people. When you and I were in high school, the surest way to get into a fight was to call someone "queer." At that point, the posturing and name-calling stopped, and you slugged it out. The idea of a man having sex with another man was considered so unspeakably abominable and perverted that hatred of those who were "queer" was accepted, and even violence against them was excused. Some of my classmates spoke casually of "trolling for queers," i.e. finding gay people and beating them.

It is truly amazing to me now to see my niece and members of her generation so freely associating with friends who are gay, lesbian, or transgender. For them, whom you love, or your gender identity, just is not an issue, and they find it outrageous to the point of incomprehensibility that such people are still the objects of hatred and discrimination. In just the few years of this century we have seen public opinion about same-sex marriage shift from strong disapproval to strong approval.[2] Fundamentalists and far-right politicians who continue to condemn and harass LGBTQ people—most recently under a bogus claim of "religious freedom"—only make themselves look ridiculous and hateful. They also incur the enmity of the business community because big corporations want to move to dynamic, open, and progressive locales, not places that still sound like ignorant, backward little cow towns. Bigotry is now bad for business.

What we have seen, then, in our lifetimes, is the bending of that "moral arc" that Barack Obama often referenced. Pluralism has always worked in this country to the extent that it has been achieved. In the Second World War, the multiethnic and non-ideological armed forces of the United States smashed the armies, navies, and air forces of Nazi Germany and Imperial Japan, societies steeped in ideologies of racial superiority. The Axis nations gambled that a society as diverse as the United States could not unite and effectively fight ethnically and ideologically homogeneous societies. Their wrecked forces and burning cities testified to their folly.

The contrast with Nazi Germany and Imperial Japan shows clearly what community in diversity really is: It is the difference between a society of rigid conformity and uniformity in which everybody is supposed to be the same versus an inclusive society in which differences are not only allowed but honored. Worship, think, speak, dress, love, and live as you please—only respect and vigorously defend everyone else's right to do the same. Community in diversity is recognizing the beauty and goodness of diversity, but achieving unity in our devotion to those ideals, those quintessentially American ideals, of justice, freedom, dignity, and opportunity for everyone. *Everyone. E pluribus unum.*

Further, it seems to be happening. Now more than ever, it seems, the "pluribus" has become more diverse, and we are increasingly living up to the ideal of making "unum" out of the many. The moral arc really is bending. Right?

Then came Donald Trump. From his first announcement in June 2015 that he would seek the presidency, Trump raised the flag of ethnic discord. He has not furled that flag since. During his campaign and his administration, by word and deed, he has waged war against the ideals of pluralism and inclusiveness. Nor is divisiveness just an adjunct or side effect of his aims. It is his main point, the sine qua non of his whole presidency.

Putting it like this makes it sound like Trump was an anomaly, an unforeseeable disaster that erupted onto the scene with no antecedents. Sadly, nothing could be farther from the truth. Alongside America's history of expanding tolerance and inclusiveness, there is the dark parallel history of hatred and intolerance, from the Alien and Sedition Acts of the early republic, to the "Know Nothings" of the nineteenth century, to the Ku Klux Klan's founding after the Civil War and its insidious revival in the twentieth century, to the Jim Crow laws of the segregated South, to today's alt-right fascists. Intolerance is as American as apple pie, baseball, and hot dogs. Donald Trump is a far more conventional figure than we would like to think.

Albert Camus's powerful novel *The Plague*, about an outbreak of bubonic plague in the Algerian city of Oran, ends with an ominous warning.[3] Camus cautions us that the plague never dies. It may be defeated in one locale or at one time, but it does not expire. It retreats and bides its time until, when the moment is right, it once more sends its rats into an unsuspecting city. Intolerance can be defeated again and again. It can be rebuked, ridiculed, shamed, and repudiated. Yet it does not die but only retreats and disappears out of sight, hiding in sewers and cesspools. Then, when the time is auspicious, as when a presidential candidate becomes the vector, the plague breaks out once again.

Yet the old divisiveness, promoted by the Klan and their ilk, mostly pitted the majority against various minorities. The old, largely racially based intolerance has not gone away, but is now largely subsumed within a broader, ideologically based divisiveness. Today's ideological schisms still correlate with ethnic and racial differences, but they also cut right across these categories, dividing neighbors and families. Last Thanksgiving there was earnest discussion about how to avoid shouting matches at the dinner table when Uncle Ed speaks up for Trump and Cousin Sue furiously rebuts. I have experienced the schism in my own extended family. Worse, Trump is only the tip of the iceberg of the deep, deep divisions that sunder us.

For want of a better term, we may call these ideological divisions the "culture wars." Some have doubted the depth or severity of our current polarization, but spend an evening watching Fox News and another watching MSNBC and I think it will be apparent that the "culture wars" are real enough. If that does not convince you, and you are of a liberal persuasion, read the platform of the Republican Party of Texas. True, the real culture warriors only constitute a minority of the population, but these are still millions of people; they are loud, and the internet and social media give them a voice and an audience such as they never had.

I spoke earlier about the sense of alienation and displacement I felt after the 2004 presidential election. I felt it even more strongly after the election of Trump. I saw a recent strip of the newspaper comic *Pearls Before Swine*. One character had a sign that was not shown and other characters walked by, saying things like "I don't know" and "No idea." The last panel showed that the sign read "What the @#@# is happening to the country I knew?"[4] My feelings exactly. My nostalgia is not for consensus. There has never been consensus in our country, and that is a good thing. Stalin had consensus. Hitler had consensus. Democracies never do. As I said earlier, vigorous, even boisterous debate is a sign of a healthy democracy. Yet there is a difference, a crucial difference, between debate and vituperation. There is a crucial difference between disagreement and contempt.

Debate, even impassioned debate, is an exchange, a mutual agreement to hear and be heard. Invective shuts off debate, and when invective becomes the common mode of exchange between opposing interests, then something precious has been lost. What has been lost is community. As noted earlier, strong, loving families sometimes argue, even vehemently, but the members never forget that everyone is still family and that what they share is much deeper than what divides them. The same should hold true of nations. When it does not, there is no nation. Iraq, for instance, is not one but three nations, the Sunnis, the Shiites, and the Kurds. Members identify with each of these religious or ethnic groups far more strongly than they identify as Iraqis, and each group wants hegemony over, or at least autonomy from, the others.

Are we seeing the "Iraqification" of the United States? It sure feels like it to me. Culture warrior Pat Buchanan famously announced/declared the war in a prime-time speech at the 1992 Republican National Convention. In the intervening years, it seems that the fissures identified by Buchanan—over issues such as abortion, gay rights, gun control, and the separation of church and state—have widened and deepened into chasms. Some have argued that the culture wars are over, but if they are they are not over because the two sides have reconciled. They are over because they no longer even deign to speak to each other. In that case, the silence is even more ominous than the noisy confrontations.

To begin the road back from polarization to community, we have to define a clear and strong notion of the common good. We will be fleshing out this notion in the remainder of this section, but let me end here with a brief delineation. A common good addresses common needs, needs that we all have. Here I could give Abraham Maslow's famous hierarchy of needs, but, in the spirit of what I have argued so far, let me offer the following Aristotle/Parsons hierarchy of needs for rational, social, animals:

I.   Animal Needs: Physical and mental health; sufficient nutritious food; fresh, clean water and air; adequate housing; a livable environment; protection from harmful agents (human and nonhuman); a modicum of other material goods (such as clothing and furniture) to live a reasonably comfortable life.

II. Social Needs: Sexual and family life (overlaps with animal needs); self-determination (i.e., limits to the demands that others may make on one's body, time, or labor); reciprocity and cooperation with others; the freedom to form voluntary friendships and associations; a sense of belonging, that is, freedom to participate fully in the political, cultural, and social life of the community; criminal and distributive justice; economic freedom, i.e., freedom to buy, sell, trade, own, rent, lend, borrow, etc. within limits that respect the common good.

III. Rational Needs: Literacy, numeracy, and other basics of education; aptitude for critical thinking; the ability to make rational choices and decisions; a wide sphere of freedom to make such choices and decisions; freedom from ambient factors (like extreme poverty) that limit intellectual growth and attainment; freedom of thought; freedom of conscience; freedom of unconformity (implied by the previous two); freedom of expression (freedom of thought and conscience would be meaningless without the freedom to express our convictions).

This list is certainly not exhaustive. Some of its elements may be debatable, which is fine. Such a listing is more of an aspiration than a definitive statement. If we can identify a set of core needs (as Aristotle was convinced we could), then this opens a wonderful possibility for us. Perhaps we can make decisions about policy and law pragmatically (i.e., empirically rather than on the basis of ideology or partisan rancor). For instance, if it can be shown by clear and solid evidence that a single-payer, universal healthcare scheme will best meet our common health needs then we can decide on that. On the other hand, if we find that free-market solutions best meet our needs, then we can opt for that. We need not start with a doctrinaire insistence on collectivist or libertarian principles, but we can actually choose on the basis of evidence. What a concept!

Ah, but there's the rub. As we saw in the first section, ideology easily trumps (this word takes on a whole new significance now) science. Ideology, of both the left and the right, creates its own "alternative facts." Historian and philosopher of science Thomas Kuhn famously said that proponents of different worldviews—what he called "paradigms"—live "in different worlds." While this statement, if taken too literally, causes mischief, it is no doubt true that people react to the world as they perceive it, not as it is.[5] If, then, people live in balkanized and hermetically sealed worldviews, it is not surprising that they not only cannot agree, but cannot even communicate. How, or whether, we can transcend ideology and let the facts dictate to us rather than vice versa, is something we will discuss.

WHAT IS COMMUNITY IN A PLURALISTIC SOCIETY?

PARIS DONEHOO

One of the sketches on the TV show *Monty Python's Flying Circus* depicts two hermits meeting each other on a hillside. As the scene progresses it becomes obvious that these "hermits" are living in the company of other hermits on whom they depend for supplies and companionship.[1] Most *Python* sketches had no purpose other than to be as silly as possible, but I always thought this one had a profound meaning, whether the writers intended it or not. The sketch says we human beings need one another, that lonely individualism is an aberration. We are created for community. In the primeval story in Genesis 2, God says, "It is not good that the man [*adam* in Hebrew] should be alone" (vs. 18). To be created in God's image means communal existence. Ancient Israel understood that to be "cut off from among the people" (Exodus 31:14 and many other passages) was tantamount to a death sentence. "Two are better than one," affirms the book of Ecclesiastes, "because they have a good reward for their toil. For if they fall, one will lift up the other; but woe to one who is alone and falls and does not have another to help. Again, if two lie together, they keep warm; but how can one keep warm alone? And though one might prevail against another, two will withstand one. A threefold cord is not quickly broken" (Ecclesiastes 4:9–12). Furthermore, in spite of the confusion and theological angst historically spawned by the Christian

231

doctrine of the Trinity, at the very least it speaks to me of a God who values community. Even the one God exists communally.

American culture, however, has always prized individualism. You and I are old enough to remember cigarette commercials on TV, and one of the most popular figures was the Marlboro Man. Usually portrayed as a cowboy, the Marlboro Man embodied the American myth of the rugged individual. He was tough, he was masculine, and he did not need others in order to be complete. (Ironically, several of the actors who portrayed Marlboro Men died of smoking-related diseases; but I digress.) The Lone Ranger was another icon of independence. Riding across the western plains with no one but his faithful friend Tonto, he swooped in to help right wrongs and fight injustice, then disappeared before anyone could even say "Thank you." The Marlboro Man, the Lone Ranger, and countless other fictional figures perpetuate the myth of *homo individuum*—a human being not beholden to anyone, who is free to interact or not interact with others of the species purely on the basis of personal choice. Almost no one, of course, desires a completely solitary life, but this myth is usually the starting point for an American's perception of his or her world.

One of my seminary professors told me about a student of hers who hailed from an Asian country, who said, "I'm having a hard time understanding you Americans. In my country, the initial personal pronouns a child learns are the words 'we' and 'us.' Here in the States it seems as if the initial pronouns a child learns are the words 'I' and 'me.'" His observation was quite astute. We need to acknowledge, therefore, that the notion of community does not come naturally to those of us who were born and raised on this side of the pond. The question, "What's in it for me?" is but the logical conclusion—albeit it a crass one—of a culture where the pronouns "I" and "me" are paramount. Indeed, Trump's vaunted foreign policy of "America First" is nothing more than American individualism writ large on the international stage.

So is community even possible in our culture? That depends on the definition of the word. For too many of us community is nothing more than what Scott Peck calls "pseudocommunity":

> In pseudocommunity a group attempts to purchase community cheaply by pretense. ... The essential dynamic of pseudocommunity is conflict-avoidance. The absence of conflict in a group is not by itself diagnostic. Genuine communities may experience lovely and sometimes lengthy periods free from conflict. But that is because they have learned how to deal with conflict rather than avoid it. Pseudocommunity is conflict-avoiding; true community is conflict-resolving.[2]

Most of what passes for community in American culture is, at best, pseudocommunity. Our avoidance of deep-seated racial bigotry, violence, poverty, consumerism, and greed (to name only a few national sins) will continue to mitigate against the formation of true community. One could argue that Americans can at least unite around symbols like Old Glory and our love of freedom, but, in practice, such unity falls apart. I value the freedom we have in this country, but I doubt Rush Limbaugh and I would define it in similar ways.

I want to appeal to our better angels. I think there is a definition of community that is simple and complicated at the same time. Jesus said, "In everything, do to others as you would have them do to you" (Matthew 7:12). Our mothers and teachers quoted those words to us often, and historians have rightly noted that a similar sentiment can be found in many cultures, over many centuries. I think there is a reason it crops up so often: It works. When you measure your actions and reactions not by "What's in it for me?" but by whether or not you would want to be treated the same way, community is born. As you say, Keith, that does not preclude different opinions or vigorous debate, but it is a much better starting point than the myth of the autonomous individual.

I think Jesus gave us a deeper definition of community when he was asked to sift through the hundreds of commandments found in the Hebrew scriptures and name the most important one. He opted for two: "The first is . . . 'You shall love the Lord your God with all your heart, and with all your soul, and with all your mind, and with all your strength.' The second is this, 'You shall love your neighbor as yourself.' There is no other commandment greater than these" (Mark 12:29–31). As a person of faith, I would argue that loving God defines what it means to love one's neighbor, but a pluralistic society such as ours means I cannot expect, much less require, a theological starting point for everyone. I can, however, suggest loving one's neighbor as an excellent definition of community. In whatever scenario I find myself, I can ask, "What is the most loving action I can take?" The answer will rarely be an easy one, and it might vary from situation to situation, but *the very act of wrestling with the question* can create a sense of communal connection with one another. What is the most loving action I can take toward the Muslim family opening a restaurant in my town? What is the most loving action I can take toward the gay couple who moved into a house down the street? What is the most loving action I can take toward the undocumented Latino man mowing my lawn? And here is the tough one: What is the most loving action I can take toward the coworker whose political persuasions are diametrically opposed to my own?

Ironically, we need community in order to build community. I cannot determine the most loving action toward others without the help of others. I must rely on interactions with various individuals and groups in order to hone and shape my practice of doing to others as I would have them do to me. I particularly need the input of people different from myself—different ethnicity, different religion (or none at all), different political persuasion, and so on. Without rubbing elbows with a cross section of humanity, I must rely solely on my own lights to figure out how to best love another, and no one is that smart. (Trump's claims to be an island of superior intellect in a sea of inferior beings notwithstanding.) Today's polarized society, in which everyone retreats to his or her own corner, listens only to people with similar perspectives, and lobs verbal hand grenades via social media, is destroying any chance for real community.

So, once again you and I come to the same place from different starting points. For you, American community can be built on the phenomenal *idea* that a nation's greatest strength is its diversity. For me, American community can be built on the *practice* of loving one's neighbor. Both are necessary. Neither is implemented without difficulty. There can be no sense of a common good without them.

Jesus pushed ideas like a "common good" against the backdrop of something he called the kingdom of God (or "kingdom of heaven" in Matthew's Gospel). It is beyond the scope of this book to explore all the nuances of that term, but suffice it to say it was the goal to which he dreamed humanity could aspire. He often began his parables by saying, "The kingdom of God is like . . ." followed by a story that usually turned conventional wisdom on its head. In my opinion, one of his most provocative stories is often referred to as the Parable of the Laborers in the Vineyard. I quote it here in its entirety:

> For the kingdom of heaven is like a landowner who went out early in the morning to hire laborers for his vineyard. After agreeing with the laborers for the usual daily wage, he sent them into his vineyard. When he went out about nine o'clock, he saw others standing idle in the marketplace; and he said to them, "You also go into the vineyard, and I will pay you whatever is right." So they went. When he went out again about noon and about three o'clock, he did the same. And about five o'clock he went out and found others standing around; and he said to them, "Why are you standing here idle all day?" They said to him, "Because no one has hired us." He said to them, "You

also go into the vineyard." When evening came, the owner of the vineyard said to his manager, "Call the laborers and give them their pay, beginning with the last and then going to the first." When those hired about five o'clock came, each of them received the usual daily wage. Now when the first came, they thought they would receive more; but each of them also received the usual daily wage. And when they received it, they grumbled against the landowner, saying, "These last worked only one hour, and you have made them equal to us who have borne the burden of the day and the scorching heat." But he replied to one of them, "Friend, I am doing you no wrong; did you not agree with me for the usual daily wage? Take what belongs to you and go; I choose to give to this last the same as I give to you. Am I not allowed to do what I choose with what belongs to me? Or are you envious because I am generous?" So the last will be first, and the first will be last (Matthew 20:1–16).

I can think of no parable of Jesus that assaults American individualism more than this one. When I read this parable in a Bible class in church, one man growled, "Sounds like communism to me!" I reminded him that his anger was misplaced. If he did not like the story he should take up the issue with the one who originally told it. He ignored me and launched into a brief tirade about how such practices would totally undermine American democracy and free enterprise. Given the widening gap between the labor force and the 1 percent who control the majority of this country's wealth, the tendency of corporations to treat employees as mere expendables, and the outright purchase of politicians by moneyed interests, I fail to see how Jesus's parable could be any more destructive to democracy than the current state of affairs.

No one, of course, wants to be treated like the laborers in Jesus's parable, especially if you are among those in the story who worked all day long. It is not fair. However, community—real community, not pseudocommunity—is built on loving actions toward one another, not fairness. I do not mean to suggest we should resign ourselves to injustice—far from it—but while we insist on leaders and captains of industry to use their power equitably, we must recognize the power we have to create community by considering others' needs alongside of, and sometimes even ahead of, our own. The landowner's question at the end of the story is an indictment upon all the barriers we erect against community: "Are you envious because I am generous?" A little background would be helpful here. A denarius (the "usual daily wage" in the translation above) was the Roman coin usually paid to a laborer for a day's work. It was not much income. In fact, it was ordinarily just enough to keep a man and his family fed for a day. Missing one day's pay often meant a man's wife and children would go hungry the following day. Thus, the laborers hired later in the parable would likely have had nothing to eat if the landowner had paid them less than a denarius. He was financially equitable toward all the workers, but he was also extremely generous to those who would have had nothing to put on the table the next day.

"Are you envious because I am generous?" American individualism invites comparisons, and I can always find someone doing better than I am, thus fueling a sense of unfair bias that short-circuits community. But if the intent of community is the *common* good, not just my *personal* good, then I must learn to be grateful for more than my own good fortune. The opposite is also true. If the intent is the common good, I must work for the welfare of others along with myself. "Do nothing from selfish ambition or conceit," Paul said, "but in humility regard others as better than yourselves. Let each of you look not to your own interests, but to the interests of others" (Philippians 2:3–4).

The aforementioned Scott Peck introduced me to a story I have told in many sermons because of how it illustrates, for me, the power of community and a sense of the common good. It's a story about a monastery that had fallen on hard times. There were only five monks left, all of them over seventy years old. Clearly theirs was a dying order. The abbot prayed and agonized over what to do, but nothing came to him. Finally, in desperation, he decided to go visit a local rabbi to see if, perhaps, he could offer some advice that might save the monastery. The rabbi said, "I know how it is. The spirit is gone out of the people. It's the same here in town. Almost no one comes to the synagogue anymore. It's sad." So the old abbot and the old rabbi wept together.

At last it was time for the abbot to leave, and he embraced the rabbi. "It has been wonderful to meet you after all these years," he said, "but is there nothing you can tell me, no piece of advice you can give me that would help me save my dying order?" "No," said the rabbi, "I'm sorry. I have no advice to give. The only thing I can tell you is that the Messiah is one of you." When the abbot returned to the monastery his fellow monks gathered around him and asked, "What did the rabbi say?" The abbot replied, "He couldn't help. He's having problems too. The only thing he did say, just as I was leaving, was that the Messiah is one of us." "What did he mean by that?" asked the other monks. "I don't know," said the abbot.

Well, the monks pondered the rabbi's statement and wondered if there was any possible significance to it. The Messiah is one of us? Could he possibly have meant one of us here in the monastery? If so, which one of us is the Messiah? Could he have meant the abbot? If anybody could be the Messiah it is the abbot. On the other hand, he might have meant Brother Thomas. Surely, he didn't mean Brother Elred! But he might have. Maybe the rabbi meant Brother Philip. Of course, he could not have meant me. I'm just an ordinary person. Yet, suppose he did mean me?

So the monks began acting differently toward one another. They treated each other with more respect. They did not complain as much. They sought ways to be helpful to one another. When they went to worship they sang with greater gusto and looked hard for new meaning in their prayers. They tried to find joy in their work and reasons to praise God more often. It didn't really seem possible, of course, but there was just the remote possibility that one among them might really be the Messiah so they acted differently toward one another. And because of the off, off chance—however slight—that each monk himself might be the Messiah, they acted differently toward themselves.

The woods where the monastery was located were beautiful, and, on occasion, a few people would come on warm, sunny days to picnic on the monastery's lawn. And as they did they began to sense something different about the place. Maybe the grounds were a little better kept, maybe they heard the monks speaking to each other in deeply respectful tones, but for some reason people felt a strange, compelling attraction to the place. Hardly knowing why, people began coming to the monastery more often to picnic, to play, even to pray now and then. They brought their friends. Those friends brought other friends. And before long some of the young men began talking with the monks, and they came back again and again to talk with them. Then a day came when one of those young men asked the monks if he could join them. Then another. And another. And within a few years the monastery was once again a thriving order, a vibrant center for light and spirituality, making a difference in the lives of everyone around.[3]

With the designation of his opponents as (to name just a few) "Crooked Hillary," "Lyin' Ted," "Pocahontas," "Rocket Man," and "Little Marco," Trump eviscerates any basis for community in American society. I much prefer wondering which of my fellow human beings could be the Messiah.

HOW HAS DIVISIVENESS BECOME SO EXTREME?

KEITH PARSONS

I loved the Monty Python skit about the hermits. That is precisely the point. Extreme individualism is a nonstarter that is simply contrary to human nature. I sometimes hear people glorifying the pioneer days when everyone was supposed to have been a "rugged individualist." Rubbish. People depended on their neighbors in those days far more than we do today. They had to. I had the privilege as a child of seeing how my grandparents lived, deep in the piney woods of south Georgia. Their nearest neighbor was a mile away, but he would drop everything, jump in his pickup, and be there in a few minutes if you needed him. Today, I hardly know any of the people in my neighborhood, even though they live their lives just a few yards from me. People do not know each other and seem to have no interest in doing so. Today's suburb dweller is far more isolated from his neighbors than my ancestors who lived in rural Georgia in the nineteenth century.

Okay, so how did we get in this situation of extreme divisiveness? The 2008 elections were a disaster for Republicans. Barack Obama won the presidency, and Democrats got a seventy-nine-seat majority in the House. However, before Obama took office in January 2009, Mitch McConnell and other Republicans, energized rather than disheartened, went into conference and devised a winning strategy, one of all-out, intransigent opposition. They would oppose anything and everything that Obama supported.[1] I saw a TV interview with Rush Limbaugh following the 2008 election but before Obama's inauguration. His message was simple: Obama must fail. That mantra became the defining strategy of the Republican Party during the Obama era, and it worked amazingly well, forestalling most of Obama's legislative initiatives, and turning voter frustration away from them and toward Democrats.

When Obama did succeed with a major project, as in passing the Affordable Care Act—with not a single GOP vote in support—Republican fury was unbounded, and repeal of the ACA became a rallying cry for Republican lawmakers. When in Obama's second term the Republicans regained control of the House, they voted dozens of times to repeal the ACA, knowing that the Democratically controlled Senate would dismiss it. Of course, as Michael Grunwald observed in *Politico*, "opposition parties always oppose, especially in a country as polarized as America."[2] Yet the fervor and consistency of the opposition was extraordinary. In fact, there were many ideas that Republicans supported *until* Obama favored them.[3] Then, predictably, when Trump came into office, Democrats in turn promised obstruction.[4]

I heard a story about Lyndon Johnson and how he would confer with Republican senator Everett Dirksen, the then Senate minority leader. According to the story, which had the ring of truth, LBJ would good-naturedly upbraid Dirksen for making defamatory remarks about him on the Senate floor, and then settle down with Dirksen to hammer out an agreement. Can we even imagine that happening in recent years? Typically now, Trump will meet with a bipartisan group of legislators to discuss, say, immigration or gun control. He will appear conciliatory and ready to make a compromise. Then, within hours, he walks back any appearance of cooperation and reverts to intransigence.

How did dysfunction become normalized? This may seem like a stretch, but consider a quote that sheds light on an even more intractable and unyielding imbroglio, one that has lasted for decades and cost many lives. Golda Meir said that progress between Israel and Palestine could only be achieved when "The Arabs will love their children more than they will hate us."[5] (Perhaps the Arabs would say the same about the Israelis; this is not my topic here.) My point is this: When it is more important to you to sustain enmity than to achieve anything of mutual benefit, then the situation has become toxic, and nothing but pain and anger will follow. When the government of a country reaches this point, the situation is very dangerous indeed. In today's hyperpartisan environment, any compromise is seen as perfidy, and frustrating the other side is valued over getting anything done.

Perhaps, though, the real serpent in the garden here, worse even than vindictive partisanship, is power. Two great epics, J. R. R. Tolkien's *The Lord of the Rings* and Richard Wagner's *Der Ring des Nibelungen*, revolve around a central, terrifying concept: A ring that gives its possessor ultimate power over all things and is therefore purely evil, eventually corrupting all who try to wield it. It is one of the greatest scenes in all of dramatic art when in *Das Rheingold* Wotan seizes the ring from Alberich, and the furious Nibelung places a terrible curse on the ring: All will lust for it and be gnawed with envy of the one who has it, but to its owner the ring will bring nothing but misery. He will guard the ring in endless anxiety, fearful that it will be taken from him. In the end, the ring's master will become its slave.

Such is the nature of power. Perhaps a better metaphor than a golden ring would be to see power as a highly addictive drug. Those who have it crave more and more, and their greatest fear is being deprived of the drug. Soon the drug rules them and they live for it.

In the opera, Wotan relinquishes the ring only when warned by Erda. Erda is the Earth itself, embodying primeval wisdom, and she is the only one who can make Wotan listen. She warns Wotan that the ring will destroy the gods and that he must give it up. Power is relinquished only when some other motivation is even stronger.

To me, one of the greatest moments in the life of our republic is on the day when a new president is inaugurated. One president stands aside as the new one is sworn in. In that moment, the world's most powerful human being watches as that power is peacefully transferred to another. Every ex-president so far has honored the Constitution and quietly surrendered power. Again, how rare this peaceful and orderly transfer of power is in the context of history! How much more often a king has waded through slaughter to a throne. Think of the rulers of Byzantium whose first act as emperor was to blind all of their brothers.

Essential to any democracy is the willingness to give up power when the voters decide that it is time. I recently read of a congressman who was defeated and bitterly complained to an aide about having to give up "his" seat. The aide reminded him that it was not his seat, but belonged to the American people. Democracy totters when those in power begin to see that power as an entitlement and an end in itself, and they stoop to manipulation and chicanery to tighten their grip. This is what we have seen in state after state when congressional districts are gerrymandered to frustrate voters and keep the dominant party in power. As many have observed, gerrymandering means that candidates get to choose their voters rather than voters choosing the candidates. This shady practice has existed throughout the history of the country, but it is now a science. Computer algorithms can draw districts with mathematical precision, packing supporters of the other party into sequestered pockets or dispersing them among districts dominated by your loyal supporters.

Similarly insidious is voter intimidation and harassment. Bogus charges of voter fraud are invoked as justification for requiring photo identification at the polls. Elderly and minority voters disproportionately lack photo IDs, and such identification is often hard for them to get. The ID requirement essentially disenfranchises them, which, of course, was its purpose.

Community is possible only if those in power are willing to lose. The determination to win at any cost makes factionalism supreme.

The founders realized that factionalism is the greatest danger to the republic. As we noted earlier, when it becomes the case that loyalty to faction is more important than loyalty to the nation, then there is no nation. There is no common good but only squalid grubbing for power, and this is where we now are in the Disunited States of America.

Note that I have phrased the problem neutrally, placing no specific blame. Of course, as a true-blue liberal and a lifetime Democrat, I place far more blame on the Republicans for our current state of disunity. However, the solution to the problem of factionalism is not an intensification of factionalism, even if you think your faction is not chiefly to blame. (By the way, Hillary Clinton's clearly and repeatedly expressed contempt for Trump voters shows that the divisiveness is not all one-sided.)

Let me pause to comment on the nature of polarization. Polarization does not mean a 50/50 split. When you look at polls of what people think, there is often broad agreement on even the hottest of hot-button issues. Consider guns. I saw a statistic just recently that only a quarter of Americans own guns, and only 3 percent own about half of the firearms in this country.[6] The NRA is estimated to have five million members.[7] Out of a population of over 300 million that is less than two percent. *Time* reports that, contrary to the hardline stand of the NRA, even most gun owners want stricter gun laws.[8] Polarization occurs when minorities who hold extreme and unyielding views gain greatly disproportionate power and influence. Their power and influence is manifested in two ways: (1) Politicians are afraid to oppose them, and (2) their views set the terms and the rhetorical temperature of public discourse. Extremist minorities who are fervent, organized, well-heeled, and loud can dominate elections and public discussion to a greatly inordinate degree.

But why are politicians so afraid of the NRA when their views are opposed by a significant majority of the people? How does the tail wag the dog? Simple: Money and primaries. The NRA and its members—

and the gun manufacturing industry—are quite willing and able to lavish large sums on politicians, and in politics money is garrulous and the public good is gagged.

As noted in a previous section, primary elections notoriously draw only a small percentage of the eligible voters. This makes it easy for highly organized and well-funded ax-grinders to mobilize large numbers of deeply committed single-issue voters who can turn primary elections. This is why Republican primaries here in Texas are basically contests to see which candidate can present himself or herself as the most ideologically pure conservative. Any hint of less than the most stringent, uncompromising orthodoxy on issues like immigration, abortion, or guns can be fatal. Attack ads running on every channel and hinting that you are soft on guns is a Republican candidate's nightmare.

Such groups are also experts in getting their message out. They can saturate TV with ads, and employ articulate, passionate, and often telegenic spokespersons who are frequent guests on Fox News and other right-wing venues. They are even the default sources for mainstream news outlets, like CNN and the networks, because they can always be depended upon to say something pithy and provocative. The NRA even has its own television network that features, among other offerings, shows on fashionable guns for women. As for the rhetorical temperature, acrimony is inevitable when, for instance, Wayne La Pierre, president of the NRA, reviled as "socialists" Democrats who called for stricter gun control in the wake of the latest assault-rifle massacre.[9]

Paradoxically, then, polarization can exist in contexts of broad consensus. If 90 percent of the people agree on an issue, but a disproportionately influential and visible 10 percent intransigently and stridently disagree, then public discourse on the issue will be angry, loud, and abusive—that is, polarized.

Here, then, is the situation we are in: When (a) partisanship is so extreme that power itself becomes the supreme value, and (b) any means fair or foul is justified if it keeps you and your party in power, and (c) remaining in power depends crucially upon the money and support of extremist groups and the voters they mobilize, then parties will align ideologically with their most extreme supporters, and polarization and division will be the order of the day. This was the situation well before Trump declared for the presidency in 2015, and both as a candidate and as president he has poured high-octane fuel on the flames of divisiveness. Trump has never displayed even the most rudimentary awareness that he is supposed to be president of all the people and not just his base. He is never happier than when he basks in the admiration of crowds at campaign-style rallies, and they eagerly applaud even his most fatuous and reckless utterances. Especially his most fatuous and reckless utterances.

There is a another, and, I think, deeper way of understanding our present divisiveness. It is a reversion to tribalism. Surely, human beings evolved in small, tribal groups, and our brains are adapted by natural selection to get along with a small in-group of familiar individuals. Nothing could be farther from our primitive social conditions than the modern pluralistic nation-state with its vast diversity of tribes. We are thrown together and expected to live together peacefully and cooperatively with people who do not look, dress, sound, or believe as we do. Tribalism may have been adaptive when we lived in tribes, but living, as we do, in a "global village," it is now severely maladaptive.

On the cover of Joshua Greene's brilliant book *Moral Tribes* is a depiction of people presumably waiting at a bus stop in what could be any large American city.[10] There is a young white man with tattoos, tie, and an untucked shirt, a Muslim woman veiled and wearing a chador, a young white woman neatly dressed and plainly coiffed, what looks like a mixed-race teenager with a skateboard, and an orthodox Jew with long black coat and black hat. This is a quintessentially American scene, something, again, rare in the context of history. Conservatives like to talk about American exceptionalism, and I think we have been exceptional at least in the fact that we have to a remarkable degree (though very far from perfectly) been able to transcend tribalism and achieve some degree of *e pluribus unum.* Now that grand and glorious achievement is in grave danger of slipping away from us.

Tribalism is still a potent and deleterious force in many parts of the world, leading to massacre, "ethnic cleansing," and genocide. When suicide bombers blow up a mosque or a church, when Hindus massacre Muslims or Muslims massacre Hindus, when Buddhists in Myanmar murder Rohingya Muslims and drive them into exile, when Tutsis were massacred by Hutus, and when white supremacists bomb, shoot, and burn, this is tribalism rampant. Tribalism has its roots in the brain, as indicated by the passages I cited previously from David Eagleman's primer of neuroscience *The Brain: The Story of You.* We have a remarkable capacity for empathy, but we also have a distressing susceptibility to seeing others as members of out-groups, and so not worthy of empathy. It is all too easy for us to slip into an "us" vs. "them" dichotomy that privileges our group and stigmatizes "others."

On January 20, 2017, Donald Trump became the Divider in Chief of an already deplorably fractured nation. By word and deed he has done all that he could to widen and deepen the divisions. The authentic drumbeat of tribalism is heard in Trump's angry 4:00 a.m. tweets. Fear-mongering is the oldest implement in the demagogue's toolbox, and Trump wields it with recklessness and crudity. He warns of rapists pouring across our southern border, and issues grossly hyperbolic claims about crimes committed by immigrants. Nativism and xeno-phobia are his stock-in-trade, but his venom is not just reserved for the ethnic groups he openly despises. Any critic is subjected to vicious, personal, and vindictive attack that recognizes no restraints of decency or dignity. In short, division is his end and hate is his means.

So, here we are, in a house divided against itself. How long can we stand?

HOW HAS DIVISIVENESS BECOME SO EXTREME?

PARIS DONEHOO

An old joke goes like this:

> Jack: Who are you voting for in the next election?
> Joe: I'll vote for the Democrat.
> Jack: Why?
> Joe: Because I'm a Democrat.
> Jack: Why are you a Democrat?
> Joe: Because my father was a Democrat, my grandfather was a Democrat, and my great-grandfather was a Democrat.
> Jack: Well, if your father was a jackass, and your grandfather was a jackass, and your great-grandfather was a jackass, would that make you a jackass?
> Joe: No, that would make me a Republican.

To be fair, I have heard permutations of the same joke with the political parties reversed, and I have heard versions that skewer Catholics and Protestants, Northerners and Southerners, and a host of other groups. Regardless of the punchline, the partisan message is clear. We laugh because we know Jack and Joe. They have always been our neighbors—sometimes they have been we ourselves—in this partisan country we call home. The Founding Fathers, as you note, warned against the dangers of factionalism, but it has been with us since the beginning. The problem now is the hyperpartisan atmosphere of our current society.

Unfortunately, it has an all-too-familiar ring to me. I mentioned earlier the Southern Baptist holy war that erupted within the denomination during the 1980s. Much like today's partisan wrangling, the squabbles were driven by extremes on both ends of the ecclesiastical spectrum, with the vast majority of pastors and parishioners wanting a middle way. I never tried to be neutral. I felt strongly that I had a dog in the fight, but I knew scores of Southern Baptist pastors who fervently desired to remain nonaligned. As the fratricide increased, however, neutrality became nearly impossible. Not taking a side was often interpreted as standing with the opposition, and some were eventually hijacked by the group that shouted the loudest.

To quote Yogi Berra, "It's déjà vu all over again." I have never tried to hide my left-leaning theology and politics from the congregations I served, but I have also tried to be fair and balanced. I have tried to be respectful of differing views, and I have always invited feedback. Every so often, however, someone would leave the church because I was "too political," which, in practice, usually meant my Christian brother or sister would have been okay with my views if they had been closer to his or her own.

The accusation that a pastor or church has become "too political" intrigues me. Is there a way for the church to be faithful to Christ and be anything other than political? Moses challenged the political leader of Egypt to end the Israelites' slavery (Exodus 5:1). The prophet Nathan confronted King David about his adultery and murder (2 Samuel 11–12). All the prophets in the Hebrew scriptures decried political and social sins. John the Baptist was beheaded because he spoke truth to power (Mark 6:18). And Pilate did not nail a sign reading "King of the Jews" to Jesus's cross in order to honor him, but to warn others about the danger of getting "too political" (Mark 15:26).

As stated earlier, I agree with Stanley Hauerwas's and William Willimon's claim that the political task of the church is to be the church.[1] There is no way to serve only one master and avoid bumping against Trump's demagogic demands for loyalty. There is no way to love one's neighbor and not advocate for immigrant rights in the face of Trump's fearmongering. There is no way to turn the other cheek without questioning Trump's threat to rain down "fire and fury" on North Korea. A sign at a recent protest rally says it all: "For I was hungry and you cut my food stamps. I was a stranger and you deported me. I was sick and you denied me healthcare. I was a child afraid to go to school, and you voted with the NRA." The "reference" was to "Matthew 25:35–36, New Hypocritical Version."[2]

The problem is not politics. As already stated, the problem is partisanship.[3] A church does not have to be partisan to be political. An individual does not have to be partisan in order to be political. To be political is to work for the common good. To be partisan is to work only for your group's good, or your own individual good. To be political is to be guided by higher principles like freedom, inclusivity, or justice for all. To be partisan is to be guided by selfish motives, or to be guided by principles that benefit only a select few. Partisanship may not be the final nail in the coffin of community, but the corpse cannot be buried without it.

Partisanship feeds a victim mentality. It grows out of a sense of being wronged by someone, by some group, by life itself, or even by God. A victim mentality looks to blame another for whatever slings and arrows are suffered. It's "their" fault that I am so miserable. For example, within days, sometimes hours, of a tragedy that captures the public's attention, the question becomes "Who is to blame?" There has to be some nefarious intent orchestrated by an evil puppet-master. There may, in truth, actually be an act of incompetence or malice behind a calamity, but the fact that we immediately look to lay blame at the feet of someone else is symptomatic of perceived victimhood that, in turn, short circuits any chance at community in a larger sense.

It should come as no surprise, therefore, that a victim mentality is fertile ground for tyrants and demagogues. One of Adolf Hitler's henchmen, Hermann Göring, appealed to a victim mentality when drumming up support for war. "All you have to do," he said, "is tell [the people] they are being attacked, and denounce the pacifists for lack of patriotism, and exposing the country to greater danger."[4] His boss, Der Führer, of course, blamed the Jews for Germany's problems. Alabama governor George Wallace, and other opponents of civil rights, blamed racial unrest in the South on "outside agitators."[5] But in Donald Trump we seem to have found a man who can play the victim card better than most. He appears to have no end of nations and groups he can blame for any perceived slight. Former secretary of state Madeleine Albright is right on target:

> What Trump is doing is making America seem like a victim. Everything is somebody else's fault: Countries are taking advantage of us. The Mexicans are sending drug dealers. Countries are not paying their dues. The trading system is unfair. And by making Americans seem like victims all the time, it then is able to, again, make the divisions stronger in terms of who is with us, who is not with us, and it's totally anti-American foreign policy. . . . I don't see America as a victim. I see America as the most powerful country in the world that has a role to play, standing up for democratic ideals and human rights across the board.[6]

Of course, some people, groups, and even countries *are* victims. There are always forces on the loose that are advancing goals at the expense of others. Jesus himself was the victim of a political system designed to keep most of the populace in subjugation, and a religious system designed to protect the privileges of an elitist class. However, even though Jesus was a victim, he never succumbed to a victim mentality. The Gospel of

John goes to great lengths to portray a Jesus who was never a mere pawn in the power games of others. "I lay down my life," he said, "in order to take it up again. No one takes it from me, but I lay it down of my own accord" (John 10:17–18). Out of context his words may sound like the dismissed employee who shouts, "You can't fire me! I quit!" but Jesus never displayed such petulance. Even when Jesus was truly a victim, he did not give in to a victim mentality. Perhaps that is why the early church made the audacious claim that Jesus's crucifixion was not a defeat but a triumph. "Thanks be to God," wrote Paul, "who gives us the victory through our Lord Jesus Christ" (1 Corinthians 15:57).

If our society is to create real community, we have to drop the victim mentality. There are multiple causes for our problems—some of them of our own making, some of them foisted upon us by others, but a victim mentality blinds us to our own agency. As long as we play the victim we will never see the potential we have to solve problems in cooperation with others. Preacher and activist Jim Wallis often meets with civic and religious leaders in town meetings around the country to discuss the problems of poverty and other social ills, and he asks who is responsible for the poor children who are falling through the cracks in their community. Immediately, the finger-pointing begins. One side says it's the fault of the Democrats and their failed programs, and the other quickly counters that it's the Republicans whose policies have abandoned the poor.

After listening to the squabbling for a while, Wallis points out that he did not ask them who is to blame. He asked them who is responsible. There is more than enough blame to go around, he says. Assigning culpability solves nothing. "Who are the leaders in your community?" he asks. After a few moments they admit, "We are." "Then who is responsible?" Wallis asks again. That is when they look at each other and acknowledge that *they* should be the ones responsible. Then the group begins to talk about "a strategy that might actually work to reduce child poverty, address real community issues like drugs and youth violence, and create safe and stable communities of opportunity and hope, instead of stagnation and despair."[7]

When a society can do nothing more than blame the Other for its troubles, there is no possibility for the mutual cooperation that is the basis of community. The reaction of Vice President Pence to the North Korean delegation at the opening ceremony of the Winter Olympic Games is emblematic of this. Sitting stone-faced, staring straight ahead, as if Kim Jong Un's sister behind him in the same box was invisible or carried some disgusting disease, he was Exhibit A for the blame game. While delegations from both ends of the Korean peninsula greeted each other warmly, and chatted about the Olympic spectacle unfolding before them, Pence displayed none of the Christian charity and goodwill he purports to believe. "Love your enemies" (Matthew 5:44)? Not if it suits your purpose to blame your enemy for international discord rather than accept responsibility for peace. Therefore, Trump's and Kim's subsequent "love fest" appears all the more self-serving and cynical.

If partisanship feeds a victim mentality, it also feeds pathological alliances. In the pursuit of your side's objectives, integrity is the first casualty, and people get hurt. One of the revelations that came from James Comey's book *A Higher Loyalty* was the way Trump and his lieutenants reacted to the news that the Russians had meddled in the 2016 election. Trump (at that time still president-elect), listened without interrupting, Comey recalls, and asked only one question: "But you found there was no impact on the result, right?" Comey replied that the officials had come to no such conclusion. What Comey noticed next was what Trump and his team did NOT ask. "They were about to lead a country that had been attacked by a foreign adversary," writes the former FBI director, "yet they had no questions about what the future Russian threat might be." All Trump and his minions did was begin discussing how they could "spin" the news in a press briefing.[8]

The potential danger to the nation, not to mention the integrity of the electoral process, did not concern the newly elected president. His only interest was how he could use the information to his own advantage. Whether Machiavelli said it or not, Trump certainly believes it: The ends justify the means.

I do not mean to imply that Trump and his followers are deliberately malevolent, like Dracula in a classic horror movie. I cannot psychoanalyze a man I have never met, and I have never spoken with any Trump supporter who has evil intent. But I keep thinking about a statement I heard from the late theologian Fred Craddock. Craddock defined the word "sin" as "something good out of place."[9] Having been raised to think of sin as the deliberate breaking of rules, I found Craddock's definition intriguing. Except for the occasional sociopath (and some have speculated that Trump fits into this category), I have never met anyone who woke up one morning and decided to ruin his or her life, wreak havoc on society, and cause general mayhem. People tend to take something good and put it in the wrong place. Sex, for example, is a wonderful gift from God, but when it is put into practice outside of a committed relationship between two people who have pledged to be faithful to one another, it can become terribly destructive.

Likewise, I am willing to give Trump the benefit of the doubt. Perhaps he honestly believes his actions and antics are for the benefit of the country. If so, he has taken a great deal of good and put it in the wrong place. Patriotism becomes the sin of loyalty to the president. National pride becomes the sin of xenophobia. And the common good becomes the sin of greed.

In the story of Jesus's temptation in the wilderness, the devil presents Jesus with the same logic. He shows him in an instant all the kingdoms of the world and says, "To you, I will give their glory and all this authority; for it has been given over to me, and I give it to anyone I please. If you, then, will worship me, it will all be yours" (Luke 4:6–7). On the surface it does not sound like a bad deal. Jesus wanted to change the world. He wanted the kingdoms of this world to turn to God, and the devil was offering him the power to get that done. What's a little worship between friends? Think of all the good Jesus could do.

John Dominic Crossan looks beneath this story by pointing out what the devil says about the kingdoms of this world. They have "been given over to me," says the devil. You would expect Jesus to contradict him. You would expect Jesus to quote a scripture like Psalm 24:1—"The earth is the Lord's and all that is in it." But the devil never said anything about the world God created. No, the devil said he had authority over "the kingdoms of the world." In other words, he had power over the world we humans have created—the world of cities and states and nations, the world of governments and institutions, the world of commerce, the world of social systems, the world of armies and military force. That's the world the devil can control and give to whoever he wants, and Jesus did not disagree with him. The devil did have sway over the kingdoms of this world, the very kingdoms Jesus wanted to redeem.[10]

But Jesus knew that the end does not justify the means. The object of one's worship matters. One's ultimate allegiance is what counts. And to worship the devil would be to buy into the system that built those kingdoms—the intrigue, the lies, the injustice, the violence, the using of people like pawns, the duping of oneself and others into thinking the end justifies the means as long as the end is what's best for everybody—especially me.

As I said earlier, the truth of this story does not lie in its literality, but in its application. The insidious nature of partisanship lies in its subtle yet profound ability to dupe us into thinking we are doing something good, when in actuality we have taken that good and put it in the wrong place. And nothing is more dangerous than a person or group convinced their actions are unquestionably the best for everyone. There is no common good because there is no mutuality in what is common to everyone, and the good is out of place.

WHAT IS THE VALUE OF COMMUNITY?

KEITH PARSONS

On June 22, 1941, Nazi Germany invaded the Soviet Union with three million men and thousands of tanks and aircraft. Employing the deadly tactics of *Blitzkrieg* against a disorganized and unprepared Red Army, the *Wehrmacht* inflicted a series of crushing defeats. In massive battles of encirclement, they surrounded and cut off whole Soviet armies, killing and capturing hundreds of thousands. Though the Russians fought back with desperate courage, by December the Germans had pushed to the gates of Moscow. The Soviet Union seemed to totter on the brink of collapse.

Yet Hitler had miscalculated. He did not count on his conquest lasting until winter, the cruel, relentless Russian winter that had been the bane of Napoleon's *Grande Armée*. Exhausted, lacking winter gear, and at the end of lengthy supply line, the Germans froze in the coldest winter of the twentieth century. The thermometer plunged to an incomprehensible minus forty-five Celsius. Stalin, meanwhile, had transferred eighteen divisions of fresh, tough, well-equipped Siberians from the east, along with 1,700 aircraft and 1,500 tanks. On December 5, the Russians launched a massive counteroffensive. Attacking in giant pincer movements, the Red Army inflicted upon the previously triumphant invaders their first bitter taste of defeat. The war would drag on another horrific three and a half years, but the Moscow counteroffensive meant that Russia would live.

In America, December 5 was a Friday. The weekend was coming

257

up, and it was holiday season. The war in Europe seemed distant and largely irrelevant. A strong isolationist movement, with its ringing doctrine of "America first," discouraged involvement in that conflict. Though most Americans felt deep sympathy for Britain and Russia, and an abhorrence of the Nazis, there was no reason to think that it would soon be our fight as well. Of course, the events of the 7th changed everything. With Pearl Harbor, in words often attributed to Admiral Isoroku Yamamoto, a sleeping giant was awakened and filled with a terrible resolve.[1]

We boomers knew the generation that fought the Second World War. They were our parents, uncles, and aunts. Every one of them testified to the sense of unity and solidarity that prevailed during the war years, and how sacrifice and rationing were borne with equanimity and even good humor. Perhaps their memories had been tainted by nostalgia, but I think that there really was a national solidarity such that those who live in our fractured times can hardly imagine. Country boys from Georgia, who had hardly been over thirty miles from home before, served alongside Italians from New York, Swedes from Minnesota, and Latinos from New Mexico. Women took over formerly masculine domains in the workplace and evinced an aggressive competence that inspired the famous "We can do it!" poster. Even some African Americans were given (far too limited) opportunities, such as the famous Tuskegee Airmen. At the end of the war, Americans could say with justifiable pride: WE did it; WE fought the good fight.

The Second World War was probably history's greatest disaster. The generally accepted figure is that sixty million human beings were killed. Yet in the United States it is still remembered as "The Good War."[2] Admittedly, the United States suffered less than any other major participant. Approximately 6,800 Americans were killed in the Battle of Iwo Jima. At Stalingrad, the Russians lost that many *every day*. The total number of Soviet citizens, military and civilian, killed in the Great

Patriotic War is unknown, but estimates are over twenty million. The only Americans killed on the US mainland as a result of enemy action were six people in rural Oregon who were killed by a Japanese balloon bomb. Yet the reason for the feeling of a "good war" was surely the pervasive sense of a people, despite our many differences, united in a great campaign, a struggle, literally, to save the world.

Is the lesson here that we need another big war to unite us again? No, the lesson is that the sense of national unity was such a good thing that even the worst war in history could be remembered as "The Good War." Sadly, after the war, African American and Hispanic veterans, some bearing decorations for bravery, returned to face the same old segregation and discrimination at home. Women who had been "Rosie the Riveter" during the war were strongly encouraged to return to domestic duties during the hyperconventional fifties. (After all, what woman could possibly resist all the marvelous new kitchen and laundry gadgets that poured from the cornucopia of postwar American industry?) So, after a brief period of unity, the entrenched forces of division, segregation, and stereotype came back with a vengeance. The civil rights, feminist, and gay rights movements that have so profoundly shaped the history of postwar America, were efforts to confront those retrograde forces, bring them into the light, and defeat them.

With respect to these social justice movements, conservatives accuse liberals of practicing "identity politics," playing off minorities and marginalized groups against the mainstream for political gain. The real reason that liberals still talk about minorities is because they realize that the dream of equality is not yet fully realized. Fifty years ago, in 1968, the report of the Kerner Commission appeared. President Johnson had appointed the panel in the previous year in the wake of the devastating riots in Detroit, Newark, and elsewhere. The commissioners were charged with investigating the causes of "urban unrest," and their uncompromising conclusion was that the underlying cause was white racism and that the consequences would be dire: "Our Nation is moving toward two societies, one black, one white—separate and unequal."[3]

When the commissioners looked at the communities where the riots had occurred, what they found was that life in the ghettos was much worse than they had imagined:

> Unemployment was pervasive, schools had insufficient funds and virtually no white students, and neighborhoods lacked access to adequate sanitation. More sobering still was the profound sense of disillusionment and anger that the commission encountered.[4]

Justin Driver, writing in the *Atlantic*, notes that, despite progress, many of these problems continue:

> While many African Americans have made momentous strides in the past five decades, cities still contain destitute neighborhoods filled with racial minorities, which—as in the late 1960s—serve as breeding grounds for despair and alienation.[5]

Perhaps the most alarming disparity is the continuing huge gap in the quality of public education. As of this writing, the Texas Education Association is threatening to take control of ten schools in the Houston Independent School District because of their poor performance. The failing schools are all—you guessed it—in inner-city minority communities.[6]

For all of the bedeviling complexities about race in America, one salient truth is simple. There is only one way forward: together. America *is* a multiethnic and multiracial society, and the demographic facts are that it is going to become more diverse, not less. There is something pathetic and desperate about the doomed efforts of demagogues to use gerrymandering and voter suppression to stem the demographic tide. It is like trying to control a tsunami with a mop and bucket. Either we achieve unity in the midst of that inevitably growing diversity, or we continue on our present course toward balkanization and hostility. (Psssst. Vladimir Putin devoutly hopes it is the latter.)

Conservatives also often also accuse liberals of putting too much emphasis on diversity, highlighting the *pluribus* at the expense of the *unum*, and I think that there is some truth to this charge. But diversity is a basic fact of life in America. People of color, gay, lesbian, and transgender people, and Muslims are not going away. In 2015 the *Houston Chronicle* reported that Latinos will soon outnumber Anglos in Texas.[7] Needless to say, some Texans don't like this development. Tough. I remember when the "tea party" movement was in full swing, a lachrymose female tea partier mourned, "I want my America back!" But the America of hardworking Christian white people of her Norman Rockwell fantasy will never be again. In fact, except in Frank Capra films and on the covers of the *Saturday Evening Post*, it never really existed in the first place.

The value of community-in-diversity should be obvious. It should be obvious that a genuinely inclusive community will be one that is happier, healthier, more productive, more innovative, and stronger. We can do more and do it better if everybody has a full opportunity to contribute, rather than only some. Besides, holding people down is hard work. I heard a quote once from educator Booker T. Washington to the effect that to hold someone in a ditch, you have to be down in the ditch with him.[8] People have a strong tendency not to quietly endure relegation to inferior status, and it takes a lot of effort to keep them there. Jim Crow laws—backed by gun, rope, and whip—kept African Americans "in their place" during the segregation era, but when so much of your society's energy is expended on oppression, other important things get left undone. To this day, the states of the former Confederacy lag behind the other states in education, life expectancy, and overall quality of life.[9]

An inclusive and open society also welcomes immigrants, a stance diametrically opposite to the virulent anti-immigrant nativism that is a defining characteristic of the Trump administration. The economic benefits of immigration are well-documented, as entrepreneur Doug Rand comments:

> Underneath the headlines about DACA and sanctuary cities, the Trump administration is quietly implementing major changes throughout the legal system, making it much harder to obtain visas and to live and work in the United States. Yet immigrants as a whole—from housekeepers to biochemists—are net job creators, grow the economy, and pay into the public treasury far more than they take out. To make the average American richer, we should encourage immigration across the board.[10]

He continues:

> Bottom line: Today's immigrant families are projected to deliver as much as $259 billion in net present value as taxpayers, including federal, state, and local taxes combined. That works out to $800 in avoided taxes (or deficits) for every man, woman and child in the United States.[11]

The children of first-generation immigrants contribute even more because of their higher educational attainment and greater earnings.[12] Nativist opposition to immigration is not only anti-American, it is economically stupid.

So the benefits of inclusiveness should be obvious to everyone, but apparently they are not. What reasons, besides simple bigotry and Trump-style fearmongering—which we can just dismiss—might someone have for opposing inclusiveness and community? The only reasonable argument I have heard goes something like this: If we are *too* inclusive, we will invite into our tolerant society individuals who are not tolerant, and who will work to make our society less open and less inclusive. In 2004, the Dutch filmmaker Theo van Gogh was murdered by a Dutch Moroccan citizen—a Muslim who was offended by Van Gogh's film *Submission*, about the status of women in Islamic societies. The Netherlands, as a very liberal, open, and tolerant society, had permitted the immigration of radical Muslims for whom free speech was not an ideal, and in whose view anyone perceived as critical of Islam deserved death.

The paradox of tolerating the intolerant is a genuine dilemma for liberal democracies. How do you address it? Do you expel Muslims and ban Muslim immigration, as rising nationalist, nativist, and racist parties in Europe demand? That, of course, would simply be to abjure one's status as a liberal democracy. This is why there has been so much outrage over Donald Trump's various proposed bans on immigration from certain Muslim countries. However, inevitably some Muslim immigrants (and others, of course) will have illiberal convictions, or become radicalized once in the country.

We must, of course, insist that anyone who comes here respect our traditions of tolerance, openness, pluralism, and free speech. However, the idea, bruited by some Muslim-baiting politicians, that Muslim immigrants want to establish enclaves of *sharia* law is just nonsense. Further, the implication that Muslim immigrants are a uniquely intolerant group is a canard. In general, for instance, as reported in the *Guardian*, American Muslims are more tolerant of gay people than are American evangelical Christians.[13] Therefore, instead of hyperventilating over Muslim immigration, we should be far more concerned that the United States not only tolerates, but elects to high office, fundamentalist Christians with records of antigay activism (Mike, cough, Pence, cough). We need to confront home-grown intolerance far more than we need to worry about importing it.

Another argument I hear is that distinctive American cultural traditions and practices will be attenuated and ultimately abandoned if we are too open to multiculturalism and too welcoming to people who do not know or value our ways. One manifestation of this fear is the annual brouhaha about a "War on Christmas," whooped up by conservative media every holiday season. Supposedly, the enforcers of political correctness, fearful of offending non-Christians, have banned Christmas parties, Christmas carols, and salutations and greetings that mention Christmas. Some people are now outraged if you wish them "Happy Holidays" instead of "Merry Christmas." In *A Charlie Brown Christmas*, Linus says, "Only you, Charlie Brown, could take a wonderful season like Christmas and turn it into a problem." Actually, it is Fox News that turns Christmas into a problem.

But the worry about cultural pollution is bogus. Houston is one of the most ethnically and culturally diverse cities on the planet, but Rodeo Houston is bigger than ever (Yee Ha!). Garth Brooks still plays to sold-out crowds of cowboys and cowgirls. There is no "War on Christmas." Besides, American culture has always been eclectic, and it is fair to say that it is this eclecticism that has given American culture its particular creativity and vibrancy. I once heard an African American commentator say, "If it weren't for black folks, white folks would still be dancing the minuet." Funny—and close to truth. Can you imagine American music without jazz, blues, or soul? How many laughs would we have missed without Jewish comedians? (No Marx Brothers?) What would American food be without French and Italian cuisine? In fact, as I am sure you recall, when we were kids local restaurants were pretty much barbecue, steak houses, and Southern style. Chinese food was unknown, and even pizza and tacos were exotic. Now, within ten minutes of my office I can get Greek, Indian, Mexican, Vietnamese, Thai, Chinese, Japanese ... and barbecue. The culinary advantages alone justify multiculturalism for me!

Maybe the best response to anyone who rejects the ideal of community in diversity is to ask what the alternative would be. Is it what we are doing now? How is that working out for us? Are we enjoying gridlock, polarization, bitterness, hatred, and resentment? Really, the choice that we face is pretty simple. Do we want to be richer, happier, nicer, and smarter, or poorer, more miserable, meaner, and dumber? If we want the good stuff, we must build a community that welcomes everyone and rejects only bigots and haters.

WHAT IS THE VALUE OF COMMUNITY?

PARIS DONEHOO

Since the early 1980s I have led numerous groups of pilgrims to Israel. I hesitate to call them "tour" groups because, for me and many others, the trip feels more like a pilgrimage than a sightseeing excursion. Because I have been traveling there for several decades, I have seen a great deal of change. The tension between Israelis and Palestinians has always been there, but the attempts to keep us away from one side or the other have become more blatant. The fissures between groups of Israelis has widened over the years as well, mirroring the fissures that have developed between Americans. When I first traveled to Israel, our bus could drive into Bethlehem and stop within a hundred yards or so of the Church of the Nativity. On more recent trips, our bus with an Israeli guide and Israeli driver was required to park outside the wall that now separates Israel from Palestinian territory so our group could transfer to a different bus, with a Palestinian guide and Palestinian driver, for a few hours visiting sites in Bethlehem.

The wall is quite imposing, with its locked gates, barbed wired strung across the top, and guard towers with armed Israeli soldiers keeping watch on both sides. On one occasion I was scanning the graffiti covering the structure, and among the hate-fueled sentiments I noticed someone had scrawled, "Pray for the peace of Jerusalem." The irony was not lost on me.

I cannot help remembering that experience every time I hear Donald Trump advocate for a wall along the Mexican-American border, or hear his supporters at rallies chant, "Build the wall! Build the wall!" The historical and cultural circumstances are different, but the results are the same—a lack of a sense of cohesiveness and common purpose that feeds a debilitating factionalism. Abraham Lincoln, the most famous son of my adopted state of Illinois, put it this way: "A house divided against itself, cannot stand."[1]

Lincoln was borrowing imagery from Mark 3:25, where Jesus addressed the charge leveled by the religious elites that he was in league with the devil, and by the devil's power he cast out demons. Implicitly, however, Jesus was referencing a foundational characteristic of the early church—community born in a unified worldview and purpose. The early followers of Jesus defined themselves in terms of community. Indeed, it was crucial to their understanding of themselves. They saw themselves as a colony within the larger culture. "Our citizenship is in heaven, and it is from there that we are expecting a Savior, the Lord Jesus Christ" (Philippians 3:20). Biblically speaking, the church is not an institution, nor a building on the corner of Main Street, but an island of one culture in the middle of another. In baptism, citizenship is transferred from one dominion to another, and Christians become resident aliens in whatever culture they find themselves.[2]

Buffeted as they were by the surrounding culture of the Greco-Roman world, those early followers of Jesus never understood community as merely being neighborly or delivering a plate of cookies to a new family down the street. For them, community was literally a matter of survival. When local authorities threatened their livelihood, or their very lives, they needed each other for subsistence as well as existence. In a broader sense, however, their survival depended upon the nurturing of the upcoming generation. Unlike the institutional church America has known throughout most of its history, they never expected the dominant society to inculcate Christian values in their ranks. Indeed, they expected the dominant culture to be openly hostile to their values. A sense of community, a sense that "we are all in this together," was pivotal for instilling Christian beliefs and practices into their ranks. Without those efforts to live as resident aliens, the church would not have lasted beyond the first century. Perhaps more perilous than persecution was the temptation of some Christians to assimilate into the dominant culture. Those who lost their distinctive community were long ago swept into the ash heap of history.

Drawing on images from the Hebrew scriptures, a late first-century Christian put it this way: "You are a chosen race, a royal priesthood, a holy nation, God's own people, in order that you may proclaim the mighty acts of him who called you out of darkness into his marvelous light. Once you were not a people, but now you are God's people; once you had not received mercy, but now you have received mercy" (1 Peter 2:9–10). Long before sociologists posited the strong pull of group identity, this writer (most scholars doubt it was the Apostle Peter) called upon the followers of Jesus to live as a colony within a culture, as a community holding a different worldview, and practicing a different ethic, from the world in which they temporarily lived.

No wonder the biblical writers enjoined unity among the faithful. One can imagine Psalm 133:1 eliciting a hearty "amen" when it was read aloud in worship: "How very good and pleasant it is when kindred live together in unity!" Purportedly writing from a jail cell, Paul said, "I therefore, the prisoner in the Lord, beg you to lead a life worthy of the calling to which you have been called . . . making every effort to maintain the unity of the Spirit in the bond of peace" (Ephesians 4:1, 3). And he reminded the Christians in Rome, "For as in one body we have many members, and not all the members have the same function, so we, who are many, are one body in Christ, and individually we are members one of another" (Romans 12:4–5).

As a student of church history, I know this unity was difficult to maintain, and was often illusory (check out Paul's Corinthian correspondence), but it was always the goal of the fledgling Christian movement. So what does this stroll down the first few centuries of church life have to do with a secular culture like America? Are there lessons here for a society founded on Enlightenment principles containing a bewildering array of belief systems alongside Christianity? I think so. First, there is a warning here against seeking unity through enforcing uniformity of belief. There are some scholars, of course, who claim that biblical and early church calls for unity were based on nothing more than a desire for consolidation. To be sure, the early Christian movement was awash in various theological perspectives, and disagreements sometimes threatened to scuttle assorted colonies of Jesus followers. However, I think the drive for unity enforced by uniformity began in earnest only when Christians on the whole began to assimilate into the dominant culture, and it reached the tipping point when Constantine—shrewd politician that he was—saw a chance to unify his empire under the banner of this burgeoning new religion. Without unity among Christians he could not use them as agents of control within the populace. When the first Council of Nicaea was called in the year 325, the die was cast.

Jesus threw open the door to a multiplicity of belief structures among his followers when he said, "Whoever is not against us is for us" (Mark 9:40). But President George W. Bush said just the opposite when he addressed the nation and the world in the aftermath of the 9/11 attacks and declared, "Either you are with us, or you are with the terrorists." Thus, America's "War on Terrorism" is the *textus receptus* by which all political and social opinions are to be weighed. Opinions swerving from the dominant orthodoxy are easily condemned as un-American, unpatriotic, uncouth, untrue, and a threat to motherhood and apple pie.

You and I cut our teeth on the "red scare" of the 1950s and 1960s, so we have seen this sort of thing before, but in Trump's America divergent beliefs are becoming just as heretical as Arianism was to the Nicene Creed. Any media outlet that disagrees with Trump's "alternative facts," or dares to question his policies is labeled "fake news" and "the enemy of the American people" (never mind that "enemy of the people" was a popular label for any person or group who disagreed with Hitler, Mao Zedong, or most Soviet leaders). When Montana senator Jon Tester questioned Trump's nominee to head the Veteran's Administration, Trump not only called the allegations a "disgrace," but went on to say, "I know things about Tester that I could say too. And if I said 'em, he'd never be elected again."[3] Needless to say, the President did not specify what he meant, and never elaborated further, but the message was clear: Keep your mouth shut and toe the line or I will ruin you. When Judge Gonzalo Curiel was set to rule on the infamous Trump University lawsuit, Trump told the *Wall Street Journal* that Curiel had "an absolute conflict" in presiding over the litigation given that he is "of Mexican heritage" and a member of a Latino lawyers' association.[4] Translation: He can't be trusted because he might disagree with me. And, to the consternation of his lawyers, Trump continues to use Twitter to attack a diverse group of people, places, and organizations, such as Democrats, fellow Republicans, television personalities, former FBI director James Comey, and television executives.[5]

Politics is always a rough-and-tumble game, and Trump's antics, and the antics of his subordinates, would be just par for the course if Trump had not broken with two centuries of American tradition when, at the Republican Convention, he did not ask Americans to place their trust in each other or in God to help him solve the country's problems, but to trust only in him. "I am your voice," he said. "I alone can fix it."[6] Everyone must be unified behind Saint Donald, and any dissenting voices are anathema.

The second warning I think America can learn from the early church is the danger of enforcing unity by fear. Here again there are voices who would claim that this is exactly what the church has done down through the centuries. In my Southern Baptist days I was no stranger to biblical references about hell, as well as revival preachers who stoked its flames so hot I could almost smell sulfur. I contend, however, that conversion via fear was, like uniformity of belief, a later development within Christianity. I am not claiming that early Christians did not believe in hell. I am claiming they did not use fear as a motivation for their work. Despite the portrayal of mass conversions due to evangelistic preaching in the book of Acts, modern social science relegates doctrinal appeals (like "Come to Jesus or burn in hell"), at best, to only a secondary role in a person's embrace of a new faith. A person becomes attached to the doctrines of his or her faith *after* conversion.[7]

For example, when various epidemics swept through huge swaths of the Greco-Roman world, most people were so fearful of getting sick they often abandoned those who were already ill, and, if they had the means, would flee to healthier regions. Christians, however, stayed to care for their own as well as persons outside their community of faith. Any medical expert, as well as any mother caring for a sick child, knows that *some* care is better than *no* care. Thus, Christians and others they cared for tended to have higher survival rates than the general population, resulting in more new adherents to the fledgling faith.[8]

Diana Butler Bass says most of us who grew up in the church assumed a certain model for Christian discipleship: *believe, behave, belong*—i.e., one *believes* the doctrines of the church (like hell awaiting nonbelievers), one learns to *behave* like a Christian, and then one can *belong* to the community of believers. By contrast, claims Butler Bass, the pre-Constantinian church followed a different model: *belong, behave, believe*—one is invited by a loving community to *belong* to the group, and in the process of living, studying, and practicing faith, one takes on their characteristics and *behaves* as they do. After a time, those behaviors become a way of thinking and one comes to *believe* the theology and doctrines of the church.[9] It is in this context one should hear these words of Jesus: "For I was hungry and you gave me food, I was

271

thirsty and you gave me something to drink, I was a stranger and you welcomed me, I was naked and you gave me clothing, I was sick and you took care of me, I was in prison and you visited me. . . . Truly I tell you, just as you did it to one of the least of these who are members of my family, you did it to me" (Matthew 25:35–36, 40).

When the church moved away from this relational approach to community and replaced it with an appeal to fear in order to keep the people in line, it sowed the seeds of the Crusades, the Inquisition, the Salem Witch Trials, and a host of other iniquities, not to mention the contempt in which it is held in much of western culture today. It pains me, therefore, to see American society now motivated by, and practicing the use of, fear in an attempt to unify the nation. Trump is famous for identifying Mexican immigrants as "murderers and rapists" when he launched his campaign for president, and he continues to employ the same tactic from the Oval Office. Commenting on the so-called caravan of migrants heading for the US border, Trump recalled his initial comment and claimed, "They're not putting their good ones . . . And remember my opening remarks at Trump Tower when I opened. Everybody said, 'Oh, he was so tough.' And I used the word 'rape.' And yesterday it came out where, this journey coming up, women are raped at levels that nobody has ever seen before. They don't want to mention that."[10] As usual, he cited no evidence for such an allegation, when, in fact, the opposite was true. It was not the migrants who were committing rapes. Many of the migrants were fleeing horrific treatment—including rape—by the authorities in their home countries, as well as suffering abuse—including rape—from smugglers, drug cartel members, and Mexican immigration agents along their route. But Trump is not constrained by mundane details like facts. As long as he can keep the American populace glancing over its shoulder in case a lusty immigrant is lurking in the shadows, he can introduce whatever ignoble policy he wants.

This fear generates attitudes and behaviors few Americans would have sanctioned not long ago. How can we sit by and allow Attorney General Jeff Sessions, in cahoots with the usual White House cabal, to separate children from their parents at the US border? It's easy when people are afraid. If the hordes purportedly streaming across the border have malevolent intent, and intend to steal jobs from good, hard-working, patriotic Americans, then such methods, while regrettable, are necessary. They also work in the other direction. Addressing the poor, tired, and hungry masses yearning to breathe free just over the line in Mexico, Attorney General Jeff Sessions snarled, "If you are smuggling a child, then we will prosecute you, and that child will be separated from you as required by law. . . . If you don't like that, then don't smuggle children over our border."[11] The message is clear: If a seven-year-old being kept away from her mother for several months is what is required as a deterrent, so be it. Ironically, the evangelicals who voted for Trump in huge numbers like to tout their belief in "family values." Those values evidently do not extend across our southern border.

Whatever else Trump may be, he is no innovator. He did not create the fear skulking through America's current psyche. He merely exploits it. The conventional wisdom after the 2016 presidential election was that Trump voters were motivated by economic anxiety—anger over opportunities lost and exclusion from economic recovery. But a study by the National Academy of Sciences suggests Trump voters are not driven by anger over the past as much they are driven by fear of what may come in the future. White, Christian, and male voters, the study suggests, turned to Trump because they felt their status in American society was at risk.[12] Tapping into this fear of what *might be*, Trump can better control the narrative of the present through reinventing the past. As George Orwell said in his classic novel *1984*, "Who controls the past controls the future. Who controls the present controls the past."[13]

Do you remember the TV show *The Outer Limits*? One of my favorite episodes was called "The Architects of Fear." A group of idealistic scientists hatches a plot to unite all the nations of earth by staging an invasion of aliens from a far-off planet. A worldwide panic, they theorize, will unite the world. The plan goes awry, of course, and the world is no more united than when they started.[14] Watching the episode after all these years I am amused by the cheap special effects, but the message is timeless: Fear is no way to unite a nation, or a world.

What can unite us is a commitment to the common good. As long as we continue to focus on the singular pronouns instead of the plural pronouns, the common good will elude us. In my experience as a pastor, people unite best in service to others. Congregations can be cantankerous groups when discussing cataclysmic issues like furniture in the vestibule or TV screens in the sanctuary, but they usually become harmonious when involved in a project that pushes them beyond their own immediate preferences and needs. Over and over I have seen people bond over a mission project or a service project that did not benefit them in any way, and then they would comment to me, "I get more out of this than the people I'm helping."

Christians have often been accused of advocating "pie in the sky by and by" theology, and, to some extent, they are guilty as charged. But the biblical mandate is not to ignore this world, but to cooperate with God to remake it as God intends it. Christians everywhere pray to God each Sunday, "Thy kingdom come, Thy will be done *on earth*, as it is in heaven" (Matthew 6:10, KJV). The church's distinctiveness, as defined above, should not be a rationale for privilege, or a cause for division, but a call to work for the common good. The only difference between a Christian's work for the benefit of others and the efforts of individuals, groups, agencies, and governments, is its basic motivation. We do it because Jesus told us to do it. To be sure, we want to make our communities, nations, and our world better places for everyone, but that is not our primary purpose. We serve others because the God we know in Christ cares about everyone, not just the rich and powerful.

Remarkably, archaeology seems to confirm this. While I never maintain that historical or scientific evidence "proves" any aspect of biblical faith, the archaeological record is interesting. When archaeologists dig into remnants of the past located beneath the ground in some places in Israel, they often find evidence of relatively egalitarian societies. Some people were better off than others, of course, but there does not seem to have been huge disparities in living conditions. In other places, however, the archaeological record is much different. The ruins of huge palatial houses are surrounded by small shacks and hovels, suggesting vast inequalities among the populace. What makes this information germane to a discussion of the common good is the dating of these sites. The sites where relative equity seems to have been the case can be dated to eras in Israel's history in which there is no record of any prophet thundering, "Thus says the Lord," followed by a call to repentance. But the sites where inequality seems to have been the case can be dated to the heyday of these prophets.[15] In the eighth century BCE, for example, the prophet Isaiah declared, "Your princes are rebels and companions of thieves. Everyone loves a bribe and runs after gifts. They do not defend the orphan, and the widow's cause does not come before them" (Isaiah 1:23).

From my theological standpoint, therefore, I contend that the value of a commitment to the common good goes beyond merely forming a more perfect union, establishing justice, insuring domestic tranquility, and securing the blessings of liberty for ourselves and our posterity. It is what God wants from us, and it does not matter if others who work for the common good believe in God or not. The end result is the same.

HOW DO WE ACHIEVE COMMUNITY IN A FRACTURED SOCIETY?

KEITH PARSONS

Your impressive erudition about church history reminds me of what a fascinating topic it is. A couple of years ago I read Paul Johnson's *A History of Christianity*, which had been sitting on my shelves unread for forty years.[1] Johnson, a Catholic, tells the story "warts and all" (and it was mostly "warts" in some places), not shying away from the ugliest and most disgraceful episodes. Johnson starts with the first real challenge to Christian unity, the confrontation between Paul and Peter that took place circa 49 CE in Jerusalem, over the issue of whether converts to Christianity had to be circumcised and obey the Mosaic laws. As Johnson shows, schism threatened Christianity repeatedly, and was a reality on a number of infamous occasions. Keeping any complex institution or society together is a real challenge, and centrifugal forces always threaten.

You draw exactly the right conclusion. Unity cannot be maintained by enforcing uniformity of belief, and neither can it be maintained by fomenting fear of outsiders. As John Locke observed in *A Letter Concerning Toleration*, when you try to enforce belief, you only succeed, at most, in producing hypocrites. Even threat of dungeon, fire, and sword can only make people conform outwardly; you do not touch the heart with threats of force.

It is just as futile to try to frighten people into unity with hateful rhetoric about the "others." This leads to paranoia and cruelty and does nothing to promote unity, as shown by the "red scare" of the fifties and Trump's "rapists and murderers" calumny today. As you say, what unites is working together for a common good, and we have seen that in this country, as when we were united to defeat Hitler and Tojo. In our lifetimes, the space program and the moon landings also promoted unity in otherwise divided times. I will suggest below some of the big projects that can now unite us.

First things first, however. The first thing we have to do is to start talking to each other again—and not through clenched teeth. American society is divided along many fault lines, such as race, ethnicity, religion, sexual preference, and class. However, the divide that really impairs our ability to communicate is doctrinal. What is the nature of this divide? The terms "liberal" and "conservative" are not very satisfactory, being vague, one-dimensional, and distorted by years of polemical rancor and hyperbole. Yet these labels are probably are the best we can do to characterize in the broadest terms the doctrinal divides that are now abyssal, with the parties on either side glaring contemptuously at each other.

Every society has its liberals and conservatives, and always will, since liberalism and conservatism are both grounded in human nature. What makes things different now in our country is the toxic level of animosity and disdain. Today's hyperpartisanship is based on the idea that any compromise with an opponent is compromise with an evil idiot. You don't compromise with evil idiots; you beat them down and keep them down by any means necessary.

Further, politics became much more vicious in the Karl Rove era of the early 2000s. In Rove's playbook, no trick was too dirty, no smear was too base, no falsehood was too egregious, and no back could not be stabbed. Is your opponent a decorated Vietnam veteran? Swift-boat him.[2] Is he running against you in the South Carolina primary? Call voters and imply that he has fathered an illegitimate African American child, as was done to John McCain in the South Carolina primary in 2000.[3] Karl Rove no longer occupies an office in the White House, but his no-holds-barred, down-and-dirty style lives on, and Donald Trump is its most accomplished practitioner.

The situation is dangerous. Things have to change, and both liberals and conservatives have to take responsibility for the necessary changes. The needle has to swing back from mutual hatred to respectful disagreement. Respect has to be based on understanding, knowing why people are liberal or conservative. (Hint: It is not because they are evil idiots.) Our guide here will be Jonathan Haidt's *The Righteous Mind: Why Good People are Divided by Politics and Religion.*[4]

We also need to realize that solutions to our biggest problems are available—if we are willing to approach these problems scientifically and pragmatically and not by grinding axes. This is argued cogently and in great detail in Steven Pinker's *Enlightenment Now: The Case for Reason, Science, Humanism, and Progress.* Pinker provides overwhelming evidence that human problems can be addressed, that progress is possible, and that the means for making progress—what has demonstrably *worked*—are solutions based on science and objective knowledge, not ideological agendas.[5]

One of the reasons that exchanges between liberals and conservatives are often so rancorous is that each seems simply obtuse to the other—that is, impervious to reason and the force of facts. You marshal your facts, get your arguments straight, and make sure that you present your case clearly and ... you have no impact at all. Reasoning that seems compelling to you makes no impression at all on them. Indeed, they appear to inhabit a realm of "alternative facts" or "fake news" that is detached from reality and dedicated to the denial of the obvious. Now there is no question that Trump's systematic lying and propensity to make major policy decisions on impulse does not create an atmosphere conducive to the nurturing of sweet reasonableness.

Further, as I have said before, persons and doctrines now labeled "conservative" would have appeared extreme or even preposterous to conservatives of a generation ago. I devoutly wish that American conservatism would undergo a "Back to Burke" or at least a "Back to Buckley" movement. If they want the rest of us to hear them, and not dismiss them as wing nuts, then they need to get rid of the wing nuts: Get rid of the conspiracy theorists, the climate-change deniers, the evolution deniers, the theocrats, the Islamophobes, homophobes, and xenophobes. Tell the neo-Nazis and alt-right racists in no uncertain terms that there is *no* place in conservatism for them. Do a thorough housecleaning, as William F. Buckley did in the sixties when he denounced the John Birch Society as extremists who undermined the conservative cause. Dust off your old copy of Edmund Burke's *Reflections on the Revolution in France* (1790) and rediscover the theoretical foundations of conservatism.

However, according to Jonathan Haidt, the fundamental differences between liberals and conservatives are not doctrinal but emotive. There may be more or less extreme forms of left-wing or right-wing ideology, but ideological differences are superficial manifestations of deeper disparities of personality, perception, and outlook. In simplest terms, our deep-seated differences in politics are matters of feeling, not reason. When presented with the same stimulus, liberals and conservatives have different spontaneous reactions. Put differently, different things elicit our reactions of pity, anger, disgust, or other such strong emotions, and it is these disparate emotional reactions, says Haidt, that underlie our political convictions.

From Haidt's perspective, we philosophers have got it all badly wrong; in fact, as wrong as can be. Philosophers propose ethical theories that purport to provide intellectual grounds for a rational set of ethical standards. Ideally, moral judgment will consist of the impartial assignment of rightness or wrongness in the light of those validated criteria. For instance, John Stuart Mill defended the Principle of Utility, which holds that actions are right or wrong in proportion to their tendency to augment or diminish human happiness. Moral judgment for a utilitarian will therefore consist of determining which course of action—or, alternatively, which set of rules—will tend to maximize happiness, or at least minimize unhappiness.

Haidt is an expert in moral psychology; that is, he studies the emotional and intellectual processes involved when people make moral judgments. Unsurprisingly, he finds that the actual way people make moral judgments is not at all like the ideally rational method recommended by philosophers. We make spontaneous judgments based upon emotion, and reason comes in not as a philosopher—preaching the ideals of objectivity—but as a lawyer advocating for the judgments made by emotions. David Hume infamously said that reason is and ought to be the "slave" of the emotions. Haidt thinks that "slave" is too strong; reason is our inner lawyer that vigorously advocates for its emotional client but also can advise the sometimes impulsive and wayward client. The philosophers' dreams of impartial reason are seemingly irrelevant. Reason is an advocate, not an umpire.

Haidt identifies six "moral foundations," innate cognitive modules or faculties designed (by evolution) to recognize and respond to certain patterns or types of social behavior.[6] When such a module detects a particular type of event, say a display of cruelty or disrespect, it automatically triggers a strong intuitive response, such as sympathy or anger, and such responses are the emotive bases of our moral judgments. Each module is therefore sensitive to its own particular object; it is a "moral taste receptor" says Haidt. The six types of moral foundations he identifies are care/harm, fairness/cheating, loyalty/betrayal, authority/subversion, sanctity/degradation, and liberty/oppression. For instance, when we have droughts in Texas (which is pretty often), water restrictions are imposed. If someone cheats and uses water when they are not supposed to, this will activate the fairness/cheating module of neighbors, who report the cheat to the authorities. The activation of our moral foundation modules therefore generates the strong emotions that prompt our moral judgments, and if we are asked to justify those judgments that is where reason comes in as our advocate, articulating and defending reasons for the intuitive judgment.

The problem is that a particular kind of event might trigger different reactions in different persons:

> Should parents and teachers be allowed to spank children for disobedience? On the left side of the political spectrum, spanking typically triggers judgments of cruelty and oppression. On the right, it is sometimes linked to judgments about proper enforcement of rules, particularly rules about respect for parents and teachers. So, even if we all share the same small set of cognitive modules, we can hook actions up to modules in so many ways that we can build conflicting moral matrices on the same small set of foundations.[7]

In fact, when plotted on a spectrum from "very liberal" to "very conservative," test subjects exhibited an overall decreasing responsiveness of the care/harm and fairness/cheating modules and an increasing responsiveness with respect to the loyalty/betrayal, authority/subversion, and sanctity/degradation modules.[8]

The differential responsiveness of moral modules would explain why, to take a notable recent case, liberals and conservatives reacted so differently to NFL players who took a knee during the pregame playing of the national anthem during the 2017 season to protest police shootings of unarmed African Americans. Conservatives were often outraged, while liberals regarded the protest as a legitimate expression of first-amendment rights. If Haidt is right, then such a sign of apparent disrespect toward the national anthem or the flag would provoke among conservatives a strong reaction by the loyalty/betrayal foundation—and perhaps the authority/subversion and sanctity/degradation modules as well. Conservatives reacted angrily when, as they saw it, pampered and privileged athletes—who had been given wealth, fame, and status—were insulting the very nation that had given them so much. To conservatives, the kneeling athletes seemed to be guilty of a squalid act of betrayal. Liberals, on the other hand, were not similarly affected. Instead, their sensitivities to harm and fairness had been strongly stimulated by the perception of police bias against African Americans, while their sense of betrayal had not been activated. To liberals, the protest seemed appropriate and justified.

If Haidt is correct, then perhaps the disparities in moral judgments between liberals and conservatives are not due to disagreements between good and smart people on one side and evil idiots on the other. All humans have the same basic moral foundations. We all respond to perceptions of cruelty, unfairness, disloyalty, etc., but our responses will be stronger or weaker from person to person, with many individual variations. If, like other traits, the distribution of the responsiveness of moral modules can be plotted on a bell curve, then some individuals will fall on one end of the curve and others on the opposite end. For instance, some people will respond to perceptions of unfairness very strongly and perceptions of disloyalty only weakly. Others will be the opposite. It will be unsurprising if people with differential degrees of responsiveness of their moral modules were prone to spontaneous and intuitive moral judgments that are very different.

An understanding of moral psychology, and how spontaneous and intuitive moral judgments underlie our political convictions, can provide a basis for mutual understanding—not agreement, but the recognition that those on the other side are not being simply perverse or pigheaded. Such an understanding will be hard for us to accept, since our spontaneous and intuitive moral feelings come with such a powerful sense of obviousness and urgency. Can't those dumbass liberals just *see* how insulting it is to take a knee during the national anthem? Duh. Can't those clueless conservatives just *see* why African Americans are so outraged by police shootings? Duh.

Maybe, though, the next time we feel our emotions running high against those other guys, we can take a deep breath and realize that our disagreements may not be due to their stupidity, ignorance, or moral failure. Perhaps we can forego the pleasure of self-righteous disdain long enough to realize that differences in judgment, even fundamental differences, may be made in good faith by good and intelligent people. This recognition should not lead us into a namby-pamby relativism or soppy sentimentalism. Liberals and conservatives will not join hands in a circle and sing "Kumbaya." Maybe, though, we can do what we recommended earlier, namely, disagree candidly but not contemptuously.

Perhaps also, guided by Haidt's insights, we can change the nature of our discourse of disagreement. Instead of aiming to put down, shut up, humiliate, and rebuke (which is what you do to an evil idiot), you might try to appeal to the moral foundations of your interlocutor. Instead of yelling at Uncle Fred when he starts to go on about "Mexicans" at the dinner table, maybe a gentle Socratic questioning would be better. Maybe see if he really knows what the conditions are like in El Salvador and Honduras (which is where many of the "Mexican" immigrants are from). Ask whether, if he found himself and his own family in a failed state with an astronomical murder rate where gangsters rule and the authorities are ineffective or complicit, he might not take the same risks and make the same decisions as the "illegals." It has to work better than calling him an idiot.

Still, as a philosopher, I have to draw a line in the sand and demand whether there is not a higher, more noble, more rational and objective role for reason in moral debates than merely to ratify or rationalize what emotion has already decided. Yes, there is. Is the philosopher's dream of reason a pipe dream? No, it isn't. Yes, we do come with an inner lawyer, one that very effectively advocates on our behalf. However, I think that if we work at it, and it does take work, we can cultivate another inner character—our inner scientist.

Developing our inner scientist is not a matter of resolving to be objective. As Haidt and many others have shown, none of us is objective. Each of us is an inveterate self-justifier, ideologue, and spin-meister. We are all suckers for confirmation bias. What we must do is recognize these facts and connect ourselves insofar as possible to what we might call "communities of objectivity," communities of scientists and scholars that base their collective judgments on methods of rigorous vetting, not personal reaction. How did Haidt come to know so much about moral psychology? He did not commission his inner lawyer to justify his intuitions about moral psychology. If we ask our inner lawyer to do science, the inner lawyer becomes our inner idiot. Haidt performed experiments and submitted his results to a skeptical scientific community that scrutinized them and tried to refute them. That is how science overcomes ideology and bias—not by sermonizing about the virtues of objectivity—but by subjecting all claims to the most rigorous tests devisable and tentatively accepting only those that survive. The objectivity of science is in its methods, not in the minds of individual scientists.

Further, as Steven Pinker argues passionately and at length in *Enlightenment Now*, science and reason demonstrably *work*. The judicious employment of human intelligence in the application of scientific methods, technology, scientific agriculture, medicine, sanitation, and rational economic policies, has produced quantifiable and robustly verifiable improvements in longevity, health, prosperity, safety, peace, and happiness. Consider, for instance, life expectancy:

A British baby who had survived the hazardous first year of life would have lived to 47 in 1845, 57 in 1905, 72 in 1955, and 81 in 2011. A 30-year-old could look forward to another thirty-three years of life in 1845, another thirty-six in 1905, another forty-three in 1955, and another fifty-two in 2011.[9]

And such gains have not just been seen in economically advanced nations like Britain, but in some of those countries disesteemed by Donald Trump: "A 10-year-old Ethiopian in 1950 could expect to live to 44; a 10-year-old Ethiopian today can expect to live to 61."[10]

Such quantifiable improvements in human well-being are non-partisan goods. Like the moon landing, though of even greater significance, these are achievements that all of us can celebrate. Such achievements permit us to take a problem-solving approach that is pragmatic, not doctrinaire. We cannot turn off our spontaneous emotional reactions, and should not try, but we can, with practice, learn to approach even hot-button issues by asking "What works?" The answer might be a rebuke to our doctrinal preferences *qua* liberal or *qua* conservative. For instance, liberals might have to admit that two-parent families really are better for children.[11] Conservatives might have to admit that the two parents might be two mommies or two daddies.[12]

One serious complicating factor is that, as we have seen, in our age of polarization even science has been politicized. Denial of human-caused climate change became a dogma of conservative orthodoxy. The academic left has had its own politically motivated anti-science vendettas—for instance, against sociobiology and evolutionary psychology. Further, our inner lawyer knows how to cherry-pick, skew, and frame scientific research to fit its own ax-grinding agenda. So, again we have a choice: We can go with tribalism, dogmatism, magical thinking, and demonization of the "other," or we can go with pragmatism, science, reason, and progress. Maybe, just maybe, enough people will choose the latter to get us out of our current mess.

HOW DO WE ACHIEVE COMMUNITY IN A FRACTURED SOCIETY?

PARIS DONEHOO

Bells and whistles went off in my head when you described "communities of objectivity." Though I do not move regularly in academic and scientific circles as you do, I am aware of the demanding standards to which conclusions are held among scholars. A consensus among learned women and men within a certain field can, usually, weed out weak assumptions and downright boneheaded ideas. Unfortunately, differing opinions and reasonable arguments are often the first casualties in the echo chamber of our current media landscape.

I will not argue that the church is, or should be, a "community of objectivity," but I have seen it become a "community of discernment" many times. By that I mean the church can become a community for vetting ideas and practices by looking at them through, first and foremost, the lens of Jesus's life and teachings, and secondarily the Bible and the spiritual sense of fellow disciples. Over forty years of ministry I saw occasions when the church took risks, made courageous decisions, and embarked on creative pathways after subjecting ideas to this discernment process. Too often, however, churches come to conclusions and take actions based on fear, or negative reactivity, or political expediency, or recourse to what author and founder of TOUCH Outreach Ministries Ralph Neighbour called "The Seven Last Words of the Church"—*We never tried it that way before*.[1]

On its better days, this community of discernment is an agent of change for the better. Of course, becoming a community of discernment implies a set of spiritual assumptions that would not apply to you, nor should they be imposed on anyone else. Such enforcement would be self-defeating. However, the confrontation between Peter and Paul you mentioned earlier points to a few lessons for creating the common good that can be instructive for all of us. As you said, one of the early tensions within the nascent Christian movement was the question of how Jewish it should be. Because the first Christians were Jews, they naturally saw their new faith as an extension of, or fulfillment of, their Jewish faith. Indeed, they proclaimed Jesus to be the promised Jewish Messiah. Relatively early on, however, non-Jewish persons began to be attracted to the church. Should these gentile believers convert to Judaism before they could be baptized as Christians? Many answered in the affirmative. "It is necessary for [gentiles] to be circumcised and ordered to keep the law of Moses," they said (Acts 15:5). Paul and his apostolic circle vehemently disagreed, saying, "Why are you putting God to the test by placing on the neck of the disciples a yoke that neither our ancestors nor we have been able to bear? On the contrary, we believe that we will be saved through the grace of the Lord Jesus, just as they will" (Acts 15:10–11).

A council to discuss the matter was called in Jerusalem. I argue that a careful reading of the text demonstrates the church acting as a community of discernment, but for my purpose here, the outcome is more important than the process. In the end, the leader of the Jerusalem church, James, the brother of Jesus (notice it was not Peter), declared, "We should not trouble those Gentiles who are turning to God, but we should write to them to abstain only from things polluted by idols and from fornication and from whatever has been strangled and from blood. For in every city, for generations past, Moses has had those who proclaim him, for he has been read aloud every sabbath in the synagogues" (Acts 15:19–21). Consequently, a letter was drafted to be sent to their fellow believers, which read, in part, "It has seemed good to the Holy Spirit and to us to impose on you no further burden than these essentials: that you abstain from what has been sacrificed to idols and from blood and from what is strangled and from fornication. If you keep yourselves from these, you will do well" (Acts 15:28–29).

Two points are relevant here. First, these followers of Jesus were savvy enough to realize there were some issues that mattered and many others that did not. What mattered was the love of God they had experienced in the life and teachings of Jesus freely offered to anyone. To place a prerequisite on such love would reduce it to rules and regulations. If one must jump through a hoop (like circumcision) to receive God's grace, then what is offered is no longer grace. Other concerns might be important, and they could have adverse effects on the community of faith, but they need not become lines in the sand. In other words, they decided what was essential and what was nonessential and built their communal lives on the former, not the latter.

I am tempted to launch into a tirade regarding the molehills many of my Christian brothers and sisters have made into mountains, contradicting the very heart of Acts 15, but the list would be too long. For my purpose here, I want to suggest a similar approach that could restore a sense of community to our fractured nation. First, we could stop acting like three-year-olds long enough to identify society's essentials. What beliefs and practices are so basic to our collective identity that we would cease being Americans without them? Freedom? Yes, but what, if any, are the limits of freedom? Inclusiveness? Fine, but where does inclusivity bleed into assimilation like the Borg Collective in *Star Trek: The Next Generation*? Government by consent of the governed? Okay, so what should we do about the outsized influences of the Koch brothers, the NRA, and other bazillionaires who can buy and sell candidates without recourse to the majority yet with the backing of the Supreme Court?

These are not easy questions to answer, and they cannot be answered if we persist in elevating the petty to the level of the profound, and ignoring the best in favor of what is good. Life is rarely a choice between good and bad. Most often it is a choice between what is good and what is best. Our current American society, however, acts as if every detail of our lives is a hill on which one must be willing to die. And when everything is crucial, selfishness becomes virtue. News outlets (Trump would call them "fake news" outlets) were shocked to learn of the comments of White House aide Kelly Sadler, who dismissed the opinions of Senator John McCain because "he's dying anyway." However, when queried about the comments made in a closed door meeting, Press Secretary Sarah Huckabee Sanders was more concerned about the story being leaked to the press than the crass, insensitive, boorish remark.[2] Evidently, saving face is a value more crucial than compassion. Until all of us openly discuss (not argue) the essentials of community, and insist that our elected leaders do the same, such triviality will continue to short-circuit any real community.

The second lesson I glean from the Acts 15 story is a recognition that community requires meaningful give-and-take instead of a winner-take-all strategy. Those church leaders gathered in Jerusalem continued to observe Mosaic law, but they did not believe it was appropriate to require non-Jews to do the same in order to be Christian. However, they also knew gentile Christians would be practicing their faith in locales with large Jewish populations who would react negatively to an in-your-face, belligerent Christianity. Merely living the ethic of Jesus already caused friction with Greco-Roman culture. Why add another layer of conflict? Consequently, they instructed their gentile sisters and brothers to abstain from practices to which Jews would be particularly sensitive—namely, ritual uncleanness through contact with blood, sexual immorality (which was offensive to Christians anyway), and eating food offered to idols in pagan temples.

This last practice seems rather esoteric to us in the modern world, but it was a thorny problem in the early church. When pagan worshippers offered food (meat was a particular delicacy) in a pagan temple it was often taken to the local marketplace and sold, or sometimes prepared on site and consumed, at a price, by passersby. Some Christians thought it sacrilegious to eat this food because it had been first given to a pagan god. Others said there was no issue because pagan gods were not gods at all. The apostle Paul agreed with the latter group. "We are no worse off if we do not eat, and no better off if we do," he reasoned (1 Corinthians 8:8). But Paul did not leave the matter there. No, Paul was a proponent of the common good, even to the point of inconvenience and personal sacrifice. He knew there could be no common good if people do not show deference to one another in matters that are nonessential. "Take care," he says, "that this liberty of yours does not somehow become a stumbling block to the weak" (1 Corinthians 8:9). "It is good not to eat meat or drink wine or do anything that makes your brother or sister stumble" (Romans 14:21). "Therefore, if food is a cause of their falling, I will never eat meat, so that I may not cause one of them to fall" (1 Corinthians 8:13).

If community is to be restored, Americans—at all social levels—must work to meet the other person where she or he may be. I am not suggesting we acquiesce to bigotry and hatred, but we must realize that we are connected even to those with whom we disagree, and maybe even find reprehensible, and reach out to them as fellow human beings. For example, African American blues musician Daryl Davis has successfully persuaded over two hundred Ku Klux Klansmen to leave their racism and hatred behind. How does he do it? After carefully studying the KKK, he now intentionally befriends Klansmen. Once they get to know him, they realize their hatred is misplaced. When a Klansman gives up his robe, Davis keeps it in his home as a reminder of what can happen when you sit down to dinner with people who hate you.

Because he takes them seriously, the Klansmen take him seriously.[3] Such compassion is a far cry from the practices of pharmaceutical company Mylan, who hiked their prices on the two-pack EpiPen from $90 to $600 simply because they could.[4] As the grandfather of a child who depends on the EpiPen to prevent her from going into potentially fatal anaphylaxis, I find this inexcusable. Did the corporate executives sit down and talk with parents, whose overarching worry is the health and safety of their children? Did they even think about meeting children whom their decision would affect, and remember their faces when they considered their options? Or did they gather in their oak-paneled conference room and contemplate only their financial bottom line and the feathering of their own nests? I think the answer is obvious.

Creating community, sustaining it, and living in it are not easy tasks. There must be ongoing conversations about what is essential and nonessential, as well as how to engage one another in our choices. Many years ago I learned a paradigm for this from Old Testament professor Ralph Klein.[5] Reflecting on the story of Tamar in Genesis 38 (check it out—it's one of the Bible's racier stories), Klein defined the word "righteousness" as "fidelity to a relationship." Most people think of righteous living (to the extent they think about it at all) as living by a set of rules such as the Ten Commandments, but Klein says the biblical concept of righteous living is faithfulness to the terms of a relationship with another human being.

If we conceive of life like a fence, Klein says, we can think of the Ten Commandments as posts in that fence (see figure 1). If I deliberately abuse my mother, I know without doubt that I have climbed over the fence and moved into behavior patterns that are counterproductive for me and for others. It is an easy call. Parental abuse is in direct violation of the fifth commandment to "Honor your father and your mother" (Exodus 20:12). Likewise, if I waltz into a restaurant and gun down a man eating supper with his wife and family, I know without a doubt I have climbed over the fence in violation of the sixth command-ment, "You shall not murder" (Exodus 20:13). Again, it is an easy call. There is no ambiguity here.

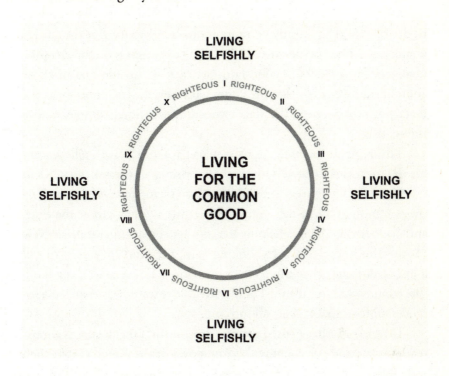

But what if I am caring for my mother as best I can while her health deteriorates and she needs skilled medical attention? What if my job is in jeopardy because I need to take so much time away from work to tend to my mother's needs? Now the situation is not so clear-cut. How do I honor my parent in this scenario? What if I own a business and one of my employees suffers from severe depression and is doing subpar work to the detriment of the rest of my staff, but I am afraid he will harm himself or someone else if I terminate him? Would I be guilty of murder even if I did not pull the trigger?

Klein says those are the moments when we act righteously—i.e., we do our best to be faithful to the relationship. What is the most loving action that has the most opportunity for the common good? There is no one-size-fits-all answer. The answer could vary from person to person, family to family, community to community. But the answer would never be a cookie-cutter rule devoid of compassion for everyone involved. It would be a good-faith attempt to handle one of those complicated scenarios that life throws at us every day. In between the fence posts, in between the places where the solution is simple, we live righteously.

Tim King, communications manager for Jim Wallis, tells a story his grandmother related to him that, I think, illustrates what Klein says about living righteously, and what I am trying to say about seeking the common good. King's grandmother was a young girl at the time, and one evening she was helping her mother cook dinner in their New Hampshire home. A scruffy-looking man, the kind they used to call a hobo, showed up at the back door of their house asking for food. The country was in the midst of the Great Depression, and such occurrences, unfortunately, were all too common.

The girl's mother invited the man to come in. The meal was almost ready, so she and her daughter sat him down at the kitchen table, then went into the pantry to get more food, a plate, and some utensils. When they came back into the kitchen the hobo was gone, along with their supper. He had absconded with the food on the stove and anything else he could carry. "We've been robbed!" the daughter shouted. "We need to get the police!" But her mother didn't respond. She quietly turned to the stove to assess how much food she had, then began to prepare a meal as best she could with what was left. The daughter was enraged. "What are you doing? This is wrong! He shouldn't get away with this!" But her mother turned to her and said these words of wisdom: "Honey, he was in need. We have enough, and we should share it."[6]

Our parents' generation looked back wistfully to the days of the Second World War as an era when America pulled together for the common goal of defeating the Axis powers. What keeps us from pulling together for the common goal of creating an egalitarian society *without* the stimulus of violence and war? It seems to me a lofty, and worthy aspiration for one of the wealthiest nations on earth. But it will require considerable social and political effort. Jesus said, "From everyone to whom much has been given, much will be required" (Luke 12:48).

CONCLUDING THOUGHTS ON COMMUNITY

KEITH PARSONS

I would like to focus on just part of a line from your last essay: "community requires meaningful give-and-take instead of a winner-take-all strategy." In a nutshell, give-and-take is what we have lost and what we must get back if we are to have community in this country. When politics and business are not approached on the basis of give-and-take, but just on the basis of take, and power and profit become our exclusive goals, then community is not possible. Our interactions become zero-sum games, where one side's gains are matched by the losses of the other. There is no notion of a common good, and no possibility of win-win outcomes, but only of victory for my faction and defeat for yours. This is close to the definition of a failed state.

I particularly appreciated your comment about the makers of the EpiPen and their enormous price hike for this lifesaving medication. Sadly, this is just one among innumerable examples of corporate greed, and not even the most egregious. Contrary to the mantra of the eighties, greed is not good. Indeed, I would say that of all the seven deadly sins, avarice is the deadliest. Lust and gluttony can be temporarily surfeited, but not avarice. Avarice knows no satiety; the more it gets the more it wants. There is literally not enough money in the world to satisfy the greedy. Community is not possible in a society where greed is not curbed.

Finally, I very much liked your take on the concept of righteousness. We atheists tend to roll our eyes when we hear the word "righteousness" because we associate it with self-righteousness. You see it as fidelity to our relationships to each other, so we are most righteous when we have to make the hard choices and stay true to our commitments even when it hurts. It follows that the opposite of righteousness is not depravity but insincerity, to have the kind of "good intentions" that, as the hard old saying goes, pave the road to hell. I am writing this just after Memorial Day, the day we honor those who gave "the last full measure of devotion." Their sacrifice should shame those who claim to be patriots but whine when they get a jury summons or invent excuses for not voting.

My concluding reflections have taken me back to the future. When you reach our age, you can reflect on what the world is like now compared to what we thought it would be like. If you had asked me in 1960 what life was going to be like by 2020, I guess I would have imagined a world like *The Jetsons*. You know—flying cars, space travel, sassy robot maids, etc. How did things work out? Well, space travel seems to be a bust, at least if you were hoping for anything beyond low-earth orbit. As for robot maids, we do have Alexa, but we still have to do the dishes and take out the garbage ourselves. I saw that Uber is developing flying taxis. Not sure this is a good idea.

One thing I would never have thought to say is that people in the future would not be so *white*. Middle-class white kids like us, like the animators of *The Jetsons*, would have just imagined a future of people who looked like us. Of course, we did know about black people, and we even had some limited interactions with them, but our world was still almost lily white. I never had an African American classmate until my senior year in high school. I never had a close black friend until I was in my forties. Needless to say, when we were kids, hardly anybody we knew was Asian or Hispanic or Middle Eastern or even Catholic. I think our class at Knollwood Elementary had one Irish Catholic girl, and that was as diverse as we got.

As we said earlier, the demographic facts are clear. America now and in the future will be multiracial, multiethnic, and increasingly diverse with respect to sexual orientation, national origin, and religion. In the wake of the #MeToo movement, and no doubt also in response to Trump's ugly misogyny, record numbers of women ran for political office in 2018. Of course, diversity does not automatically mean equality. As this is being written, cover stories in both *Time* and the *Atlantic* discuss the rise of the new meritocratic upper class, which is predominately white and has rigged the system to maintain its privileges for the foreseeable future.[1] Perhaps, though, the best hope for de-rigging the system is the rise of a much more diverse America, populated by people not willing to be marginalized.

The demographic facts being what they are, Trump's fulminations against Mexicans and Muslims will not matter in the long run, and those who back Trump in hopes that he will restore the white America of their collective fantasy will be disappointed. In the short run, nativism, xenophobia, and racism can be very damaging. It is easy to be discouraged when you witness the daily parade of the grotesque, the appalling, the absurd, and the tawdry that is the Trump administration. How should we react? Should we hate him?

I hated George W. Bush passionately, and my hatred was not a flickering light, but burned always with a hard gemlike flame. Funny thing, though, my hatred only hurt me and not Bush. I am not particularly a fan of TV pop psychologists, but "Dr. Phil" once made a very wise observation. He said to someone who was obsessed with an enemy, "You're letting him live rent-free in your head!" Writers far older and wiser than Dr. Phil have shown us the terrible things that happen to us when we give in to hate. We sometimes speak of people as "consumed" with hate, and this is an appropriate metaphor. In the *Oresteia*, Aeschylus portrays Clytemnestra as so obsessed with vengeance that her hatred devours her from within like a horrible parasite until her very humanity is consumed. Hate just is not worth it.

We can oppose Trump with all our might without letting him freeload in our heads. How? "When they go low, we go high," advised Michelle Obama. Every time you think Trump can go no lower, he surpasses himself, so he gives us endless opportunities to follow her advice. How do we "go high" when Trump plumbs the depths? We do it by standing up for the things that Trump is tearing down, like truth, civility, and community. Do not lie, prevaricate, or shill, and call out those who do. Do your best to talk civilly with all of those who will talk with you. Make it your default assumption that those who disagree with you are rational, decent people, and not evil idiots. Don't harm yourself by obsessively hating even the evil idiots.

How do we individually and collectively promote community in the age of Trump? There are many things large and small we can do. Do not underrate the small things; they add up to something big. I recently heard of an office where white and black people worked together harmoniously, but then, when they had a Christmas party, the white people all sat at one table and the black people all sat at another. Wouldn't it have been great if, say, just one white person had walked up to the table with all black people and asked if he or she could join them? Sometimes all it takes is for one person to do something to make everyone more aware. Treat people who are often targets of hatred, like Muslims and LGBTQ people, with respect and dignity. Don't be ostentatious about it; just do it. Speak up when people say bigoted, misogynistic, or hateful things.

One of the many nodes of agreement that you and I have discovered is here. Christian teaching emphasizes that small courtesies and considerations matter. Jesus says (Matthew 5:47) that if you only greet those who greet you, you haven't shown any merit. Even the heathen do that. I don't think he was recommending effusiveness or officiousness. The compulsively perky put me in curmudgeon mode and make me wonder if they are up to something. Also, far too many Christians take far too great an interest in minding their neighbors' business. I think Jesus's point (if an atheist may venture an exegesis!) is simply that our ordinary, mundane interactions with people matter. It really matters whether your typical interactions with people are mannerly, pleasant, and considerate rather than rude, condescending, and arrogant. In this age of Trumpian boorishness, merely being mannerly is an act of resistance.

Finally, since we wrote this book in a spirit of finding common ground between secular and religious worldviews, let me end on that note. One of the sharpest divides in our current polarized milieu is between believers and nonbelievers. It is easy and fun to be mean. I confess to having succumbed to the temptation far too often. It is viscerally satisfying to make sweeping condemnations of the other side.[2] I have heard even generally responsible and respectable writers say that people become atheists so that they can indulge guilt-free in sexual sin. Some Christian authors have written whole books depicting atheists as morally degenerate and intellectually bankrupt.[3] Their understanding of Christian charity must be, "Love thy neighbor, unless he disagreeth with thee, and then mayest thou revile him utterly." Needless to say, some atheists reciprocate with equally censorious judgments. One of the "new" atheists has said that raising children as Catholic is a form of child abuse.[4] Ugh. Come on. Do we really have to be so nasty?

At this point, though, when I would like to offer irenic admonitions, we seem to run into the same old conundrum: Are there not some persons on the "other" side who truly are despicable and worthy of censure? What about Paige Patterson, the Southern Baptist bigwig recently ousted as head of Southwestern Baptist Seminary? He was fired after some very embarrassing remarks were publicized, including expressions of lip-smacking salaciousness about a hypothetical sixteen-year-old girl, and advice to abused women to stick with their spouses and endure continued physical abuse. What about creationists and other crackpots who subvert science and, in general, "darken counsel by words without knowledge (Job 38:2)?" What about homophobes who travel to African countries to promote the violent persecution of gays?[5] What about Catholic apologists who continue to downplay, deny, or minimize the horrific depredations of pedophile priests?[6] Don't such obscurantists, fanatics, theocrats, hypocrites, and bigots deserve condemnation in the clearest and most severe terms?

Indeed they do. Here, though, is, I think, a central truth: The best antidote to bad religion is good religion. When I, as an atheist, criticize anything said or done by a religious person, my critique, however cogent, will be viewed in consideration of its source: "Of course that is what *he* would say." When, however, the critique comes from one whose religious credentials are obvious and impeccable, then such a criticism is much harder to dismiss. The over-zealous Catholic apologist will easily and contemptuously disregard my opinion, but if, say, rebuked by Pope Francis, he will have to take this chastisement much more seriously. As I said earlier, when you, Paris, lower the boom on the hypocrites of the religious right, challenging them to be *more* scriptural and *more* Christian, you threaten them much more than the most eloquent condemnations of Richard Dawkins or Christopher Hitchens.

My advice to atheists, then, is to recognize that some religious people are not your enemies but your most valuable allies in your struggles against fundamentalists, creationists, theocrats, homophobes, and the other denizens of the Kingdom of Darkness. Don't listen to those atheists whose only desire is to debunk religion at all costs, even at the cost of not understanding it. To be part of the solution instead of part of the problem, find that common ground, as I have tried to do here.

CONCLUDING THOUGHTS ON COMMUNITY

PARIS DONEHOO

There was an Irish Catholic girl at Knollwood Elementary in Decatur, Georgia? I never knew. I was aware that the lunch ladies always served fish sticks on Friday because Catholics were required in those pre-Vatican II days to eat fish on Fridays, but I certainly did not know any Catholics who thus avoided committing a sin in the cafeteria. Everybody in the world you and I inhabited was at least nominally Baptist, Methodist, or Presbyterian. I did not meet a Catholic until ninth grade. My high school was not racially integrated until 1966—a full twelve years after the Supreme Court's *Brown v. Board of Education of Topeka* ruling—and it would be another year before I became friends with an African American. My mother had a Polish hairdresser who still bore the hideous number tattooed on his forearm as a souvenir from a Nazi concentration camp, but there were no other Poles or Jews in my purview. Hindus, Buddhists, and Muslims were people who lived on the other side of the world and needed a missionary (preferably a Southern Baptist one) to go and snatch them from the jaws of hell before it was too late.

Like you, I could not have conceived of the world we live in today. The congregation from which I retired, for example, is located in Elgin, Illinois, a municipality that is almost 50 percent Hispanic, with smaller concentrations of black, Asian, and other races within its environs. Along with Catholics and Protestants, the congregation and I worked, studied, and cared for our town beside Jews, Muslims, Buddhists, Hindus, and Baha'i. As children, you and I could easily envision encounters with Martians, but not the real human encounters that have become commonplace.

When Trump ties illegal immigrants to the vicious MS-13 gang, he is blatantly playing on the fears of those who look on America's current diversity as a threat to be resisted, not a strength to be celebrated. Behind the xenophobic language of our current political discourse there is a wistfulness for that simpler society you and I knew as children, and demagogues like Trump know how to manipulate it. All it takes is a Trumpian bellows to fan the flames of nostalgia into overheated anxiety, and people scatter to their respective camps to fire missiles of insult and half-truths across the no-man's-land between us. Thus, community dies, "Not with a bang but a whimper."[1]

Therefore, as tempting as it is to point the finger at Trump and his followers, I am reminded of the saying I heard from my mother and numerous Sunday School teachers: "When you one point a finger at someone, you have three more fingers pointing back at you." If we are to rediscover the joys and challenges of real community, we must realize it starts with us. Our elected officials are ultimately reflections of the society that put them in office. It is too easy to blame the politicians for our present-day schisms. If "we the people" had wanted leaders who cooperate with one another and look first to the common good, we would have practiced it first ourselves. Instead, again and again we have bought into the serpent's lies (see remarks on Genesis 3) that "the one who dies with the most toys wins," "second place is the first loser," and "God, guns, and guts made this country great." I once heard someone claim that many Christians believe we all must be twin brothers and sisters, or we cannot be brothers and sisters at all. In other words, those who are not mirror images of ourselves theologically, spiritually, and practically cannot be claimed as fellow members of the Christian family. Unfortunately, the same sentiment has taken hold across non-Christian as well as Christian America. We fear the Other, and, whether consciously or unconsciously, we elect politicians who will justify our trepidation.

Activist and author Adrienne Maree Brown says that racist realities in America "are not getting worse. They are getting uncovered. We must hold each other tight and continue to pull back the veil."[2] I fear she is correct on a number of fronts, not just the racial one. The chasms between us were widening long before Trump took office. As government became more and more dysfunctional we should have pulled back the veil to see the root causes of discontent and quoted the famous words from Walt Kelly's comic strip *Pogo*: "We have met the enemy, and he is us."

Perhaps I could characterize our current approach to social discourse as a type of pornography. The insidious aspect of sexual pornography is its reduction of a human being to nothing more than an object for personal pleasure. It matters not whether the woman or man has feelings, needs, hopes, dreams, struggles, or people who care for him or her. All that counts is the satisfaction a voyeur gets from watching. Likewise, when I paint an opponent with a malevolent brush, and sweep him or her into my pile of "dingbats" and "morons," or "enemies of the people," it feels good for the moment, but I have not given the other person the right to be just as human as I am, nor have I—from my theological point of view—recognized the person as a creation of God, loved just as much as God loves me. Social pornography, in the long run, is counterproductive. Community cannot be built on the ruins of decency.

Perhaps I am expecting too much. I am only too aware of the intractability of certain people and opinions. I left the Southern Baptist church because I grew tired of offering to listen and engage with fundamentalist Christians who, in return, only wanted to deride my thinking and cast me "into the outer darkness, where there will be weeping and gnashing of teeth" (Matthew 25:30). In their minds I was required to be a twin brother or not a brother at all. But, as you point out, narrowmindedness is not the exclusive domain of religion. I have encountered the same eye-rolling, paternalistic, "Oh, someday you'll come to your senses" smirk from atheists and agnostics, too. I confess to my own blind spots in dealing with others as well. I have often been too quick to label some believers as "toxic Christians" and many politicians as "right-wing nut jobs."

So what is to be done? How can we restore community in this fractured society? Here I circle back to your observation that ordinary, mundane interactions with people matter. At a rally against gun violence in schools, I marched through town carrying signs denouncing the NRA and the proliferation of assault weapons, as well as giving the "thumbs up" sign to drivers who honked their horns in support. One man, however, stood on the sidelines with counterprotest signs, while shouting to all of us about his constitutional right to bear arms. What did I do as I walked by him? Shouted my slogans even louder. But a lady from my church stopped and engaged the man in conversation. She did not change his mind, and he did not change hers, but for a few beautiful moments they listened to each other, and a potentially perilous situation was averted. On that day, the parishioner taught the pastor a lesson.

After worship one Sunday I joined two of my grandchildren at the ubiquitous coffee hour in the fellowship hall. When they had piled their plates with snacks, I asked, "Where do you want to sit?" My granddaughter, Natalie, surveyed the room and saw Sam (not his real name). Sam is a homeless man who wanders into the church building almost every Sunday, sits in the hall, and waits for drinks and goodies to appear between and after services. He rarely ventures into the sanctuary for worship, and when he does he usually falls asleep and snores— loudly. Sam was a fixture around the building. Natalie noticed Sam at a table surrounded by other tables filled with parishioners. "Let's go sit with Sam," she said. "He's all by himself."

Seems like I remember reading something about "a little child shall lead them" (Isaiah 11:6). On such small, apparently insignificant actions, community is built. The writer of the book of Hebrews admonishes, "Let us consider how to provoke one another to love and good deeds" (Hebrews 10:24). Some translations say, "Let us consider how to *stir up* one another," but I like the word "provoke" better. It is a stronger sentiment for a crucial time. I am not suggesting we mandate love and good deeds, but I am suggesting we be bold in our words and actions for the common good. The lady who talked with the counter-protester "provoked" me to do better. My granddaughter "provoked" me to do better. Should we be silent in the face of injustice? By no means. But we can practice the kind of community described in the Bible: "And we urge you, beloved, to admonish the idlers, encourage the faint-hearted, help the weak, *be patient with all of them*" (1 Thessalonians 5:14, emphasis mine).

CONCLUSION
AN UNABASHEDLY ALARMIST CODA

In the tumultuous 1960s, cabinet secretary John W. Gardner addressed the graduating class at Cornell University and noted that many American institutions were "caught up in a savage crossfire between unloving critics and uncritical lovers."[1] In these pages we have tried to avoid both extremes while observing that the same savage crossfire is wreaking havoc again. We believe, however, that our current situation is worse. In fact, the present situation frightens us. We have argued that truthfulness, civility, and community are not luxuries or superficialities, not baubles merely desirable but inessential. On the contrary, a society where these qualities are no longer valued and practiced is a society in name only. It is not awaiting dissolution but has dissolved already. It may lumber along, but it is a zombie society, still capable of physical movement, but devoid of mind or conscience.

At rock bottom, what keeps any group of people together, from a family to a nation, is a sense of identity and belonging, a sense that *this is who we are and this is where we belong.* These relationships may be formalized into pacts, laws, and constitutions, but these are mere form once the substance is gone, once the binding ties are loosed. Tolstoy said that all happy families are alike, but that each unhappy family is unhappy in a different way. Really, though, many dysfunctional families present the same picture. There is no mutual respect, but either tacit or blatant contempt; members lie, deceive, and manipulate to get what they want; there is no notion of shared or common good, but each member is out for himself or herself.

Dysfunctional nations have the same outline: The operant definition of "true" becomes "what my side says"; disagreement is taken as
proof of stupidity or wickedness; the good of the whole is immate-
rial, and what matters is success for myself and people like me. Every
grubby little lie, every sneering tweet, every ugly racist slur, does its
small bit to unravel the social fabric, adding another drop of division
and alienation to the poisonous mix. And what is the upshot? Well, it
isn't pretty, as we know from history.

Several times we have referred to the Civil War and the circumstances leading to it. Sober historians would probably regard comparisons between our present situation and the period prior to the
Civil War as exaggerated and alarmist. No doubt they would point
to many relevant dissimilarities between then and now, and, indeed,
history does not literally repeat itself. However, though history does
not repeat, as Mark Twain said, it does rhyme. We think that some
of today's events are rhyming with some of the more notorious ones
of the past. As for being alarmist, as the title to this conclusion indicates, we are willing to run that risk. We feel a responsibility to point to
what we regard as a real and imminent danger, and if we are wrong, and
the situation is not nearly as dire as we indicate, then we will be most
relieved to know it. In the meantime, we have to call it as we see it, so
we look to the period leading up to the Civil War for analogies to our
current dysfunction.

For decades before the first cannon shell arced through the
predawn sky toward Fort Sumter on April 12, 1861, North and South
had engaged in rhetorical war, a war that was waged in newspapers,
journals, books, and in Congress. We will focus on just one notorious
event, to which we have alluded earlier—the inflammatory speech
delivered by Senator Charles Sumner of Massachusetts, and his subsequent caning at the hands of Congressman Preston Brooks of South
Carolina. This is an often-told tale. Bruce Catton, preeminent histo-

rian of the Civil War of a previous generation, opens his book *This Hallowed Ground* with a vivid account of the incident.[2] We think it bears telling again as an illustration of how verbal vehemence can prefigure physical violence.

Senator Charles Sumner was hard to ignore or dismiss. His physical presence was imposing, his speaking voice was sonorous, and he bore himself with the gravitas of those noble Romans familiar to the classically educated Sumner. His contemporaries often also regarded him as self-important and egotistical, an impression he seems to have done little to dispel. On May 19, 1856, he rose on the floor of the Senate to begin the delivery of a very long speech titled "The Crime against Kansas." This was during the "bleeding Kansas" conflict in which proslavery and free-soil forces were, in effect, fighting a proxy war in the Kansas Territory.

Sumner, an ardent abolitionist, employed all of the florid grandiloquence of nineteenth-century oratory to condemn in harshest tones and terms those he deemed responsible for the "crime." Interestingly, for an age often identified as inhibited, oratory abounded in sexual imagery. One common trope, perhaps taking a cue from the book of Revelation, was to compare anything deeply despised to a prostitute. Thus, Senator Andrew Butler of South Carolina was accused of pimping for the harlot slavery:

> The Senator from South Carolina has read many books of chivalry, and believes himself a chivalrous knight, with sentiments of honor and courage. Of course he has chosen a mistress to whom he has made his vows, and who, though ugly to others, is always lovely to him; though polluted in the sight of the world, is chaste in his sight—I mean the harlot Slavery. For her his tongue is always profuse with words. Let her be impeached in character, or any proposition made to shut her out from the extension of her wantonness, and no extravagance of manner or hardihood of assertion is then too great

for this senator. The frenzy of Don Quixote in behalf of his wench Dulcimer del Taboos is all surpassed.[3]

Not only is Senator Butler a pimp, he is a deluded knight errant, and the fair lady whose honor he seeks to uphold is really nothing but a whore. In the mid-nineteenth century, these were fighting words.

At this point Sumner was really just warming to his subject, and he continued at great length. The published speech went to ninety five pages. There is no need to follow the rest of the oration since its drift is clear. One person who got its drift was Congressman Preston Brooks of South Carolina, a cousin of Senator Butler. (Senator Butler was not in attendance.) Brooks regarded the oration as a mortal insult to his family's honor, the kind of insult that no Southern gentleman could forget or forgive.

Brooks at first considered challenging Sumner to a duel, but you dueled only with social equals, and Brooks did not consider Sumner to be a gentleman, so he decided to whip him like a cur. On May 22, Brooks approached Sumner as he sat at his desk on the Senate floor. Brooks lashed him repeatedly with a thick cane topped with a gold head. Trapped in his heavy desk, which was bolted to the floor, Sumner could not avoid the blows rained repeatedly onto his head. Finally, Sumner ripped the desk from the floor and staggered up the aisle, blinded by his own blood, until he fell unconscious. Brooks continued to beat the unconscious Sumner until the cane broke.

It took years for Sumner to recover from his severe injuries, but he did eventually return to the Senate to finish a lengthy and distinguished career. No official action was taken against Congressman Brooks. Northerners responded to the incident with copious outrage, calling Brooks "cowardly" and "Bully Brooks" and comparing the violence on the Senate floor to the violence in Kansas. Southerners celebrated what they considered the just chastisement of an arrogant and vulgar traducer of Southern honor. Brooks received hundreds of canes from all over the South to replace the one he had broken; one was inscribed "Hit him again!"

Thomas A. Bailey, author of the popular textbook *The American Pageant: A History of the Republic*, brilliantly summarized the significance of the event:

> The Sumner-Brooks clash and the ensuing reactions revealed how dangerously inflamed passions were becoming, North and South. It was ominous that the cultured Sumner should have used the language of a barroom bully, and that the gentlemanly Brooks should have employed the tactics and the tools of a thug. Emotion was displacing thought. The blows rained on Sumner's head were, broadly speaking, among the first blows of the Civil War.[4]

Do these events from over 160 years ago have a familiar ring—or rhyme? We think they do. As this is being written, two female comedians, Samantha Bee and Roseanne Barr, have gotten into trouble for abusive and offensive comments. Barr tweeted comments to the effect that Valerie Jarrett, a black woman who had worked in the Obama administration, looked like the offspring of "The Muslim Brotherhood" and "Planet of the Apes." In her weekly program, Bee characterized Ivanka Trump with an obscene term for female genitals. (Not the term used by Trump in the *Access Hollywood* video. The other one.) When Barr, a conservative, was fired by her network and her series canceled, and Bee, a liberal, was not, the White House predictably responded with outrage, charging that a "double standard" exists that punishes conservatives for offensive remarks but permits liberals to attack Trump and the Trump family in the most scurrilous terms.

Whether or not these incidents do or do not reveal the existence of a double standard is not relevant to our point here. We think that there are some things that *no* decent person should ever say. We can think of no circumstances that would justify calling any African American the off-spring of an ape or calling any woman by the term used by Bee. The fact that these things were said, in public (before a cheering audience in Bee's case), indicates that a degree of reckless incivility has metastasized in our society. Of course, both Bee and Barr apologized quickly and no doubt sincerely, but the fact that such things were said at all indicates to us that, as Bailey said above about the period prior to the Civil War, passions are dangerously inflamed and emotion has replaced thought.

When Rick Perry, currently Trump's secretary of energy, was governor of Texas, he tossed some red meat to his hard-core supporters by making comments that flirted with the idea of secession.[5] After the 2004 presidential election, a map was circulated showing Canada and the states that had gone for Kerry. These were depicted in blue and labeled "The United States and Canada." The southern and western states that had gone for Bush were shown in red and labeled "Jesus land." The map was a joke, of course, and it is hard to believe that Perry was entirely serious. Yet the deep divisions are real and no laughing matter.

Will there be another civil war? Will the deep red states of South and the West secede, with Texas leading the charge? We think that this is unlikely, but history turns on so many contingencies and imponderables, that only the foolish will spell out detailed scenarios. We do think that the current situation is untenable, and that Trump is making it much worse. As we have argued here, his utter disregard for truth, his extreme incivility, and his relentless divisiveness undermine the values and virtues that constitute the fundamental cohesiveness of society. There can be no organization founded upon cooperation when the members cannot trust what the others tell them, address each other in terms of abuse and contempt, and favor their own or their faction's advantage over a common good that includes everyone.

We conclude then with an appeal to every person of good will, secular and religious, liberal and conservative, Clinton voters or

Trump voters: Tell the truth, and do not tolerate those who do not. Support scientists and all those who strive for truth, and oppose those who obfuscate for the sake of ideology or profit. Make civility, not contempt, your default mode of interaction with those who disagree with you. Observe standards of decency and restraint even when dealing with those whom you regard as genuinely contemptible. Recognize and honor the diversity of your fellow citizens, and struggle always to make the motto *e pluribus unum* more of a living reality. Reject all who sow hatred and division, and stand against the devastating effects of Mahatma Gandhi's Seven Deadly Social Sins:

1. Politics without principle
2. Wealth without work
3. Commerce without morality
4. Pleasure without conscience
5. Education without character
6. Science without humanity
7. Worship without sacrifice[6]

We would like to end as we began—on a personal note. We were teenagers and young adults during the eras of Vietnam and Watergate. We sat and watched together as extreme violence erupted during the Democratic National Convention in Chicago in 1968. We were seniors in high school when antiwar demonstrators were gunned down at Kent State, and then called "bums" by Richard Nixon. We both reluctantly registered for the draft in August 1970, unwilling to fight in a war we regarded as grossly unjust. Patriotism came easily for our parents' generation, but not for ours. Our parents had been united in the mighty endeavor to save the world from monstrous tyrannies. We watched as presidents told us about the "light at the end of the tunnel" in Vietnam, and we heard Nixon proclaim himself "not a crook." When your national leaders feed you a steady diet of cynical lies, you tend to become cynical also, and not overflowing with patriotic feeling.

It is a sad truth that you often do not realize how much something means to you until you are in danger of losing it. As we noted at the beginning, for us, writing this book has reminded us of how much we love this country and how strongly we want to have one nation with liberty and justice for all. We think the founders' vision (tweaked and purified over the course of American history) of a society with equal rights for all and special privileges for none is an ideal worth fighting and dying for. We think that civil liberties and civil rights are precious and must be protected against any encroachment or abridgement. We think that the United States of America is an ongoing project that must always be guided to a more complete realization of its ideals.

It is because we have rediscovered our patriotism that we are so appalled by Donald Trump, whose words and deeds we regard as not merely un-American but as anti-American, and as gravely dangerous. Here we have focused on his untruthfulness, his incivility, and his divisiveness. There are many other, perhaps even more serious, issues: He is a would-be autocrat whose attacks on the FBI and his own Department of Justice undermine the rule of law. As this is being written, Trump has claimed that he has the unlimited right to pardon himself, and his lawyers have argued that, by definition, the president cannot obstruct justice. Further, Trump is a symbol of self-aggrandizing corruption who refuses to draw a bright line between his private business interests and the responsibilities of his public office. He opposes the freedom of the press, demonizes journalists, and blatantly tries to bully and intimidate all critics. Finally, and perhaps most despicably, he has abandoned basic humanity and decency with his cruel policy of separating small children from parents who arrive illegally. Trump's reply, when confronted with outrage over such inhumanity, is to blame the Democrats. This lie is egregious even for Trump, the most prolific of presidential liars.[7] If this book can to any degree whatsoever unite good people to support what is best about this country, and oppose what is worst, as typified by Donald Trump, then our efforts here will be abundantly rewarded.

We hope we have demonstrated in these pages that different viewpoints—in our case born from contrasting belief systems—need not be mutually exclusive or lead to rancor and division. Our purpose, from the outset, has never been to prove one of us right and the other one wrong. Our purpose has been to exhibit the kind of cooperation that is absolutely essential to healing the divides in our country that are becoming more and more dangerous each day. The cynics and pessimists abroad in the land may think such commonality is not possible, even if desired. Perhaps this book is a step toward dispelling this misconception. We would be thrilled indeed to someday discover that our long-term friendship had, in some small way, helped to create a new commitment to truth, a rebirth of civility, and a sense of real community in this nation we love.

BIBLIOGRAPHIC ESSAY

PARIS DONEHOO

Because of the proliferation of bogus news outlets, one must be careful citing contemporary sources, particularly those found on the internet. Therefore, I have tried to be careful in my search for documentation of news items. The *New York Times*, the *Washington Post*, the Associated Press, and other classic journalistic outlets can still be trusted for fair and balanced reporting, regardless of Trump's labeling them "fake news." The pace of breaking stories over the past couple of years has been a veritable boon for this project, as there was never any shortage of material. Some days it seemed as if the news was tailored for whatever we happened to be writing about at that moment. For insightful perspectives on society from a progressive religious viewpoint the *Christian Century* is always relevant. It is also useful for introducing works by theologians and religious authors who cut through the superficiality of what often passes for faith in modern America.

Rodney Stark's *The Rise of Christianity* brings a sociologist's perspective to the formation of the church in its first few centuries of life, and ably demonstrates how the behavioral, rather than doctrinal, practices of the early church contributed to its profound impact on the Greco-Roman world. *Destroyer of the Gods* by Larry Hurtado delves deeper into the characteristics of early Christians, and explains how their distinctiveness ultimately became their most powerful asset. John Dominic Crossman's *The Greatest Prayer* is not a devotional treatise on the words of Jesus called the "Lord's Prayer," but an exploration of the radical nature of the prayer in its historical/social context, and its implications for contemporary faith practices. Crossan's *God and Empire* examines the nonviolent nature of Jesus's teaching on the kingdom of God, and lays bare the church's justification of war since the days of Constantine. *Excavating Jesus* and *In Search of Paul*, both coauthored by Crossan and Jonathan Reed, are fascinating glimpses behind the curtain of the Bible to rescue it from obscurantism and misappropriation. Walter Wink's masterful series on the "principalities and powers" mentioned often in the Pauline epistles remain some of the most seminal works on the relationship between faith and power in the ancient world and our own. *Naming the Powers*, *Unmasking the Powers*, *Engaging the Powers*, and *The Powers That Be* should be digested by anyone seeking a biblical faith which confronts the current status quo.

When Stanley Hauerwas and William Willimon wrote *Resident Aliens* in 1989 they exposed the capture of American Christianity by American culture, and they gave a voice to scholars and practitioners who longed to reinvent the church along more biblical lines. Tony Campolo, as a sociologist, teacher, and preacher, has also called for reform in various settings. Because he has bona fides in scholarly, evangelical, and progressive Christian circles he is often an authoritative witness to what is wrong with modern faith, and what is also right with modern faith. In particular, his book *Power Delusions* was instrumental in "something like scales" falling from my eyes during the Southern Baptist holy war of the 1980s. So-called "Red Letter Christianity" and "Emergent Church" movements are heavily influenced by Campolo. When the Great Recession hit in 2008, Jim Wallis's book *Rediscovering Values* spawned an entire series of sermons for my Elgin, Illinois, congregation, called "Being a Disciple When the Economy Stinks." *God's Politics* is also a great resource for Christlike engagement in society.

Though based on a study by the conservative Barna Group, *Unchristian* by David Kinnaman and Gabe Lyons is a sobering examination of the beliefs and practices of many Christians that are driving away the millennial generation. Kinnaman's subsequent *You Lost Me* provides practical suggestions for waking up the American church to its present reality. Diana Butler Bass has a unique ability to assess the religious landscape of the twenty-first century, and *Christianity After Religion* calls on Christians to ask the tough questions about their individual and corporate understanding of themselves in an era when the old rules do not apply anymore. *The Practicing Congregation* and *Christianity for the Rest of Us* provide examples for churches that want to meet these challenges head on. Anthony Robinson's *Transforming Congregational Culture* was the first book to help me shift my paradigms for living discipleship in the modern world. Subsequent works such as *Changing the Conversation* and *What's Theology Got to Do with It?* push readers to envision new forms of faith for the future. I have been greatly blessed by the writings of fellow United Church of Christ minister Michael Piazza. One could say *Liberating Hope!* (co-authored with Cameron Trimble) picks up where Butler Bass's *Christianity After Religion* leaves off, providing practical ideas for congregational renewal. I am particularly grateful to Michael for allowing my congregation to use his book *Vital Vintage Church* even before it was officially published, as a guide for reinventing ourselves for the modern age.

For anyone who desires to hang on to faith—particularly biblically based faith—but cannot embrace its outdated constructs, I highly recommend *If Grace Is True*, and the follow-up volume, *If God Is Love*, both by Philip Gulley and James Mulholland. Finally, though I have only referred to one of his sermons in these pages, John Claypool began shaping my thoughts on discipleship while I was a seminary student, and continues to do so now in my retirement. *Tracks of a Fellow Struggler* has been especially helpful during my life's most difficult moments.

BIBLIOGRAPHIC ESSAY

KEITH PARSONS

The philosophy of religion can be a fiercely technical field, requiring, for instance, expertise in modal logic or Bayesian confirmation theory to tackle some points. Among the works that argue for atheism in a way that is accessible yet philosophically sophisticated, three that can be most strongly recommended are: Nicholas Everitt, *The Non-Existence of God* (London: Routledge, 2004), J. L. Mackie, *The Miracle of Theism: Arguments for and Against the Existence of God* (Oxford: Oxford University Press, 1982), and Michael Martin: *Atheism: A Philosophical Investigation* (Philadelphia: Temple University Press, 1990). The level of argument in these books is far above that in the "new atheist" tomes, and the tone is not censorious.

In my view, there is no more qualified or skilled practitioner of the philosophy of religion than Graham Oppy. His grasp of the issues is thorough, and his arguments are penetrating and rigorous. Some of his books are too technical to recommend for laypersons, but his recent work on naturalism, Graham Oppy, *Naturalism and Religion: A Contemporary Philosophical Investigation* (London: Routledge, 2018), is accessible and highly recommended. Here Oppy takes on recent theistic attacks on naturalism and provides careful and cogent rebuttals.

The most important recent work in the philosophy of religion is John Hick, *An Interpretation of Religion: Human Responses to the Transcendent*, 2nd ed. (New Haven, CT: Yale University Press, 2004). Hick's knowledge of both Western and Eastern religious traditions is unsurpassed. He argues forcefully for religious pluralism; that is, that all the great religious traditions are human efforts to respond to the transcendent, and that no such tradition can claim exclusive truth. It is a profound work backed by astounding erudition. As an atheist, I appreciate the fact that Hick admits that naturalism is a fully reasonable option. The world, he says, is "religiously ambiguous"—that is, it can be reasonably interpreted in a naturalistic or religious way. I think he is absolutely right.

For the truly intrepid who want to know the details about the theories of truth, see Richard J. Kirkham, *Theories of Truth: A Critical Introduction* (Cambridge, MA: MIT Press, 1992). A shorter and more elementary introduction is Frederick F. Schmitt, *Truth, A Primer* (Boulder, CO: Westview Press, 1995). For a more up-to-date, but significantly more technical introduction, see Alexis G. Burgess and John P. Burgess, *Truth* (Princeton: Princeton University Press, 2011). The authors also defend a deflationist approach to truth; namely, that saying "P is true" is really just equivalent to saying "P."

Michael P. Lynch shows that philosophical writing need not be an impenetrable nest of technicalities, utterly inaccessible to laypersons. His *True to Life: Why Truth Matters* (Cambridge, MA: MIT Press, 2005) offers what, for my money, is the most lucid and plausible understanding of the nature of truth, and, more importantly, he gives compelling arguments for the importance and irreplaceability of truth.

All who love the truth and deplore those who muddy the waters owe an enormous debt to George Orwell. His classic essay, "Politics and the English Language" in *The Orwell Reader: Fiction, Essays, and Reportage by George Orwell* (New York: Harcourt, Brace, and World, 1956), pp. 355–66, was written in the aftermath of the Second World War. Its account of how bombast and polysyllabic misdirection can obscure truth is more relevant today than ever.

The contributions of Daniel Kahneman and Amos Tversky to

our understanding of human irrationality and its intractability are immense and significant. Their studies, published in academic journals over many years, are engagingly summarized by Massimo Piattelli-Palmarini in *Inevitable Illusions: How Mistakes of Reasoning Rule our Minds* (New York: John Wiley, 1994). See also Michael Shermer, *The Believing Brain* (New York: Henry Holt, 2011). Better yet, read Kahneman himself: *Thinking Fast and Slow* (New York: Farrar, Straus, and Giroux, 2013).

I have had the privilege of meeting Naomi Oreskes and interacting with her at a couple of academic conferences. She impressed me as a truly incisive intellect, someone who is both an accomplished scholar with notable publications in the history of science, and a highly effective public intellectual. Her book with Erik M. Conway, *Merchants of Doubt: How a Handful of Scientists Obscured the Truth on Issues from Tobacco Smoke to Global Warming* (New York: Bloomsbury Press, 2010) is a brilliantly written and thoroughly researched exposé of the big business of creating doubt—that is, of how scientific conclusions are obscured to protect vested interests. The greatest danger to science in our day is the big money that is spent to oppose it when its conclusions threaten profit. Oreskes and Conway drag the perpetrators from the shadows into the light and reveal their tactics.

That climate "skepticism" (i.e., dogmatic denial) no longer has any scientific respectability is shown most clearly by the Skeptical Science site: https://www.skepticalscience.com/global-warming-scientific-consensus-intermediate.htm.

Likewise, the emptiness of crackpot claims against vaccines is made crystal clear by the CDC: https://www.cdc.gov/vaccinesafety/concerns/autism.html.

Politicians have been playing tricks with truth since ancient times. No source illustrates this in more amusing and memorable ways than Herodotus's *Histories*. The best edition by far is Robert B. Strassler, ed., *The*

Landmark Herodotus: The Histories, trans. Andrea L. Purvis (New York: Anchor Books, 2007). On the sophists, see Anthony Gottlieb's immensely readable, *The Dream of Reason: A History of Western Philosophy from the Greeks to the Renaissance* (New York: W. W. Norton, 2000). I use this book in my Great Philosophers classes, and it is esteemed by my students.

Lying is now a sophisticated art, even a science. Lies have been weaponized, as shown by Daniel Levitin in *Weaponized Lies: How to Think Critically in the Post-Truth Era* (New York: Dutton, 2016). One of the most effective ways of lying is to lie with statistics. Darrel Huff's classic *How to Lie with Statistics* (New York: W. W. Norton, 1954) is still a reliable and hugely entertaining guide. If I may indulge in a bit of self-promotion, I think that my own logic text has some good tools for dealing with weaponized lies: Keith Parsons, *Rational Episodes: Logic for the Intermittently Reasonable* (Amherst, NY: Prometheus Books, 2010).

The classic source for understanding the anti-intellectual tradition in America is still Richard Hofstadter, *Anti-Intellectualism in American Life* (New York: Vintage, 1966). Far from receding, the tide of anti-intellectualism has flooded in recent years—to the extent that scientific illiteracy and general ignorance are not only tolerated but admired in some quarters. How this happened and the dire consequences are detailed in such works as Chris Mooney and Sheril Kirshenbaum, *Unscientific America: How Scientific Illiteracy Threatens our Future* (New York: Basic Books, 2009), Mark Bauerlein, *The Dumbest Generation: How the Digital Age Stupefies Young Americans and Jeopardizes our Future.* (New York: Jeremy P. Thatcher/Penguin, 2008), and, most trenchantly, in Charles P. Pierce, *Idiot America: How Stupidity Became a Virtue in the Land of the Free* (New York: Anchor, 2010). Pierce has the remarkable talent of being hilarious and horrifying at the same time.

The lapse of the Republican Party from a moderate-to-conservative party in the sixties to the party of birtherism, conspiracy theories, phobias, and general lunacy is detailed in Mike Lofgren, *The Party Is*

Over: How Republicans Went Crazy, Democrats Became Useless, and the Middle Class Got Shafted (New York: Viking, 2012). Lofgren is a lifelong Republican who spent twenty-eight years working in Congress, including sixteen years as a senior analyst with the House and Senate Budget committees. This critique by a former insider is truly devastating. To see how far into the truly bizarre Republicans have fallen, the whole "Jade Helm" fiasco is truly illustrative. See the PolitiFact Texas report: http://www.politifact.com/texas/article/2018/may/03/jade-helm-15-greg-abbott-texas-state-guard-hayden-/.

Ronald Reagan's deviations from truth were amusingly documented by Mark Green and Gail MacColl in *There He Goes Again: Ronald Reagan's Reign of Error* (New York: Pantheon Books, 1983). The real story behind Linda Taylor, the "Welfare Queen" of Reagan's most famous tale, is fascinatingly told by Josh Levin in *Slate*, published on December 19, 2013: http://www.slate.com/articles/news_and _politics/history/2013/12/linda_taylor_welfare_queen_ronald _reagan_made_her_a_notorious_american_villain.html. Taylor really was a despicable person, but Reagan's story turned a small-time criminal into a cheater of mythic proportions.

Also, you really should watch the video of Bush addressing the up-and-in and calling them "my base": https://www.c-span.org/video/?c4506459/haves-mores. This was probably the most honest statement made by Bush during his whole presidency. It is remarkable to see a Republican politician—the president of the United States, no less—proclaiming his willingness to carry water for the rich.

The Bush administration's lying reached its peak (or plumbed its depths) with the lead-up to the Second Gulf War. One of the best accounts of the lies and deceptions leading to that war is in Frank Rich, *The Greatest Story Ever Sold: The Decline and Fall of Truth* (New York: Penguin, 2006). Rich leaves no question about the delusions and duplicity that led to thousands of American deaths and many times that number of Iraqi deaths. The definitive account of the Bush administration's manipulation of public opinion through the employment of spin tactics is Ben Fritz, Bryan Keefer, and Brendan Nyhan, *All the President's Spin: George W. Bush, the Media, and the Truth* (New York: Simon & Schuster, 2004). The insidious nature of spin, making truth more deceptive than any lie, is made plain in this study.

Trump's outrageous lies about immigrant crime are debunked by Alex Nowrasteh, "Everything Is Bigger in Texas—Except the Illegal Immigrant Crime Rate," *Houston Chronicle*, March 12, 2018, p. A11, https://www.houstonchronicle.com/opinion/outlook/article/ Everything-is-Bigger-in-Texas-Except-the-12747805.php. Nowrasteh, of the libertarian Cato Institute, shows that both conviction and arrest rates for undocumented immigrants is lower than that for the native-born population. Donald Trump, whose image of Mexicans seems to be derived from the Frito Bandito, painted a lurid picture of swarms of drug dealers, rapists, and murderers pouring into the United States. Nowrasteh explodes this malicious lie, and, in the libertarian periodical *Reason*, responds to his critics: https://reason.com/ archives/2018/02/01/immigrants-and-crime.

Trump's lies are so numerous that just keeping track of them is a herculean task. Nevertheless, David Leonhardt and Stuart A. Thompson of the *New York Times* attempted to document Trump's lies in his first six months of office: https://www.nytimes.com/interactive/2017/06/23/opinion/trumps-lies.html.

A follow-up story showed that in his first ten months in office Trump told nearly six times as many lies as Obama told in his whole presidency: https://www.nytimes.com/interactive/2017/12/14/opinion/ sunday/trump-lies-obama-who-is-worse.html.

Richard Rhodes, in *The Making of the Atomic Bomb* (New York: Simon & Schuster, 1985), superbly tells the story of how beautiful physics and the highest scientific genius produced a weapon of horrific destruction. Stephen Jay Gould, in *The Mismeasure of Man* (New York: W. W. Norton, 1981), tells another sort of cautionary tale. He shows how scientists can be easily led to erroneous conclusions by their own biases and predispositions. Perhaps motivated in part by reflections on the power of science to produce weapons of mass destruction (as shown by Rhodes) and to perpetuate racial bias (as shown by Gould), there arose among academic leftists a strong anti-science movement in the 1980s. This movement was brilliantly confronted by Paul Gross and Norman Levitt in *Higher Superstition: The Academic Left and its Quarrels with Science* (Baltimore: Johns Hopkins University Press, 1994). Gross and Levitt mercilessly expose the ignorance, bias, and illogic of the attacks on science. The "Sokal Hoax" further revealed the incompetence and ignorance of the would-be debunkers of science. Sokal gives his account in Alan Sokal, *Beyond the Hoax: Science, Philosophy and Culture* (Oxford: Oxford University Press, 2008).

It is one of the ironies of our age that an anti-science activist could head the House Science Committee. James Osborne, writing in the *Houston Chronicle* on April 9, 2017, shows how Rep. Lamar Smith attacks science: "Lamar Smith Sows Disorder as Climate Debate Rages," https://www.houstonchronicle.com/business/article/Lamar-Smith-sows-disorder-as-climate-debate-rages-11061772.php.

Donald Trump is just as ignorant of and hostile to science as Rep. Smith, as Barbara J. King reported for National Public Radio on January 22, 2017: "Fact Check: Science and the Trump Administration," https://www.npr.org/sections/13.7/2017/01/22/510384513/fact-check-science-and-the-trump-administration.

Writing in the *New Yorker* on March 4, 2018, Alan Burdick deftly and succinctly summarizes Trumps bizarre ideas and his "know-nothing" science budget: "Donald Trump's Know-Nothing Science Budget," https://www.newyorker.com/news/daily-comment/donald-trumps-know-nothing-science-budget.

The professionalization of lying is alarmingly detailed by Ari Rabin-Havt and Media Matters in *Lies Incorporated: The World of Post-Truth Politics* (New York: Anchor Books, 2016). Lying is now big business, and professional liars have it down to a science. They can command big bucks from businesses that have an interest in hiding the truth. Rabin-Havt shows how ideologues and shills have blown smoke into just about every major public issue, from guns to gay marriage.

Perhaps the best indication of the way that ideology can promote pseudoscience and anti-science is the fact that a large percentage of Americans—about one-third—deny evolution. On the percentage of Americans who do not accept evolution see: http://www.pewresearch.org/fact-tank/2017/02/10/darwin-day/.

Jerry Coyne's superb *Why Evolution Is True* (New York: Viking, 2009) is a brilliant summary of the evidence for evolution. What is really remarkable is that in the twenty-first century such a book would still need to be written. Neil Shubin's *Your Inner Fish: A Journey into the 3.5-Billion-Year History of the Human Body* (New York: Pantheon Books, 2008) is the second-best book I have ever read on evolution— second only to *The Origin of Species*. Of course, religious fundamentalism and creationist pseudoscience account for the rejection of evolution. Dozens of books and hundreds of articles have demolished creationist arguments point by point. A thorough presentation of creationist (including "intelligent design") arguments and the sources for debunking them is: Mark Isaak, *The Counter-Creationism Handbook* (Berkeley: University of California Press, 2007).

On the Heartland Institute and the many other organizations devoted to promoting corporate agendas over science, see Oreskes and Conway. Again, this is a remarkable book that names names and does not pull its punches. It details the greatest threat to science in our day, namely the influence of corporate cash—allied with ideology—to undermine climate science and to promote the big polluters.

The most famous statement in support of human dignity is the second formulation of the Categorical Imperative in Immanuel Kant's *Grounding for the Metaphysics of Morals.* Kant essentially says that we should not use people as means to our ends, but regard them as ends in themselves. Kant's work is difficult, but a more powerful defense of the dignity of rational beings has never been written. There are many editions of the work. The one I use in my classes is the translation by James W. Ellington, third edition (Indianapolis: Hackett, 1993).

Liberal critiques of Trump are easily dismissed by his defenders. One book that they will not easily dismiss is Charles J. Sykes's *How the Right Lost Its Mind* (New York: St. Martin's Press, 2017). Sykes's conservative credentials are impeccable. He was a leading conservative talk-show host, and he has written a number of solidly conservative books. He argues that traditional conservative ideas and values are now ignored by the right and that a cult of personality has arisen in its place. With the rise of Trump, Sykes argues, all the crazy ideas that had been at the margins of conservatism for years have now become mainstream. Thoughtful conservatism has been replaced by a proudly ignorant extremism. I could not agree more.

There are many good books on the way that upper management has grotesquely enriched itself at the expense of ordinary workers. One of the most effective—and enraging—is Arianna Huffington's *Pigs at the Trough: How Corporate Greed and Political Corruption Are Undermining America* (New York: Crown, 2003). Warning: Make sure you are taking your blood pressure medication when you read this! The level of corruption and greed is truly blood-boiling.

With the nuclear threat raising its hideous head again, it is good to be reminded of what thermonuclear weapons are and what they can do. PBS's interview with Dr. Harold Agnew, one of the physicists who developed the hydrogen bomb, is most enlightening. The interview is accessible at the website for the outstanding episode, "The World's Biggest Bomb," of the PBS series *Secrets of the Dead*: http://www.pbs.org/wnet/secrets/the-world%E2%80%99s-biggest-bomb-about-this-episode/846/.

How are humans capable of committing gross atrocities against other humans? How can we suspend our empathy and look upon other people as less than human? Remarkably, we now have the insights of neuroscience into how the brain shuts off empathy and how it switches from thinking of people as people and instead views them as objects. David Eagleman's wonderful *The Brain: The Story of You* (New York: Pantheon Books, 2015), pp. 147–58, details this process lucidly and alarmingly. This is the book to accompany the PBS series of the same name. It is available on DVD.

As I say in the text, I am an Aristotelian. I think that Aristotle basically got it right in *The Nicomachean Ethics*. That is, the good for human beings depends on the nature of the human organism. We are, by nature, rational and social beings, and human flourishing therefore must involve the achievement of a state of moral and intellectual excellence. The states of character that allow us to achieve such excellence are the intellectual and moral virtues. Ethics therefore involves the development of such virtues. Further, the objective nature of human flourishing provides an objective criterion for ethical assessment, that is, actions are good in proportion to their tendency to promote human flourishing (and, I think, the well-being of all sentient creatures). There are many good editions and translations, but a recent one that has received much praise is Robert C. Bartlett and Susan D. Collins, *Aristotle's Nicomachean Ethics* (Chicago: University of Chicago Press, 2011).

Contempt is the toxin that poisons our current political discourse. Our default response is to regard those who disagree with us as evil or idiots or both. Psychologist Alison Gopnik's "A Cure for Contempt," *Atlantic,* April 2018, pp. 39–41, makes the remarkable observation that families can remain healthy and whole even when the members sometimes disagree strongly and arguments become heated. A family cannot survive when its members view each other with contempt. What applies to families applies to nations and societies. Americans have always disagreed, often heatedly, yet have been able to set aside differences on many occasions. Most of us remember the pervasive sense of unity following 9/11. Today, the level of mutual disdain is so high, that I do wonder whether even a 9/11 would bring us together now.

The problem, of course, is that there really are some contemptible people who richly merit our disdain. For instance, Scott Pruitt, who served as Trump's first head of the Environmental Protection Agency, is a climate-change-denying crackpot who spent much of his previous career attacking the very agency he headed. In his role as EPA administrator he faithfully served the interests of polluting industries and gutted environmental regulations, as detailed by Rebecca Leber in her chilling article "Toxic Avenger," *Mother Jones,* March/April 2018, pp. 22–31. Leber also reveals Pruitt's religious motivations for trashing the planet.

On the early Romans and their techniques for increasing their population, see the classic source, Livy's *The Early History of Rome*, trans. Aubrey de Sélincourt (London: Penguin Classics, 2002), pp. 39–40. Don't worry about whether these stories are true or not. Just enjoy terrific tales told by one of the greatest storytellers of ancient times.

I read Albert Camus's *The Plague* (1947) in college, and it left an abiding impression. I think it is a much better book than his more famous *The Stranger.* The concluding words of the novel are a profound meditation on the intractability of evil. It can suffer defeat again and again, but it never dies. It bides its time waiting to strike again. As a case in point, however often the white supremacist movement is knocked down, it never dies, but lies dormant until, as with the election of Donald Trump, it is energized to spread its disease again.

The most influential work in the philosophy of science written in the twentieth century was Thomas Kuhn's *The Structure of Scientific*

Revolutions, third ed. (Chicago: University of Chicago Press, 1996), initially published in 1962. I think this book has certainly done more good and bad than any other work in the field. In my view, it combines deep insights with equally deep errors. On the one hand, it demonstrated the need to take the history of science seriously, so that we see how science *really* operates (warts and all) as opposed to mythologized and sanitized accounts. On the other hand, it did much mischief by encouraging, whether intentionally or not, extreme relativism and the view that science is merely a social construct. For a thorough critical discussion of Kuhn's strengths and weaknesses, see my book *It Started with Copernicus: Vital Questions about Science* (Amherst, NY: Prometheus Books, 2015).

How the GOP became the "Party of No" is explained by Michael Grunwald in *Politico*, December 4, 2016: https://www.politico .com/magazine/story/2016/12/republican-party-obstructionism -victory-trump-214498.

Future books of American history will point to Mitch McConnell as the Machiavellian manipulator of this era. All of his maneuvers, from the policy of 100 percent opposition to Obama to stealing the Supreme Court seat by refusing to hold hearings for Obama's nominee, are pure power plays. His hyperpartisan manipulations have had one goal only—the increase in Republican power. In that aim he has been fiendishly effective.

The reversion to tribalism in American public discourse is one of the most obvious and alarming features of the current cultural and political milieu. Joshua Greene in *Moral Tribes: Emotion, Reason, and the Gap between Us and Them* (New York: Penguin, 2013) explains how and why we so easily fall into this dichotomy of "us" versus "them." He argues that tribalism inheres in the way our brains spontaneously operate—that is, by emotional responses to potentially threatening people or situations. We also have a capacity for objective reasoning, but it has to battle uphill against value judgments based on emotion. He says that we can learn when to trust our instincts and when we should trust reason instead. Greene's book is an excellent companion to the Eagleman book cited above and the Haidt book discussed below. Studs Terkel's *The Good War* (New York: New Press, 1997) is a Pulitzer Prize–winning oral history of the experience of Americans in the Second World War. The title is a reflection of the sense that, despite its horrors, the war was a time when Americans had a strong sense of "us" that contrasts starkly with the extreme state of division that we are in today.

The Kerner Commission was appointed in 1967 by Lyndon Johnson to investigate the causes of the conditions and circumstances that led to the horrific riots that had taken place in American cities like Detroit, Newark, and Los Angeles. Johnson hoped that the commission would basically affirm his "war on poverty" policies and offer a generally optimistic assessment. When the report came out in 1968, however, it reached the stark conclusion that racism was the cause of the circumstances leading to the riots. Justin Driver, writing in the *Atlantic*, discusses how things have changed—and how they have not—in the fifty years since the report was released: Justin Driver, "The Report on Race that Shook America," *Atlantic* 321, no. 4 (May 2018): 34.

Except for Native Americans, America is a nation of immigrants. Nativism, the opposition to immigrants in favor of "real Americans" is therefore a bizarre phenomenon; yet, as I say in the text, it has been with us since nearly the beginning of our country. One common argument is that immigrants will take jobs away from "natives." In fact, immigrants create wealth for all of us, as entrepreneur Doug Rand explains in "Want to Get Rich? Embrace Foreign Workers," *Houston Chronicle*, April 15, 2018, p. A34. This is really just common sense. People who come here generally do so to have opportunities that were denied them in their country of origin. They are here to take advantage of educational and occupational opportunities, and they make the best of them. Donald Trump's smears could not be more wrong.

The history of Christianity is largely a history of the struggle by the church to maintain unity in the face of schismatic forces. Doctrinal disputes, by their very nature, tend to be intractable and often bitter. Attempts to impose unity by force led to much futile bloodletting. Paul Johnson's *A History of Christianity* (New York: Atheneum, 1977) is a superbly written and brutally honest history of Christianity. Nobody can accuse Johnson, a Catholic, of sugarcoating or whitewashing. The picture that comes through is of an all-too-human institution that has struggled and evolved to face innumerable challenges, and thereby has survived in recognizable form for two thousand years.

Jonathan Haidt's *The Righteous Mind: Why Good People Are Divided by Politics and Religion* (New York: Vintage, 2013) is an indispensable book for anyone who wants to *understand* the divide between liberals and conservatives and not merely indulge in partisan polemics. Haidt is a social psychologist, and his research shows how and why people divide into political camps. He argues that there are innate dispositional differences between people, such that we have different spontaneous emotional reactions to ethically charged situations. For instance, as I explain in the text, the NFL players who took a knee during the playing of the national anthem excited very different responses from liberals and conservatives. We can understand that difference by seeing how the moral intuitions of liberals and conservatives differ.

Haidt's book provides important insights, and I think that if we take his claims seriously we may be less inclined to demonize or dismiss those who disagree with us. We can see that those who respond differently are also morally motivated, but that our moral feelings push us in different directions. While I appreciate Haidt's insights and think that they are genuine, I cannot agree completely with his thesis. He essentially holds that the differences in our emotional responses are genetically based.

Genes shape brains and brains generate emotions. However, this does not explain certain obvious facts, such as the gender and racial disparities in voting. White men, for instance, vote more conservatively than black women. Haidt gives no reason for thinking that genetic dispositions toward conservatism or liberalism would be correlated with race or sex, so social and cultural explanations seem more plausible here.

Steven Pinker is correctly recognized as one of the most important public intellectuals. His recent book *Enlightenment Now: The Case for Reason, Progress, Humanism, and Science* (New York: Viking, 2018) is a stupendously researched case for Enlightenment practices and values. That is, he holds that scientific methods and techniques and the application of technology has enabled humans to make enormous strides in improving the conditions of human life. Compared to a few centuries ago, we live much longer, are healthier, wealthier, and suffer less crime and warfare. The particular value of Pinker's book for our project here is that it shows that there are real, pragmatic solutions to problems and that these are hindered by intrusions of dogma and ideology—whether from the left or the right. Unfortunately, in recent decades both the postmodernist academic left and big-money funded anti-science on the right have undermined such progress.

A level playing field with equal opportunities for upward mobility is necessary if we are to achieve genuine community. Unfortunately, recent cover articles in both the *Atlantic* and *Time* argue that current inequality has greatly restricted opportunity and reinforced the position of the (predominately white) well-off: Matthew Stewart, "The Birth of a New American Aristocracy," *Atlantic* 321, no. 5 (June 2018): 48–63; and Steven Brill, "My Generation Was Supposed to Level the Playing Field. Instead, We Rigged it for Ourselves," *Time*, May 28, 2018, pp. 32–39. The hope is that with inevitably increasing demographic diversity, people of color will gain the power to demand that the system be de-rigged.

In writing a book like this one that attempts to bridge the gap between believers and nonbelievers, we have to fight uphill against zealots on either side. Deeply unhelpful are books like Anthony DeStefano's *Inside the Atheist Mind* (Nashville: Thomas Nelson, 2018). Equally unhelpful are hyperbolic pronouncements from "new" atheists, like the infamous statement of Richard Dawkins that raising a child as a Catholic is a form of mental child abuse, perhaps worse than physical abuse: https://www.richarddawkins.net/2013/01/physical-versus-mental-child-abuse/.

While I think that Dawkins does raise legitimate worries about the inculcation of terrifying doctrines like an eternal punitive hell, the inflammatory manner of expression was unnecessary and counterproductive.

I first heard of the famous beating of Senator Sumner by Preston "Bully" Brooks in Bruce Catton's *This Hallowed Ground* (New York: Doubleday, 1956). Catton was an outstanding writer, and though, of course, his work has been superseded by more recent historians, his books remain both informative and enjoyable. Sumner's speech was published at the time: *The Crime against Kansas* (Boston: John P. Jewett & Company, 1856), and is accessible at the United States Senate website: https://www.senate.gov/artandhistory/history/minute/The_Crime_Against_Kansas.htm.

The speech is a jewel of nineteenth-century oratory, a time when great orators were the rock stars of the day, performing (in the days before microphones and amplifiers) before audiences of thousands. The great orators had stentorian voices, the endurance of a marathoner, the skills of an actor, and the verbal fluency of a playwright. The significance of the Brooks/Sumner affair is admirably summed up in Thomas A. Bailey's *The American Pageant: A History of the Republic,* 4th ed. (Lexington, MA: D. C. Heath, 1971), p. 424. This was my textbook in the eleventh grade, and I still read it for pleasure today. Too bad all textbooks cannot be this witty, insightful, and informative.

ACKNOWLEDGMENTS

PARIS DONEHOO

"Of making many books there is no end" (Ecclesiastes 12:12). The preacher's words should caution me about adding more verbiage to our information-glutted society, but I must express my gratitude for the experiences and support that have influenced these pages.

First, I must acknowledge the help and support of my coauthor, Keith Parsons. Our collaboration has been a delight throughout this process. I am in awe of his brilliance, wit, and thought-provoking insights. I had written for publication in the past, but the discipline has changed over the years, and Keith was patient with me as I dipped my toe into this brave new world. I treasure his friendship.

A weekly Sunday deadline over four decades has been an invaluable forum for developing ideas and honing ways to express them. Much of the material contained in these pages is the result of preaching and teaching real people, who have listened, complimented, complained, questioned, suggested, and supported me over the years. Therefore, I would like to thank the congregations of the Sardis Baptist Church in Palmetto, Georgia; the Lost Mountain Baptist Church in Powder Springs, Georgia; the Park Ridge Community Church in Park Ridge, Illinois; and the First Congregational United Church of Christ in Elgin, Illinois, for their contributions to this book. Their presence in the pews week in and week out has helped me to find my theological footing.

When I heard Ralph Klein verbally describe the connection between the Ten Commandments and the biblical concept of righteousness, I scribbled out a diagram not much better than a stick figure and used it in various teaching scenarios over the years. For use in this book, I knew I would need a much better rendition. Enter my good friend, Lindsay Iverson, who made it look incredibly professional and readable.

I am grateful for the memory of Brantley Seymour, who served as pastor of my home church, the First Baptist Church of Roswell, Georgia. Brantley not only provided a nurturing environment for my unfolding faith, but when I declared my intention to enter ministry, he took me under his wing and taught me more about being a pastor than I learned in seminary. His commitment to the Bible, and his social conscience, left an indelible mark on my life and my thinking.

Though I have never been under their direct tutelage, several theologians and preachers have been filtered through my mind to these pages. Tony Campolo gave me a voice for faith that engages society in progressive and inclusive ways while simultaneously being unapologetically Christian. John Claypool gave me the capacity for seeing a biblical passage like a prism that could be turned in the light for facets I would normally overlook. Fred Craddock gave me the gift of seeing life, and ultimately my writing about life, in narrative terms. I owe each of them my undying gratitude.

I am thankful for my colleague at the Elgin church, Lois Bucher, with whom I worked closely through my sixteen-year tenure. In between discussions about church programs, administrative details, and which parishioner had made us laugh, cry, or cuss that week, we bounced ideas off of each other as we struggled with how to be a church in these rapidly changing times. For several years we met together once a week to read scripture, pray, meditate, and explore our respective spiritual pilgrimages. Those moments shaped my thoughts for this book more than any committee meeting ever could.

I would be remiss if I did not acknowledge the indirect contributions of my parents—John and Peggy Donehoo—to this book. Almost from the beginning of my life, my mother sensed that I was destined for a life in ministry. She never breathed a word to me about it for fear of tugging me in a direction I was not meant to travel. The only nod she gave to her thoughts was the gift to me of a Bible at Christmas when I was six years old. When I came to her many years later to say I was pondering a life in ministry, she said, "I was wondering when you would come to me about this." My dad (God rest his soul) and I did not agree with each other on many issues—political, social, or theological—but he bestowed many gifts to me nonetheless. From him I learned the value of humor, the beauty of language, and the power of stories told well. His life also taught me that a faith without passion is no better than a museum artifact. I once gave him a book about the making of the King James Bible, and wrote on the flyleaf a line I adapted from Fred Craddock: "The Bible gave me The Word, but you gave me the words."

Finally, I am blessed with a wonderful family. My daughters, Meg Pfister and Kathryn Keenon, and my step-children, Rachel Georgakis and Matt Holihan, have been so supportive of this project. And my beautiful, intelligent, compassionate, feisty, Sicilian-born wife, Penny, has been encouraging me for many years to broaden the scope of my writing. She has always believed I had something worthwhile to say in the pulpit as well as beyond the pulpit. Her love and encouragement are two of God's greatest gifts to me.

ACKNOWLEDGMENTS

KEITH PARSONS

Of course, first thanks go to Paris for his eagerness to work with me on this project and, really, for being an ideal coauthor. It has been a genuine pleasure to interact with him over the past year, and an especially great pleasure reading his contributions. I once heard that great preaching "comforts the afflicted and afflicts the comfortable." Nobody does this better than Paris. In each of his contributions, the depth of his values, the power of his faith, and the strength of his intellect shine through. Also, like any good Southern preacher, he has a wealth of terrific stories that nail the point dead center.

I have worked with Prometheus Books on many occasions, and I am always deeply impressed by the professionalism of my longtime editor Steven L. Mitchell and his staff. Steven's uncompromising commitment to quality of content and to the highest production values surely has made Prometheus into the outstanding publishing venue that it is. Special thanks to Sheila Stewart for her fine job of copyediting.

As always, thanks to my wife, Carol Molina, who recognizes that even on weekends I must sequester myself for many hours at a time when working on book projects. My colleagues at the University of Houston–Clear Lake must also be thanked because writing is very time consuming, and that means that I shirk as many committees and service obligations as I can in good conscience. I try to do my fair share of committee work—but no more than that. I appreciate it when they take on more than their share.

342

My intellectual debts are so numerous that I would not know where to begin. Maybe my greatest debt is to the late, great John Hick. His introduction to the philosophy of religion was the first book I read on the subject, and its excellence hooked me. Much later in life, when reading *An Interpretation of Religion*, I found it truly eye-opening. Hick articulated my thoughts—inchoate at the time—that, while the project of natural theology was dead, and while my atheism was right for me, there are still fully rational people who remain religious. Hick showed me how that could be, and for that I will always be grateful. Everyone who truly wants to *understand* religion, and why some people are religious and others not—and not just pound the polemical drums—needs to sit down with Hick.

NOTES

INTRODUCTION

Donehoo

1. Anne Lamott, *Traveling Mercies: Some Thoughts on Faith* (New York: Pantheon Books, 1999), p. 135.

2. Will D. Campbell, *Brother to a Dragonfly* (1977; Jackson: University Press of Mississippi, 2018), p. 187.

3. Dietrich Bonhoeffer, *The Cost of Discipleship*. New York: Macmillan Paperbacks, 1963, pp. 45–48.

4. Philip Gulley and James Mulholland, *If Grace Is True: Why God Will Save Every Person*. (New York: HarperOne, 2003), p. 191.

5. Ibid., p. 140.

6. Unless stated otherwise, all scripture references are taken from the *New Revised Standard Version Bible*, copyright © 1989 the Division of Christian Education of the National Council of the Churches of Christ in the United States of America. Used by permission. All rights reserved worldwide.

7. John Claypool, *Tracks of a Fellow Struggler: Living and Growing Through Grief*, rev. ed. (Harrisburg, PA: Morehouse, 1995), p. 16.

INTRODUCTION

Parsons

1. Nicholas Everitt, *The Non-Existence of God* (London: Routledge, 2004); J. L. Mackie, *The Miracle of Theism: Arguments for and Against the*

Existence of God (Oxford: Oxford University Press, 1982); Michael Martin: *Atheism: A Philosophical Investigation* (Philadelphia: Temple University Press, 1990); Graham Oppy, *Naturalism and Religion: A Contemporary Philosophical Investigation* (London: Routledge, 2018).

2. John Hick, *An Interpretation of Religion: Human Responses to the Transcendent*, 2nd ed. (New Haven: Yale University Press, 2004).

WHAT IS TRUTHFULNESS?

Parsons

1. For a thorough study of the theories of truth, see Richard J. Kirkham, *Theories of Truth: A Critical Introduction* (Cambridge, MA: MIT Press, 1992). A shorter and more basic introduction is Frederick F. Schmitt, *Truth: A Primer* (Boulder, CO: Westview Press, 1995). A somewhat more technical but also more up-to-date introduction is Alexis G. Burgess and John P. Burgess, *Truth* (Princeton: Princeton University Press, 2011).

2. Michael P. Lynch, *True to Life: Why Truth Matters* (Cambridge, MA: MIT Press, 2005).

3. George Orwell, "Politics and the English Language," in *The Orwell Reader: Fiction, Essays, and Reportage* (New York: Harcourt, Brace, and World, 1956), pp. 355–66.

4. For an excellent summary of Kahneman and Tversky's work and other research on cognitive illusions, see Massimo Piattelli-Palmarini, *Inevitable Illusions: How Mistakes of Reasoning Rule Our Minds* (New York: John Wiley & Sons, 1994). See also Michael Shermer, *The Believing Brain: From Ghosts and Gods to Politics and Conspiracies—How We Construct Beliefs and Reinforce Them as Truths* (New York: Henry Holt, 2011).

5. Scott Adams, "Rent a Weasel," *Dilbert*, October 31, 2007, http://dilbert.com/strip/2007-10-31.

6. Naomi Oreskes and Erik M. Conway, *Merchants of Doubt: How a Handful of Scientists Obscured the Truth on Issues from Tobacco Smoke to Global Warming* (New York: Bloomsbury Press, 2010).

7. "The 97% Consensus on Global Warming," Skeptical Science, last updated January 29, 2017, https://www.skepticalscience.com/global -warming-scientific-consensus-intermediate.htm.

8. The CDC makes it clear that vaccines do not cause autism: "Vaccines Do Not Cause Autism," Centers for Disease Control and Prevention, last updated November 23, 2015, https://www.cdc.gov/ vaccinesafety/concerns/autism.html.

WHAT IS TRUTHFULNESS?

Donehoo

1. Peter B. Panagore, *Two Minutes for God: Quick Fixes for the Spirit* (New York: Touchstone Faith Books, 2007), p. 73.

2. Eugene Scott, "Trump Believes in God, But Hasn't Sought Forgiveness," CNN Politics, July 18, 2015, https://www.cnn.com/2015/ 07/18/politics/trump-has-never-sought-forgiveness/index.html.

ARE WE IN THE POST-TRUTH ERA?

Parsons

1. See Robert B. Strassler, ed., *The Landmark Herodotus: The Histories*, trans. Andrea L. Purvis (New York: Anchor Books, 2007), p. 35.

2. Plato uses this phrase several times. One place is in the *Apology*, *The Dialogues of Plato*, trans. Benjamin Jowett, vol. 1 (New York: Random House, 1937), p. 402.

3. On the sophists, see Anthony Gottlieb, *The Dream of Reason: A History of Western Philosophy from the Greeks to the Renaissance* (New York: W. W. Norton, 2000), pp. 109–28.

4. Daniel Levitin, *Weaponized Lies: How to Think Critically in the Post-Truth Era* (New York: Dutton, 2016).

5. See also the classic by Darrell Huff, *How to Lie with Statistics* (New York: W. W. Norton, 1954).

6. Keith Parsons, *Rational Episodes: Logic for the Intermittently Reasonable* (Amherst, NY: Prometheus Books, 2010).

7. Richard Hofstadter, *Anti-Intellectualism in American Life* (New York: Vintage Books, 1966).

8. Chris Mooney and Sheril Kirshenbaum, *Unscientific America: How Scientific Illiteracy Threatens Our Future* (New York: Basic Books, 2009); Mark Bauerlein, *The Dumbest Generation: How the Digital Age Stupefies Young Americans and Jeopardizes our Future* (New York: Jeremy P. Tarcher/ Penguin, 2008).

9. Charles P. Pierce, *Idiot America: How Stupidity Became a Virtue in the Land of the Free* (New York: Anchor Books, 2010).

10. See PolitiFact Texas: W. Gardiner Selby, "Did Greg Abbott Activate Texas Troops to Monitor Jade Helm 15?" PolitiFact, May 3, 2018, http://www.politifact.com/texas/article/2018/may/03/jade-helm-15 -greg-abbott-texas-state-guard-hayden-/.

11. Mike Lofgren, *The Party Is Over: How Republicans Went Crazy, Democrats Became Useless, and the Middle Class Got Shafted* (New York: Viking, 2012).

12. Mark Green, "The Great Communicator or the Great Prevaricator?" introduction to *There He Goes Again: Ronald Reagan's Reign of Error*, by Mark Green and Gail MacColl (New York: Pantheon Books, 1983), pp. 8–19.

13. Green and MacColl, *There He Goes Again*, p. 85.

14. Josh Levin, "The Welfare Queen," *Slate*, December 19, 2013, http:// www.slate.com/articles/news_and_politics/history/2013/12/linda_taylor _welfare_queen_ronald_reagan_made_her_a_notorious_american_villain.html.

15. Green and MacColl, *There He Goes Again*, p. 44.

16. "Al Smith Memorial Dinner," C-SPAN, October 19, 2000, video, 0:20, https://www.c-span.org/video/?c4506459/haves-mores.

17. One of the best accounts of the lies and deceptions leading to the Second Gulf War is Frank Rich, *The Greatest Story Ever Sold: The Decline and Fall of Truth from 9/11 to Katrina* (New York: Penguin, 2006).

18. "Does Your Dog Bite?" *The Pink Panther Strikes Again*, directed by Blake Edwards (Amjo Productions, 1976).

19. The definitive account of the Bush administration's manipulation of public opinion is Ben Fritz, Bryan Keefer, and Brendan Nyhan, *All the President's Spin: George W. Bush, the Media, and the Truth* (New York: Simon & Schuster, 2004).

20. Alex Nowrasteh, "Everything Is Bigger in Texas—Except the Illegal Immigrant Crime Rate," *Houston Chronicle*, March 12, 2018, p. A11, https://www.houstonchronicle.com/opinion/outlook/article/ Everything-is-Bigger-in-Texas-Except-the-12747805.php. Nowrasteh, of the libertarian Cato Institute, shows that both conviction and arrest rates for undocumented immigrants is lower than that for the native population. Trump's image of swarms of drug dealers, rapists, and murderers streaming across the border to do mayhem in the United States is a malicious lie. Nowrasteh replies to his critics in *Reason* magazine: Alex Nowrasteh, "Restrictionists Are Misleading You about Immigrant Crime Rates," *Reason*, February 1, 2018, https://reason.com/archives/2018/02/01/ immigrants-and-crime.

21. David Leonhardt and Stuart H. Thompson, "Trump's Lies," *New York Times*, December 14, 2017, https://www.nytimes.com/ interactive/2017/06/23/opinion/trumps-lies.html.

A follow-up story showed that in his first ten months in office Trump told nearly six times as many lies as Obama told in his whole presidency: David Leonhardt, Ian Prasad Philbrick, and Stuart A. Thompson, "Trump's Lies vs. Obama's," *New York Times*, December 14, 2017, https://www .nytimes.com/interactive/2017/12/14/opinion/sunday/trump-lies-obama -who-is-worse.html.

ARE WE IN THE POST-TRUTH ERA?

Donehoo

1. Dave Tabler, "A School for Subversives and Communists?" *Appalachian History: Stories, Quotes, and Anecdotes,* January 19, 2015, http://www.appalachianhistory.net/2015/01/school-for-subversives-and-communists.html.

2. For this insight into the Genesis narrative I am indebted to a sermon delivered by the late John Claypool at the Furman University Pastor's School sometime in the mid-1980s. The exact date has been lost to me in the mists of time.

3. Melissa Quinn, "Trump Praises Greg Gianforte: 'Any Guy That Can Do a Body Slam, He's My Kind of Guy,'" *Washington Examiner,* October 18, 2018, https://www.washingtonexaminer.com/news/trump-praises-greg-gianforte-any-guy-that-can-do-a-body-slam-hes-my-kind-of-guy.

4. David A. Fahrenthold, "Trump Recorded Having Extremely Lewd Conversation about Women in 2005," *Washington Post,* October 8, 2016, https://www.washingtonpost.com/politics/trump-recorded-having-extremely-lewd-conversation-about-women-in-2005/2016/10/07/3b9ce776-8cb4-11e6-bf8a-3d26847eeed4_story.

5. Jeremy Diamond, "Trump: I Could 'Shoot Somebody and I Wouldn't Lose Voters,'" CNN, January 24, 2016, https://www.cnn.com/2016/01/23/politics/donald-trump-shoot-somebody-support/index.html.

6. Steve Reilly, "Hundreds Allege Donald Trump Doesn't Pay His Bills," *USA Today,* June 9, 2016, https://www.usatoday.com/story/news/politics/elections/2016/06/09/donald-trump-unpaid-bills-republican-president-laswuits/85297274/.

7. Gregory A. Smith and Jessica Martinez, "How the Faithful Voted: A Preliminary 2016 Analysis," Pew Research Fact Tank, Washington, DC, November 9, 2016, http://www.pewresearch.org/fact-tank/2016/11/09/how-the-faithful-voted-a-preliminary-2016-analysis/.

8. George Bernard Shaw, *Man and Superman* (1903; London: Penguin Books, 2000), p. 257.

9. *Seinfeld*, season 6, episode 15, "The Beard," directed by Andy Ackerman, written by Carol Leifer, aired February 9, 1995, on CBS.

WHAT IS THE VALUE OF TRUTH?

Parsons

1. Richard Rhodes, *The Making of the Atomic Bomb* (New York: Simon & Schuster, 1985), p. 675. Rhodes's account of the Trinity test is possibly the greatest piece of historical writing that I have ever read.

2. Cited in Michael P. Lynch, *True to Life: Why Truth Matters* (Cambridge, MA: MIT Press, 2005), p. 95.

3. Stephen Jay Gould, *The Mismeasure of Man* (New York: W. W. Norton, 1981).

4. Paul Gross and Norman Levitt, *Higher Superstition: The Academic Left and Its Quarrels with Science* (Baltimore: Johns Hopkins University Press, 1994).

5. Alan Sokal, *Beyond the Hoax: Science, Philosophy, and Culture* (Oxford: Oxford University Press, 2008).

6. James Osborne, "Lamar Smith Sows Disorder as Climate Change Debate Rages," *Houston Chronicle*, April 9, 2017, https://www.houston chronicle.com/business/article/Lamar-Smith-sows-disorder-as-climate -debate-rages-11061772.php.

7. "Rep. Lamar Smith—Texas District 21: Top Industries 2015– 2016," OpenSecrets.org, data released November 27, 2017, https://www .opensecrets.org/members-of-congress/industries?cid=N00001811& cycle=2016.

8. Seth Shulman et al., *Smoke, Mirrors, & Hot Air: How ExxonMobil Uses Big Tobacco's Tactics to Manufacture Uncertainty on Climate Science* (Cambridge, MA: Union of Concerned Scientists, January 2007), https://

www.ucsusa.org/sites/default/files/legacy/assets/documents/global
_warming/exxon_report.pdf.

9. "How the NRA Suppressed Gun Violence Research," *The Disinformation Playbook*, Union of Concerned Scientists, https://www
.ucsusa.org/suppressing-research-effects-gun-violence#.W9CosktKiUk.

10. Shawn Otto, *The War on Science: Who's Waging It, Why It Matters, What We Can Do About It* (Minneapolis: Milkweed Editions, 2016), pp.
314–16.

11. Ted Barrett, "Inhofe Brings Snowball on Senate Floor as Evidence Globe Is Not Warming," CNN, February 27, 2015, https://www.cnn
.com/2015/02/26/politics/james-inhofe-snowball-climate-change/index
.html.

12. Otto, *War on Science*, p. 318.

13. National Center for Science Education, https://ncse.com/.

14. Barbara J. King, "Fact Check: Science and the Trump Administration," NPR, January 22, 2017, https://www.npr.org/
sections/13.7/2017/01/22/510384513/fact-check-science-and
-the-trump-administration.

15. Alan Burdick, "Donald Trump's Know-Nothing Science Budget," *New Yorker*, March 4, 2018, https://www.newyorker.com/news/
daily-comment/donald-trumps-know-nothing-science-budget.

WHAT IS THE VALUE OF TRUTH?

Donehoo

1. James Weldon Johnson, "The Creation," in *God's Trombones: Seven Negro Sermons in Verse* (New York: Penguin Books, 1976), p. 15.

2. John Dominic Crossan, *God and Empire: Jesus against Rome, Then and Now* (New York: HarperOne, 2007), p. 28.

3. "The Virtues We Need in a Post-Truth World," *Christian Century* 134, no. 1 (January 4, 2017): 7.

4. Ibid.

5. Lawrence Cunningham, "Stairways to Heaven" *Notre Dame Magazine*, Autumn 2002, https://magazine.nd.edu/news/stairways-to-heaven/.

6. Michael White, Graham Chapman, John Cleese, Eric Idle, *Monty Python and the Holy Grail*, directed by Terry Gilliam (Culver City, CA: National Film Trustee Company, Python [Monty] Pictures, 1974).

7. Darlene Superville, "Trump Addresses Faith and Freedom Coalition Conference During Comey Testimony," PBS, June 8, 2017, https://www.pbs.org/newshour/politics/watch-live-trump-addresses-faith-freedom-coalition-conference-comey-testimony.

8. Anthony Robinson, *Transforming Congregational Culture* (Grand Rapids, MI: William B. Eerdmans, 2003), p. 25.

9. David Kinnaman and Gabe Lyons, *Unchristian: What a New Generation Really Thinks about Christianity* (Grand Rapids, MI: Baker Books, 2007), pp. 29–30.

10. Peter Beinart, "Breaking Faith," *Atlantic*, April 2017, https://www.theatlantic.com/magazine/archive/2017/04/breaking-faith/517785/.

HOW DO WE RESTORE RESPECT FOR TRUTH AND TRUTHFULNESS?

Parsons

1. Michel de Montaigne, "Of Cripples," *The Essays* (*Les Essais*) (Paris: Abel Langelier, 1588), book 3, chap. 11.

2. Ari Rabin-Havt and Media Matters, *Lies, Incorporated: The World of Post-Truth Politics* (New York: Anchor Books, 2016), p. 190.

3. On the percentage of Americans who do not accept evolution see David Masci, "For Darwin Day, 6 Facts about the Evolution Debate," Fact Tank, Pew Research Center, February 10, 2017, http://www.pewresearch.org/fact-tank/2017/02/10/darwin-day/.

On the truth of evolution see Jerry A. Coyne, *Why Evolution Is True* (New York: Viking, 2009).

One of the best books on evolution is Neil Shubin, *Your Inner Fish: A Journey into the 3.5-Billion-Year History of the Human Body* (New York: Pantheon Books, 2008).

A thorough presentation of creationist arguments and sources for debunking them is: Mark Isaak, *The Counter-Creationism Handbook* (Berkeley: University of California Press, 2007).

4. See, for example, Kenneth R. Weiss, "Washington Talk; States Circle Their Wagons for the Money Wars," *New York Times*, April 25, 1989, https://www.nytimes.com/1989/04/25/us/washington-talk-states-circle -their-wagons-for-the-money-wars.html.

5. On the Heartland Institute, see Naomi Oreskes and Erik M. Conway, *Merchants of Doubt: How a Handful of Scientists Obscured the Truth on Issues from Tobacco Smoke to Global Warming* (New York: Bloomsbury Press, 2010).

6. See Rabin-Havt and Media Matters, *Lies Incorporated*, pp. xi–xvii.

HOW DO WE RESTORE RESPECT FOR TRUTH AND TRUTHFULNESS?

Donehoo

1. Tony Campolo, "What's a Red Letter Christian?" Beliefnet, February 2006, https://www.beliefnet.com/faiths/christianity/2006/02/ whats-a-red-letter-christian.aspx.

2. Rod Dreher, "Trump Can't Save American Christianity," *New York Times*, August 2, 2017, https://www.nytimes.com/2017/08/02/opinion/ trump-scaramucci-evangelical-christian.html.

3. Ralph Drollinger, interview by Jennifer Wishon, "Bible Studies at the White House: Who's Inside This Spiritual Awakening?" Christian Broadcasting Network, July 31, 2017, http://www1.cbn.com/cbnnews/ politics/2017/july/bible-studies-at-the-white-house-whos-at-the-heart-of -this-spiritual-awakening.

4. Dietrich Bonhoeffer, *Letters and Papers from Prison* (New York: Simon and Schuster Touchstone ed., 1997), p. 8.

5. Rod Dreher, "Trump Can't Save American Christianity," *New York Times*, August 2, 2017, https://www.nytimes.com/2017/08/02/opinion/trump-scaramucci-evangelical-christian.html.

6. Stanley Hauerwas and William H. Willimon, *Resident Aliens: A Provocative Christian Assessment of Culture and Ministry for People Who Know That Something Is Wrong* (Nashville: Abingdon, 1989), p. 32.

7. Ibid., p. 38.

8. Michael Piazza and Cameron B. Trimble, *Liberating Hope!: Daring to Renew the Mainline Church* (Cleveland: Pilgrim, 2011), Kindle, loc. 3177 of 3519.

9. Bonhoeffer, *Letters and Papers from Prison*, p. 9.

10. Tony Campolo, *Let Me Tell You a Story: Life Lessons from Unexpected Places and Unlikely People* (Nashville: W. Publishing Group, 2000), pp. 117–19.

CONCLUDING THOUGHTS ON TRUTH

Donehoo

1. Adam Sternbergh, "Stephen Colbert Has America by the Ballots," *New York Magazine*, October 16, 2006, http://nymag.com/news/politics/22322/.

2. "The Word—Truthiness," *The Colbert Report*, October 17, 2005, video, 2:55, http://www.cc.com/video-clips/63ite2/the-colbert-report-the-word---truthiness.

3. Samantha Schmidt and Lindsey Bever, "Kellyanne Conway Cites 'Bowling Green Massacre' That Never Happened to Defend Travel Ban," *Washington Post*, February 3, 2017, https://www.washingtonpost.com/news/morning-mix/wp/2017/02/03/kellyanne-conway-cites-bowling-green-massacre-that-never-happened-to-defend-travel-ban/?utm_term=.d4eefe99de9a.

4. "'That Day in Bowling Green' Written by Dave Stinton," YouTube

video, 2:12, posted by Nick and Gabe, February 3, 2017, https://www
.youtube.com/watch?v=-api7B5x9E0.

WHAT IS CIVILITY?

Donehoo

1. Mike Lester, "Death of Civil Discourse," *The Moderate Voice*, April 1, 2010, http://themoderatevoice.com/death-of-civil-discourse/.
2. David Goldfield, *America Aflame: How the Civil War Created a Nation* (New York: Bloomsbury), Kindle, p. 116.
3. Tradition ascribes authorship of this book to the apostle Paul. Most modern scholars, however, think it more likely to have been written later, perhaps by one of Paul's followers.
4. Eliza Relman, "Sarah Huckabee Sanders Defends Trump's Attacks on Mika Brzezinski: 'When the President Gets Hit, He's Going to Hit Back Harder,'" *Business Insider*, June 29, 2017, https://www.businessinsider.com/sarah-huckabee-sanders-defends-trump-tweets-on-mika-brzezinski-facelift-2017-6.

WHAT IS CIVILITY?

Parsons

1. This, of course, is Kant's second formulation of the Categorical Imperative in *Groundwork of the Metaphysics of Morals* (1785).
2. Jonathan Haidt, *The Righteous Mind: Why Good People Are Divided by Politics and Religion* (New York: Vintage Books, 2012).
3. Vincent Fitzpatrick, *H. L. Mencken* (Macon, GA: Mercer University Press, 1989), p. 141.

HAS CIVILITY BROKEN DOWN IN OUR DAY?

Donehoo

1. David Bianculli, *Dangerously Funny: The Uncensored Story of* The Smothers Brothers Comedy Hour (New York: Simon & Schuster 2009), p. 317.

2. Burt Constable, "Guns and Christmas an Unholy Mix for One Advocate," *Daily Herald* (Suburban Chicago), November 9, 2017, https://www.dailyherald.com/news/20171109/constable-guns-and-christmas-an-unholy-mix-for-one-advocate.

3. Philip Gorski, "Becoming America," *Christian Century* 134, no. 5 (March 1, 2017): 29.

4. Ibid., p. 30.

5. Steve Peoples, "GOP Leaders Bolt from Moore after Sex Claim," *Daily Herald* (Suburban Chicago), November 9, 2017, https://www.dailyherald.com/article/20171109/news/311099836/.

6. Nicole Gaouette, "Despite Haley Threat, UN Votes to Condemn Trump's Jerusalem Decision," CNN Politics, December 22, 2017, https://www.cnn.com/2017/12/21/politics/haley-un-jerusalem/index.html.

HAS CIVILITY BROKEN DOWN IN OUR DAY?

Parsons

1. Keith M. Parsons, "Message to My Freshman Students," *Huffington Post*, May 14, 2015, https://www.huffingtonpost.com/keith-m-parsons/message-to-my-freshman-st_b_7275016.html.

2. I am not going to try to document each of these incidents. They were extremely well publicized during the campaign and are only a click or two of a mouse away if anyone wants to confirm their occurrence.

3. Arianna Huffington, *Pigs at the Trough: How Corporate Greed and Political Corruption Are Undermining America* (New York: Crown, 2003).

WHY IS CIVILITY SO IMPORTANT?

Donehoo

1. Patrick Buchanan, "1992 Republican National Convention Speech," August 17, 1992, http://buchanan.org/blog/1992 -republican-national-convention-speech-148.

2. Sarah Pulliam Bailey, "Southern Baptist Seminary Drops Bombshell: Why Paige Patterson Was Fired," *Washington Post*, June 1, 2018, https://www.washingtonpost.com/news/acts-of-faith/wp/2018/06/01/ southern-baptist-seminary-drops-bombshell-why-paige-patterson-was-fired.

3. Quoted in Ralph Douglas West, *Finding Fullness Again: What the Book of Ruth Teaches Us about Starting Over* (Nashville: Broadman and Holman, 2006), p. 38.

4. Alan Fram and Jonathan Lemire, "Trump: Why Allow Immigrants from 'Shithole' Countries?" Associated Press, January 12, 2018, https:// www.apnews.com/fdda2ff0b877416c8ae1c1a77a3cc425.

5. Brent D. Griffiths, "Trump: 'I Am the Least Racist Person You Have Ever Interviewed,'" *Politico*, January 14, 2018, https://www.politico .com/story/2018/01/14/trump-least-racist-person-340602.

6. Melissa Guillebeau, Facebook post, January 12, 2018. Used by permission.

7. Edward Helmore, "Trump New York Co-Chair Makes Racist 'Gorilla' Comment about Michelle Obama," *Guardian*, December 24, 2016, https://www.theguardian.com/us-news/2016/dec/23/donald -trump-carl-paladino-michelle-obama.

8. Scripture taken from *The Message*. Copyright © 1993, 1994, 1995, 1996, 2000, 2001, 2002. Used by permission of NavPress Publishing Group.

9. C. S. Lewis, *The Great Divorce* (New York: Macmillan, 1946), pp. 18–19.

10. Events recreated by recollections and conversations with Rev. Gary Blobaum. Used by permission.

11. Alexander Bolton, "Schumer: Negotiating with Trump

'Like Negotiating with Jell-O,'" *Hill*, January 20, 2018, https://thehill
.com/homenews/senate/369929-schumer-working-with-trump
-like-negotiating-with-jello.

   12. Walter Wink, *Engaging the Powers: Discernment and Resistance in
a World of Domination* (Minneapolis: Augsburg Fortress Press, 1992), pp.
175–84.

   13. Cheryl Phibbs, *The Montgomery Bus Boycott: A History and
Reference Guide.* (Santa Barbara, CA: ABC-CLIO, 2009), p. 65.

WHY IS CIVILITY SO IMPORTANT?

Parsons

   1. Leslie Casimir, "Data Show Nigerians the Most Educated in the
U.S.," *Houston Chronicle*, January 12, 2018, https://www.chron.com/news/
article/Data-show-Nigerians-the-most-educated-in-the-U-S-1600808.php.

   2. As this book was being completed, Trump and Kim Jong Un
met for talks at Singapore on June 12, 2018. However, it appears that very
little of substance was gained by these talks. I predict that they will be back
sneering at each other within months. A photo-op meeting is not enough to
get leopards to change their spots.

   3. The interview was in the episode "The World's Biggest Bomb,"
season 11, episode 7, of the program *Secrets of the Dead*, written by
Andy Webb, aired May 16, 2011 (Arlington, VA: PBS, 2011). It can be
accessed at: http://www.pbs.org/wnet/secrets/the-world
%E2%80%99s-biggest-bomb-about-this-episode/846/.

   4. David Eagleman, *The Brain: The Story of You* (New York:
Pantheon Books, 2015), pp. 147–58.

HOW DO WE RESTORE CIVILITY?

Donehoo

1. Matt Sedensky and Maryclaire Dale, "Synagogue Attack Shatters Safety of Longtime Jewish Enclave," AP News, October 28, 2018, https://www.apnews.com/1a8c6af98e254aaa85d987bf8fc89e54.

2. Gregory Korte, "Trump Blasts 'Treasonous' Democrats for Not Applauding at His State of the Union Address," *USA Today*, February 5, 2018, https://www.usatoday.com/story/news/politics/2018/02/05/trump-blasts-treasonous-democrats-not-applauding-his-state-union-address/301962002/.

3. William Jones, sermon, Furman University Pastor's School, Greenville, SC, 1979.

4. Jim Wallis and Chuck Colson, "Conviction and Civility," *Christianity Today*, January 24, 2011, https://www.christianitytoday.com/ct/2011/januaryweb-only/convictioncivility.html.

5. Ibid.

HOW DO WE RESTORE CIVILITY?

Parsons

1. There are many good editions and translations, but a recent one that has received much praise is Robert C. Bartlett and Susan D. Collins, *Aristotle's Nicomachean Ethics* (Chicago: University of Chicago Press, 2011).

2. These restrictions apply not just to anger, but to all of our emotions. See Book II, chapter 5 of the *Nicomachean Ethics*.

CONCLUDING THOUGHTS ON CIVILITY

Donehoo

1. Mark Twain, *Letters from the Earth* (New York: Harper Perennial, 2013), EPUB, pp. 187–88.
2. *New International Version*, copyright © 1973, 1978, 1984, 2011 by Biblica, Inc., used by permission. All rights reserved worldwide.
3. Rick Bragg, "The Best of Who We Are," *Southern Living*, October 2017, p. 136, https://www.southernliving.com/culture/rick-bragg -charlottesville.
4. Ibid.

CONCLUDING THOUGHTS ON CIVILITY

Parsons

1. Alison Gopnik, "A Cure for Contempt," *Atlantic*, April 2018, pp. 39–41.
2. Brady Dennis, "Pollution Kills 9 Million People Each Year, New Study Finds," *Washington Post*, October 19, 2017, https://www .washingtonpost.com/news/energy-environment/wp/2017/10/19/ pollution-kills-9-million-people-each-year-new-study-finds/?utm_term =.dbd0e3e94368.
3. Rebecca Leber, "Toxic Avenger," *Mother Jones*, March/April 2018, pp. 22–31, https://www.motherjones.com/politics/2018/02/ scott-pruitt-profile-epa-trump/.

WHAT IS COMMUNITY IN A PLURALISTIC SOCIETY?

Parsons

1. Sadly, this passage was written before the massacre at the Tree of Life synagogue in the beautiful Squirrel Hill neighborhood where I used to walk. The alleged shooter is a crazed anti-Semite who was apparently acting on hateful lies promulgated by Trump and other right-wing promoters of conspiracy theories. Religious tolerance is still one of our society's greatest achievements, even though all it takes to violate it is one unhinged and heavily armed fanatic who believes and acts on the words of hatred.

2. "Changing Attitudes on Gay Marriage," Pew Research Center, Washington, DC, June 26, 2017, http://www.pewforum.org/fact-sheet/changing-attitudes-on-gay-marriage/.

3. Albert Camus, *The Plague* (New York: Vintage, 1991).

4. Stephan Pastis, "What Is Happening to the Country I Knew?" *Pearls Before Swine*, March 9, 2018, https://www.gocomics.com/pearls beforeswine/2018/03/09.

5. For a thorough and critical discussion of Kuhn's claims about "paradigms" and "different worlds," see Keith Parsons, *It Started with Copernicus: Vital Questions about Science* (Amherst, NY: Prometheus Books, 2015).

WHAT IS COMMUNITY IN A PLURALISTIC SOCIETY?

Donehoo

1. Graham Chapman, John Cleese, Terry Gilliam, et al., *The Complete Monty Python's Flying Circus: All the Words*, vol. 1 (New York: Pantheon Books, 1989), pp. 102–103.

2. Scott Peck, *The Different Drum: Community Making and Peace* (New York: Simon and Schuster, 1987), p. 88.

3. Ibid., pp. 13–15.

HOW HAS DIVISIVENESS BECOME SO EXTREME?

Parsons

1. Michael Grunwald, "The Victory of 'No,'" *Politico*, December 4, 2016, https://www.politico.com/magazine/story/2016/12/republican-party-obstructionism-victory-trump-214498.

2. Ibid.

3. Amy Lynn Smith, "10 Ideas Republicans Loved Until Barack Obama Became President," *Eclectablog*, August 22, 2013, http://www.eclectablog.com/2013/08/10-ideas-republicans-loved-until-barack-obama-became-president.html.

4. Eric Mack, "Politico: Democrats Going Full Obstructionist," Newsmax, April 30, 2017, https://www.newsmax.com/politics/democrats-obstruct-trump-no/2017/04/30/id/787260/.

5. Wikipedia, s.v. "Golda Meir," last edited April 9, 2018, https://en.wikiquote.org/wiki/Golda_Meir.

6. Youyou Zhou, "Three Percent of the Population Own Half of the Civilian Guns in the US," *Quartz*, October 6, 2017, https://qz.com/1095899/gun-ownership-in-america-in-three-charts/.

7. Christopher Ingraham, "Nobody Knows How Many Members the NRA Has, But Its Tax Returns Offer Some Clues," *Washington Post*, February 26, 2018, https://www.washingtonpost.com/news/wonk/wp/2018/02/26/nobody-knows-how-many-members-the-nra-has-but-its-tax-returns-offer-some-clues/?utm_term=.1d2b8cf01915.

8. Bloomberg, "Most Gun Owners Support Stricter Laws—Even NRA Members," *Time*, March 13, 2018, http://time.com/5197807/stricter-gun-laws-nra/.

9. Lauren Fox, "NRA Chief Accuses Democrats of Pushing 'Socialist' Agenda in Wake of Florida Shooting," CNN, February 23, 2018, https://www.cnn.com/2018/02/22/politics/wayne-lapierre-cpac-speech-nra/index.html.

10. Joshua Greene, *Moral Tribes: Emotion, Reason, and the Gap between Us and Them* (New York: Penguin, 2013).

HOW HAS DIVISIVENESS BECOME SO EXTREME?

Donehoo

1. Stanley Hauerwas and William H. Willimon, *Resident Aliens: A Provocative Christian Assessment of Culture and Ministry for People Who Know That Something Is Wrong* (Nashville: Abingdon, 1989), p. 38.

2. Bridget Mary Meehan, "For I Was Hungry and You Cut My Food Stamps . ." *Bridget Mary's Blog*, Association of Roman Catholic Women Priests, March 26, 2018, http://bridgetmarys.blogspot.com/2018/03/for-i-was-hungry-and-you-cut-my-food.html.

3. Michael Piazza, "Our Silence Will Not Save Us," *Liberating Word*, March 15, 2018, http://web-extract.constantcontact.com/v1/social_annotation?permalink_uri=2DrhOfj&image_url=https%3A%2F%2Fmlsvc01-prod.s3.amazonaws.com%2Fbb2deeec001%2Fbee02d0c-6b81-4c8a-b6f3-6aa93a288e36.jpg%3Fver%3D1521061042000.

4. Found only in the 1947 version of Gustave Gilbert, *Nuremberg Diary* (New York: Farrar, Straus), last paragraph of chap. 12, "Frank's Defense."

5. "George Wallace on Segregation, 1964," *History Now*, Gilder Lehrman Institute of American History, https://www.gilderlehrman.org/content/george-wallace-segregation-1964.

6. Terry Gross, "Madeleine Albright Warns: Don't Let Fascism Go 'Unnoticed Until It's Too Late,'" *Fresh Air*, NPR, April 3, 2018, https://www.npr.org/2018/04/03/599120190/madeleine-albright-warns-dont-let-fascism-go-unnoticed-until-its-too-late.

7. Jim Wallis, *God's Politics: Why the Right Gets It Wrong and the Left Doesn't Get It* (San Francisco: HarperCollins, 2005), p. 225.

8. John Bowden, "Comey Says Trump Reacted to News of Russian Meddling by Asking If It Changed Election Results," *Hill*, April 14, 2018, https://thehill.com/homenews/administration/383205-comey-says-trump-reacted-to-news-of-russian-meddling-by-asking-if-it.

9. Fred Craddock, *Preaching as Storytelling*, Furman University Pastor's School, Greenville, SC, 1981, audio CD.

10. John Dominic Crossan, *The Greatest Prayer: Rediscovering the Revolutionary Message of the Lord's Prayer* (New York: HarperOne, 2010), Kindle, pp. 171–72.

WHAT IS THE VALUE OF COMMUNITY?

Parsons

1. The quote, "I fear all we have done is to awaken a sleeping giant and fill him with a terrible resolve," is portrayed in the film *Tora! Tora! Tora!* directed by Richard Fleischer, Toshio Masuda, and Kinji Fukasaku (Los Angeles, CA: 20th Century Fox, 1970).

2. The phrase "the good war" is from the Pulitzer Prize-winning oral history of the Second World War, Studs Terkel, *The Good War: An Oral History of World War II* (New York: New Press, 1997).

3. Quoted in Justin Driver, "The Report on Race That Shook America," *Atlantic* 321, no. 4 (May 2018): 34, available online at https://www.theatlantic.com/magazine/archive/2018/05/the-report-on-race-that-shook-america/556850/.

4. Ibid., p. 35.

5. Ibid., p. 36.

6. Shelby Webb, "Could Texas Take Over Houston ISD? And Why Are People So Upset?" *Houston Chronicle*, April 25, 2018, https://www.houstonchronicle.com/news/education/article/Q-A-What-s-happening-in-Houston-ISD-12863537.php.

7. Dylan Baddour, "Latinos Soon to Outnumber Whites in Texas," *Houston Chronicle*, July 10, 2015, https://www.houstonchronicle.com/news/article/Latinos-soon-to-outnumber-whites-in-Texas-6378873.php.

8. Booker T. Washington, *An Address on Abraham Lincoln: Delivered Before the Republican Club of New York City on the Night of February Twelfth, 1909*, https://archive.org/details/addressonabraham00wash, pp. 6–7.

9. Karsten Strauss, "The Most—and Least—Educated States in the US in 2018," *Forbes*, February 1, 2018, https://www.forbes.com/sites/karstenstrauss/2018/02/01/the-most-and-least-educated-states-in-the-u-s-in-2018/#3aa44ddb51e1; Wikipedia, s.v. "List of US States and Territories by Life Expectancy," last edited September 16, 2018, https://en.wikipedia.org/wiki/List_of_U.S._states_and_territories_by_life_expectancy; "Best States Rankings: Measuring Outcomes for Citizens Using More than 75 Metrics," *U.S. News & World Report*, last updated May 14, 2018, https://www.usnews.com/news/best-states/rankings.

10. Doug Rand, "Want to Get Rich? Embrace Foreign Workers," *Houston Chronicle*, April 15, 2018, p. A 34, available online as "Want to Get Rich? Let in More Immigrants," https://www.houstonchronicle.com/opinion/outlook/article/Want-to-get-rich-Let-in-more-immigrants-Opinion-12836559.php#photo-15400316.

11. Ibid.

12. Ibid.

13. Moustafa Bayoumi, "How the 'Homophobic Muslim' Became a Populist Bogeyman," *Guardian*, August 7, 2017, https://www.theguardian.com/commentisfree/2017/aug/07/homophobic-muslim-populist-bogeyman-trump-le-pen.

WHAT IS THE VALUE OF COMMUNITY?

Donehoo

1. Abraham Lincoln, "House Divided Speech," Springfield, IL, June 16, 1858, http://www.abrahamlincolnonline.org/lincoln/speeches/house.htm.

2. Stanley Hauerwas and William H. Willimon, *Resident Aliens: A Provocative Christian Assessment of Culture and Ministry for People Who Know That Something Is Wrong* (Nashville: Abingdon, 1989), p. 12.

3. Jill Colvin and Zeke Miller, "Trump Says Democrat Should Quit

over VA Nomination Brouhaha," AP News, April 28, 2018, https://www
.apnews.com/906125fd63044879912c8c57ffc5ec36.

4. Tom Kertscher, "Donald Trump's Racial Comments about
Hispanic Judge in Trump University Case," PolitiFact Wisconsin, June
8, 2016, https://www.politifact.com/wisconsin/article/2016/jun/08/
donald-trumps-racial-comments-about-judge-trump-un/.

5. Kevin Quealy, "Trump Is on Track to Insult 650 People, Places,
and Things on Twitter by the End of His First Term," *New York Times*, July
26, 2017, https://www.nytimes.com/interactive/2017/07/26/upshot/
president-trumps-newest-focus-discrediting-the-news-media-obamacare
.html.

6. Yoni Appelbaum, "I Alone Can Fix It," *Atlantic*, July 21, 2016,
https://www.theatlantic.com/politics/archive/2016/07/trump-rnc
-speech-alone-fix-it/492557/.

7. Rodney Stark, *The Rise of Christianity: How the Obscure, Marginal
Jesus Movement Became the Dominant Religious Force in the Western World
in a Few Centuries* (San Francisco: HarperCollins, 1997), p. 14.

8. Ibid., pp. 82–93.

9. Diana Butler Bass, *Christianity after Religion: The End of Church
and the Birth of a New Spiritual Awakening* (New York: HarperCollins,
2012), Kindle, pp. 200–14.

10. Aaron Blake, "Trump Conjures a New Immigrant Rape Crisis,"
Washington Post, April 5, 2018, https://www.washingtonpost.com/news/
the-fix/wp/2018/04/05/trump-conjures-yet-another-immigrant-rape
-epidemic/?utm_term=.8392500d816d.

11. Philip Bump, "Why Separate Immigrant Children from Parents?
The Politics of Fear—Just Indirectly," *Washington Post*, May 11, 2018,
https://www.washingtonpost.com/news/politics/wp/2018/05/11/why-
separate-immigrant-children-from-parents-the-politics-of-fear-just
-indirectly/?utm_term=.cae99d363509.

12. Niraj Chokshi, "Trump Voters Driven by Fear of Losing Status,
Not Economic Anxiety, Study Finds," *New York Times*, April 24, 2018,
https://www.nytimes.com/2018/04/24/us/politics/trump-economic
-anxiety.html.

13. George Orwell, *1984* (1949; Planet ebook online edition), p. 44.

14. Wikipedia, s.v. "The Architects of Fear," last edited August 12, 2018, https://en.wikipedia.org/wiki/The_Architects_of_Fear.

15. Jim Wallis, *Rediscovering Values: On Wall Street, Main Street, and Your Street* (New York: Howard Books, 2010), p. 81.

HOW DO WE ACHIEVE COMMUNITY IN A FRACTURED SOCIETY?

Parsons

1. Paul Johnson, *A History of Christianity* (New York: Atheneum, 1977).

2. In the 2004 presidential campaign, decorated Vietnam War veteran John Kerry was made the target of a campaign of slurs against his service on swift boats during the war. Hence, to "swift boat" means to attack someone by lying about their best achievements or strongest virtues.

3. See Richard Gooding, "The Trashing of John McCain," *Vanity Fair*, November 2004, https://www.vanityfair.com/news/2004/11/mccain200411.

4. Jonathan Haidt, *The Righteous Mind: Why Good People Are Divided by Politics and Religion* (New York: Vintage, 2013).

5. Steven Pinker, *Enlightenment Now: The Case for Reason, Progress, Humanism, and Science* (New York: Viking, 2018).

6. Haidt, *Righteous Mind*, pp. 150–79.

7. Ibid., p. 145.

8. Ibid., p. 184.

9. Pinker, *Enlightenment Now*, p. 59.

10. Ibid.

11. In the 1980s, Candace Bergen starred as the title character in the hit show *Murphy Brown*. In one episode, Murphy announced that she was going to be a single mom. This prompted a rebuke from then vice president J. Danforth Quayle, who chastised the character and asserted that two

parents were better than a single parent. Quayle, regarded as an intellectual lightweight by liberals, was dismissed with derisive laughter. Turns out he was right, as the *Washington Post* reported: Isabel Sawhill, "20 Years Later, It Turns Out Dan Quayle Was Right about Murphy Brown and Unmarried Moms," *Washington Post*, May 25, 2012, https://www.washingtonpost .com/opinions/20-years-later-it-turns-out-dan-quayle-was-right-about -murphy-brown-and-unmarried-moms/2012/05/25/gJQAsNCJqU_story .html?utm_term=.c0789d5ebbae.

12. For an enlightening case study of how activists opposing same-sex marriage employed a junk and debunked study to argue that children are worse off with same-sex parents, see Ari Rabin-Havt and Media Matters, *Lies Incorporated: The World of Post-Truth Politics* (New York: Anchor, 2016), pp. 167–87.

HOW DO WE ACHIEVE COMMUNITY IN A FRACTURED SOCIETY?

Donehoo

1. Ralph W. Neighbour Jr., *The Seven Last Words of the Church: "We Never Tried It That Way Before"* (Nashville: Baptist Sunday School Board, 1979).

2. Ken Thomas, "Sanders: Aide's McCain Comment Shouldn't Have Been Leaked," Associated Press, May 12, 2018, https://www .usnews.com/news/politics/articles/2018-05-12/sanders-aides -mccain-comment-shouldnt-have-been-leaked.

3. "Invitation to Dinner," *Christian Century* 134, no. 19 (September 13, 2017): 8.

4. Dan Mangan, "Mylan Hit with Racketeering Suit Over Big Price Hikes of EpiPen," CNBC, April 3, 2017, https://www.cnbc.com/2017/04/03/ mylan-hit-with-racketeering-suit-over-big-price-hikes-of-epipen.html.

5. Ralph Klein, "Great Love Stories of the Bible" (unpublished lecture; Furman University Pastors' School, Greenville, SC, July 1982).

6. Jim Wallis, *Rediscovering Values: On Wall Street, Main Street, and Your Street* (New York: Howard Books, 2010), pp. 241–42.

CONCLUDING THOUGHTS ON COMMUNITY

Parsons

1. Matthew Stewart, "The Birth of a New American Aristocracy," *Atlantic* 321, no. 5 (June 2018): 48–63, available online as "The 9.9 Percent Is the New American Aristocracy," https://www.theatlantic.com/magazine/archive/2018/06/the-birth-of-a-new-american-aristocracy/559130/; Steven Brill, "My Generation Was Supposed to Level the Playing Field. Instead, We Rigged It for Ourselves," *Time*, May 28, 2018, pp. 32–39, available online as "How Baby Boomers Broke America," http://time.com/5280446/baby-boomer-generation-america-steve-brill/.

2. A few years ago I said, in public, "Two thousand years of Christianity are enough!" I forget what exactly set me off, but I now regard such remarks as unfair and intemperate. Reading John Hick's *An Interpretation of Religion: Human Responses to the Transcendent*, 2nd ed. (New Haven: Yale University Press, 2004) showed me that a religious worldview can indeed be rational. Another thing that has made me back away from incendiary remarks is the recognition that some atheists are as fanatical and fundamentalist in spirit as any Bible-beater. Indeed, over years of blogging, the nastiest treatment I have ever gotten did not come from religious people but from zealous atheists who were driven into a frothing rage when I said some nice things about Christians and dared to criticize some atheists. Mostly, though, it was renewing my discussions with Paris that made me realize that my enemy was not religion per se but fundamentalism—whether religious or atheistic.

3. One of the nastiest and most poorly argued is Anthony DeStefano, *Inside the Atheist Mind: Unmasking the Religion of Those Who Say There Is No God* (Nashville: Thomas Nelson, 2018).

4. Richard Dawkins, "Physical versus Mental Child Abuse," Richard Dawkins Foundation, January 1, 2013, https://www.richarddawkins.net/2013/01/physical-versus-mental-child-abuse/.

5. Nathalie Baptiste and Foreign Policy in Focus, "It's Not Just Uganda: Behind the Christian Right's Onslaught in Africa," *Nation*, April 4, 2014, https://www.thenation.com/article/its-not-just-uganda-behind-christian-rights-onslaught-africa/.

6. Adam Peck, "Bill Donohue: It's 'a Lot Less Expensive' to Fight Victims of Pedophile Priests," ThinkProgress, March 13, 2012, https://thinkprogress.org/bill-donohue-its-a-lot-less-expensive-to-fight-victims-of-pedophile-priests-feff518383e3/.

CONCLUDING THOUGHTS ON COMMUNITY

Donehoo

1. T. S. Eliot, "The Hollow Men," *The Complete Poems and Plays* (New York: Harcourt, Brace, and World, 1971), p. 59.

2. "Call to Action," *Christian Century* 134, no. 19 (September 13, 2017): 8.

CONCLUSION: AN UNABASHEDLY ALARMIST CODA

1. David B. Julen, "My Police Officer Friend: Caught between 'Unloving Critics' and 'Uncritical Lovers,'" *Charlotte Observer*, October 14, 2016, https://www.charlotteobserver.com/opinion/op-ed/article 108325412.html.

2. Bruce Catton, *This Hallowed Ground: A History of the Civil War* (New York: Vintage, 2012).

3. Charles Sumner, *The Crime against Kansas* (Boston: John P. Jewett, 1856), p. 9. Accessible at the United States Senate website: Charles

Sumner "The Crime against Kansas," US Senate, May 19, 1856, https://www.senate.gov/artandhistory/history/minute/The_Crime_Against_Kansas.htm.

4. Thomas A. Bailey, *The American Pageant: A History of the Republic*, 4th ed. (Lexington, MA: D. C. Heath, 1971), p. 424.

5. Alexander Mooney, "Texas Governor Says Secession Possible," *Political Ticker* (blog), CNN, April 16, 2009, http://politicalticker.blogs.cnn.com/2009/04/16/texas-governor-says-secession-possible/.

6. Jim Wallis, *Rediscovering Values: On Wall Street, Main Street, and Your Street* (New York: Howard Books, 2010), p. 4.

7. Trump quickly reversed his policy of family separation when the level of public outcry became overwhelming—after thousands of children had been abducted. It is hard to say who looked worse in this whole debacle. Was it Attorney General Jeff Sessions who invoked the Bible as a cover for his cruelty? Was it the Secretary of Homeland Security, Kirstjen Nielsen, who said that her agency was merely doing its job—a claim eerily reminiscent of the Nazis who said that they were "only following orders"? Was it the former Trump staffer, who, when told of a child with Down's Syndrome who had been separated from her parent, responded only with a mocking "womp"? Was it other Republicans, who were too weak and cowardly to stand up to Trump, even over this? Those who defend the indefensible are odious; those who know what is wrong but refuse to speak up are even worse.